D1165761

Such a Simple Little Tale

Critical Responses
to
L. M. Montgomery's
Anne of Green Gables

Mavis Reimer, Editor

**The Children's Literature Association
and
The Scarecrow Press, Inc.
Metuchen, N. J. & London
1992**

British Library Cataloguing-in-Publication data available

Library of Congress Cataloging-in-Publication Data

Such a simple little tale : critical responses to L.M. Montgomery's
    Anne of Green Gales / edited by Mavis Reimer.
      p.   cm.
    Includes index.
    ISBN 0-8108-2560-0
    1. Montgomery, L. M. (Lucy Maud), 1874-1942. Anne of Green
Gables. 2. Children's stories, Canadian—History and criticism.
I. Reimer, Mavis.
PR9199.3.M6A6537 1992
813'.52—dc20   92-7392

Contents

Acknowledgments

Temma F. Berg, "*Anne of Green Gables*: A Girl's Reading," *Children's Literature Association Quarterly* 13 (1988): 124-8. Reprinted with the permission of the author.

Susan Drain, "Community and the Individual in *Anne of Green Gables*: The Meaning of Belonging," *ChLAQ* 11 (1986): 15-19. Reprinted with the permission of the author.

Carol Gay, "'Kindred Spirits' All: Green Gables Revisited," *ChLAQ* 11 (1986): 9-12. Reprinted with the permission of Dr. Thomas Gay.

Nancy Huse, "Journeys of the Mother in the World of Green Gables," *Proceedings of the Thirteenth Annual Conference of the Children's Literature Association held at the University of Missouri—Kansas City, May 16-18, 1986,* ed. Susan R. Gannon and Ruth Anne Thompson (ChLA, 1988) 60-63. Reprinted with the permission of the author.

Eve Kornfeld and Susan Jackson, "The Female *Bildungsroman* in Nineteenth-Century America: Parameters of a Vision," *Journal of American Culture* 10.4 (1987): 69-75. Reprinted by permission of the Popular Press. The authors wish to dedicate this article to their mothers.

T. D. MacLulich, "L. M. Montgomery's Portraits of the Artist: Realism, Idealism, and the Domestic Imagination," *English Studies in Canada* 11 (1985): 459-73. Copyright 1985 by the Association of Canadian University Teachers of English. Reprinted by permission of the author and the Association.

Perry Nodelman, "Progressive Utopia: Or, How to Grow Up Without Growing Up," *Proceedings of the Sixth Annual Conference of the Children's Literature Association, University of Toronto, March 1979,* ed. Priscilla A. Ord and Margaret P. Esmonde (Villanova, PA: Villanova U, 1980) 146-54. Reprinted with the permission of the author.

Catherine Ross, "Calling Back the Ghost of the Old-Time Heroine: Duncan, Montgomery, Atwood, Laurence, and Munro," *Studies in Canadian Literature* 4.1 (1979): 43-58. Reprinted by permission of the author and *Studies in Canadian Literature.*

Mary Rubio, "*Anne of Green Gables*: The Architect of Adolescence," *Touchstones: Reflections on the Best in Children's Literature,* ed. Perry Nodelman, vol. 1 (West Lafayette, IN: Children's Literature Association, 1985) 173-87. Reprinted with the permission of the author.

Marilyn Solt, "The Uses of Setting in *Anne of Green Gables*," *ChLAQ* 9 (1984-85): 179-80, 198. Reprinted with the permission of the author.

Gillian Thomas, "The Decline of Anne: Matron vs. Child," *Canadian Children's Literature* 3 (1975): 37-41. Reprinted by permission of the author and *Canadian Children's Literature.*

Janet Weiss-Townsend, "Sexism Down on the Farm?: *Anne of Green Gables,*" *ChLAQ* 11 (1986): 12-15. Reprinted with the permission of the author.

Muriel A. Whitaker, "'Queer Children': L. M. Montgomery's Heroines," *Canadian Children's Literature* 3 (1975): 50-59. Reprinted by permission of the author and *Canadian Children's Literature.*

Introduction

The Anne-Girl and the Anne Book

"Anne, Anne, you little red-headed monkey," wrote Lucy Maud Montgomery in her journal on November 29, 1910, "you are responsible for much!" (2:32). Montgomery inserts the exclamation into her detailed account of her first trip to Boston, a trip arranged by publishers Lewis and George Page as a tribute to, and promotion of, one of their best-selling authors. Wined, dined, and fêted by people of note in the city's social and literary circles, the young woman from rural Prince Edward Island felt that she had "lived more, learned more, enjoyed more" of life in fourteen days than she had in the previous twelve years (2:19). Eighty years after Montgomery's first novel was issued, the heroine whose transformation from carrot-haired urchin to Titian beauty is the subject of *Anne of Green Gables* continues to be "responsible for much."

But just how much notice and affection Montgomery's character has generated came as a surprise to me when I began this project. *Anne of Green Gables* went through seven printings within the first six months of its publication in June 1908 and was soon taken up for translation into Swedish, Danish, and Polish. Such success prompted the Pages to press Montgomery to write sequel stories as quickly as she was able and more quickly than she would have liked. Interest in Anne's story has not waned in the years since then, as Mary Rubio demonstrates in her article reprinted in this collection. The facts Rubio lists indicate the enduring and, apparently, rising popularity of the novel in places quite unlike Canada's Prince Edward Island and quite unlike each other.

In Canada, the renown of "that Anne-girl," to use Miss Josephine Barry's name for the character, is such that she has taken on a life outside Montgomery's text. I found myself repeatedly tripping over Anne while I was working on the novel. "Anne of Green Gables, never change. We love you just this way," sang my son as he walked in the door from school choir practice one day. Selections from the musical version of Anne's story, it seemed, were to be included on the spring concert program. My daughter was chosen to play Miss Stacy in her class's production of the same musical a year later. A visit to a local children's bookstore brought me home with an entry form for a contest; the first prize was a trip to "Green Gables." (That name has been given to the restored Cavendish house Montgomery identified as the prototype for the fictional house, although it is not the house in which she lived.) The calendar in my kitchen at the time was decorated with scenes from the Sullivan Productions films of Anne's story. A ballet about the girl from Green Gables is a standard Christmas presentation of the principal dance company in my city. Spin-offs both from the novel and the films seemed to be everywhere: I could have bought Anne of Green Gables dolls, cookbooks, address books, birthday books, diaries, coloring books, and a variety of abridged and rewritten versions of the novel.

If Anne intruded into my life independently of the text which created her, Montgomery herself was being redefined in terms of texts. (In fact, she is a character in a recent Canadian girls' book, Bernice Hunter's *As Ever, Booky*.) The publication of the first two volumes of Montgomery's private journals in 1985 and 1987 provoked considerable commentary on book review pages. Reviewers were usually confused, sometimes disappointed, but invariably intrigued by the discrepancies between the sunny, expansive world of Montgomery's best-known novels and what one reviewer called the "dark, little room" of her life (Powell C5). During the fall of 1987, a curious story involving one of Montgomery's adult novels preoccupied the literary media in Canada (and, reportedly, in England and Australia as well). Shortly after the publication that year of *The Ladies of Missalonghi* by popular Australian novelist Colleen McCullough, rumors began to circulate that McCullough's story bore a strange resemblance to Montgomery's *The Blue Castle*, first published in 1926. Commentators were anxious to avoid suggesting that the borrowing had been deliberate, but they continued to reiterate their perplexity at what one called "the density of the coincidence" between the two books (Garvey). Not only were the stories structurally similar, but also such details as the names of characters, elements of the setting, and unusual phrases from *The Blue Castle* were replicated in *The Ladies of Missalonghi.* McCullough's response to the controversy swirling around her— that she had read *The Blue Castle* as a child of ten or eleven and could only guess that it had somehow "imprinted" itself on her subconscious—offered a tantalizing hint of the power of the language of a novelist who, as a children's writer and a sentimentalist, practiced forms of fiction that are often disparaged as less than serious writing.

Critical notice of a literary text does not necessarily follow popular enthusiasm, but both audiences have paid attention to *Anne of Green Gables.* In fact, the interest of many literary critics seems to have been piqued by what Carol Gay, in her article in this volume, calls "the problem of the enduring classic that retains its popularity through the years without much evidence of what is usually defined as literary merit." Montgomery herself referred to her story as "such a simple little tale" in her journal (1:339); professional readers, attempting to account for the appeal of Montgomery's novel, have called each element of that description into question.

The amount of erudition generated by *Anne of Green Gables* prompted Perry Nodelman, then editor of the *Children's Literature Association Quarterly,* and Jill May, then head of the Publications Committee of the Children's Literature Association, to propose this compilation of critical essays. They realized that, during the years of their editing scholarship and criticism in the discipline of children's literature, they had published more articles on Montgomery's book than on any other children's book. Nodelman and May suggested that assembling these discussions in a single volume would make for an interesting casebook on the strategies critics choose to read children's fiction. I agreed and took on the task of gathering the articles for a collection the ChLA Board soon dubbed "the Anne book."

My search for other criticism and scholarship on Montgomery's novel was launched with the intention of using this work only to identify the place of the ChLA articles in Montgomery criticism. Early in my research, however, I began to suspect that a collection on children's literature and critical strategy that used *Anne of Green Gables* as its case in point would have to take a somewhat different shape.

Among the writers addressing Montgomery's novel are many who take little notice of the deliberations of other scholars. The phenomenon of commentators assuming that they are forging new ground in discussing a work that is already colonized territory is a familiar one to critics of children's literature. As a relatively new and unprestigious field of literary study, children's literature is only now becoming the province of experts who are concerned to identify the texts that constitute the canon of their discipline and who regularly recognize the importance of each other's work. As the bibliographies in the "Suggestions for Further Reading" demonstrate, the place of *Anne of Green Gables* in literature has been debated since it was first published. To bring to the attention of readers and critics a selection of the important work that has already been done on the novel, I decided, would be one of the purposes of this collection.

Second thought convinced me that the lack of cross-references in the criticism was not so much a fact to be deplored as explored for what it suggests about the fundamental differences in the assumptions readers make about how to read *Anne of Green Gables*. For, if the essayists seldom cite each other, they do point to a fascinating and wide range of secondary material, critical, historical, and theoretical.

The difference that first struck me was that between Canadian and American critical approaches to the novel. Published in the United States in 1908, *Anne of Green Gables* is often discussed as an American novel by critics and, indeed, seems to be readily assumed into those literary contexts. In plotting, characterization, and theme, Montgomery's novel fits snugly into well-known traditions of late nineteenth- and early twentieth-century American books: critics have described *Anne* as an example of the literature of local color popular in turn-of-the-century New England, as a girls' book, as a series book, as domestic fiction, and as sentimental fiction. In much of the Canadian literature on Montgomery's first novel, on the other hand, *Anne* is seen as a singular, if not anomalous, achievement. Canadian critics have discussed *Anne of Green Gables* as the best novel of the Anne series, have studied *Anne* as uniquely successful among Montgomery's characters, and have celebrated or—just as heartily—denigrated Montgomery's durable, far-flung, and uncommon popularity. It is a second objective of this collection to alert readers of Montgomery in both countries that claim *Anne* as part of their literary heritage to the conversations under way in the other country.

But differences between the Canadian and American approaches to *Anne* are tendencies rather than definite divergences. Some essayists write from outside the North American context entirely, and many essayists write from perspectives that complicate any attempt to type their pieces simply by national origin. For example, several critics (among them Catherine Ross and Thomas MacLulich in this volume) cite *Anne of Green Gables* in discussions of mainstream Canadian literature. It is ironic that, because novels for adults are often valued for their uniqueness and *Anne of Green Gables* is commonly read as *one* of a kind in Canada, the continuity of Montgomery's themes, characters, and structures with other Canadian fiction can be seen. Montgomery's novel is read by common readers, some of them children, as well as professional readers, and so qualifies for discussion as popular fiction. Explicated in terms of its appeal to audiences widely separated in time and place, *Anne* loses its circumscribed national and historical personality: critics considering Montgomery's novel as popular fiction argue either that the novel displays mythic archetypes or entrenched cultural stereotypes. Critics who read the novel in the light of research into the separate traditions of women's literature describe Montgomery's accomplishments as inheritor and innovator differently again. And, many of the critics invoke more than one context in the course of their discussions.

Given these multiple and quite different points of departure for commentators on Montgomery's novel, I realized that my initial assumption—that Montgomery's novel would be read, first and foremost, as children's fiction—might itself be a choice that excluded some readings, if not some reading strategies. It was a choice, too, that determined how I read the articles published in children's literature journals: in fact, only some of those writers explicitly consider the relation of the novel to an audience of children. I finally decided that a group of essays on *Anne of Green Gables* would be most useful if it paid attention to as many perspectives as possible and included articles that, either by their assumptions or by their procedures, call into question the assignment of the novel to children's lists. The articles reprinted in this volume first appeared in a variety of publications; some, such as the papers previously published only in conference proceedings, were relatively inaccessible to many Montgomery readers. Each of the articles breaks some new ground in *Anne of Green Gables* criticism.

At the core of this collection are the eight articles on Montgomery's novel first published by ChLA. They do, indeed, illustrate a wide range of reading strategies. In current discussions, critics of children's literature are addressing the question of whether children's literature is naturally allied to particular reading strategies.[1] It is a problem usefully kept in mind when reading the ChLA articles, in which the writers have used methods from structuralism, formalism, and psychoanalysis, and theories of feminism, reading, and genre to make meaning of a single children's book.

In an argument first presented at a ChLA conference, Perry Nodelman examines the structure of a number of girls' books and discovers that all tell the same story. That story is a version of ideal female childhood which Nodelman suspects contemporary feminists might well find objectionable. Marilyn Solt's formalistic analysis of setting in *Anne* focuses on Montgomery's expert use of detail. One of the editors of Montgomery's journals, Mary Rubio, writes a psychoanalytic study of the novel, considering the connections between Montgomery's life and her story. Carol Gay begins her essay by decrying "the male-centered terms" of the questions we indiscriminately ask of all literature; she chooses to read *Anne of Green Gables* rather as a female utopia. Janet Weiss-Townsend queries the usefulness of the label, "girls' books," and ventures a definition of children's literature that includes both girls' books and boys' books. In her thematic discussion of the novel, Susan Drain argues that Montgomery refuses simple or single concepts of community, individuality, and belonging. Nancy Huse's feminist reading of the Anne series concentrates on Montgomery's images of motherhood. Temma Berg proposes a theory of reader response that would account for the disparity between her recollection of Montgomery's novel and her reaction to the Sullivan Productions films of Anne's story.

Two other critics in this volume, like the ChLA writers, present their arguments as part of a discussion of children's literature. These are the two pieces from the 1975 special Montgomery issue of *Canadian Children's Literature:* Muriel Whitaker's comparative study of characterization in four of Montgomery's books—one from each of the three series of girls' books and *The Blue Castle*— and Gillian Thomas's evaluation of the characterization of Anne through the eight novels of the Anne series. Both Whitaker and Thomas judge the Anne of *Anne of Green Gables* to be among Montgomery's most successful creations. But, in considering the reasons for that success, they set *Anne of Green Gables* beside different texts and find different explanations for Montgomery's achievement in her first novel.

Also reading Montgomery as a Canadian writer, but not as a children's writer, are Catherine Ross and Thomas MacLulich. The article by Ross, first published in *Studies in Canadian Literature,* places Montgomery beside other Canadian women novelists of the twentieth century in her use of structural irony. Thomas MacLulich's article, which first appeared in *English Studies in Canada,* positions Montgomery in relation to her contemporaries and the theories of fiction current in Canada at the turn of the century.

Eve Kornfeld and Susan Jackson, in a piece first published in the *Journal of American Culture,* discuss Montgomery as a nineteenth-century American writer; they demonstrate that *Anne of Green Gables* shares many features with other novels of female development published in the United States after mid-century.

There are, of course, many other ways of linking and opposing the arguments articulated in these articles. For example, do the structural analyses of Nodelman, Huse, and Ross confirm or contradict each other? What are the intersections and what the disjunctions of the feminist readings of Gay, Huse, Berg, Kornfeld and Jackson? The articles in this volume appear in the order in which they were first published. Are there assumptions and concerns that critics writing during the same years share with each other? Questions such as these arise from reading the arguments contained within this volume in relation to one another. Other queries surface when these arguments are set within the context of Montgomery criticism as a whole. In a number of the articles summarized in the "Suggestions for Further Reading," for example, critics have used psychoanalytic approaches to read the novel; Rubio's description of Montgomery as "The Architect of Adolescence" illuminates and is illuminated by those other arguments.

But whether readers are convinced to privilege as truth one, several, or none of the critics' arguments is finally of little significance. Criticism is more often moved forward by disputation than by agreement. Such energetic debate is exemplified by a series of the ChLA articles reprinted here which runs counter to the tendency in Montgomery criticism to working with the text alone. The argument Nodelman outlines in his paper was the basis for a classroom lecture he gave on the novel. Student Weiss-Townsend, taking umbrage at some of his analysis, sought out other ways of reading the novel and found a review of Gerda Lerner's *The Female Experience,* written by Carol Gay, which pointed her in a new direction. Neither Gay nor Nodelman finally persuaded her, but each made it necessary for Weiss-Townsend to think about, and to accommodate into her reading, matters she had earlier ignored. The process of her reevaluation is the subject of "Sexism Down on the Farm?: *Anne of Green Gables.*" (Gay's suggestions, first made in *ChLAQ* in 1982, were later amplified in the article also reprinted here.) Berg's reading of Gay, Weiss-Townsend, and Drain in turn spurred her to remember her own immersion in the world of Green Gables as a girl and to inquire into the reasons for her passionate attachment to Montgomery's novel.

Many readers—particularly girls and women—identify the sort of fervent involvement Berg describes as a primary response to *Anne of Green Gables.* The preponderance of articles about the novel are authored by women; indeed, Gay suggests that "Montgomery's Avonlea books are a common bond shared by women of our century." These facts will no doubt continue to compel the interest of feminist critics and scholars who are exploring the functioning of gender in reading and writing and who are retrieving the experiences of women from the silences of history. The attention of young readers will surely make it necessary for critics of children's literature to account for Montgomery's novel as they develop theories of the genre. Since the success of the two recent films of Anne's story, *The Story Girl,* another of Montgomery's novels for children, has been serialized for television as *The Road to Avonlea.* There are many questions that should be asked about the relationship of commercial, consumer culture and children's literature that might focus around this Montgomery revival. Montgomery's journals, which continue to be published, might well reward close readings by theorists and critics newly interested in the art and meaning of self- and life-writing.

But whatever directions the research and inquiry into the meanings of L. M. Montgomery's first novel take, the essays in this volume deserve to be part of the critical conversation. For each can provoke readers into rereading *Anne of Green Gables*, thinking about their responses to it in other terms, and—perhaps best of all—clarifying or complicating their own arguments.

Many friends not only cheered me on to the completion of this project but also prompted me to rethink aspects of it; the assistance of a number of them must not go unacknowledged. Thanks to Jill May and Tony Manna, who, as heads of the Publications Committee of the Children's Literature Association, gave me both practical and moral support; to Barbara Garner and Mary Harker, who allowed me to see their annotated bibliography in manuscript; to Patricia Srebrnik, Neil Besner, Roderick McGillis, and Jeanne Perreault for conversations and advice on a variety of issues; to Perry Nodelman, for listening carefully and critically as I articulated problems and sought solutions; and to the members of my family—Maria, Andrew, Carlton, and Garth—for all the ways in which they helped the Anne book to grow. The Department of English at the University of Winnipeg provided me with support services; special thanks are due Patty Hawkins, who prepared the typescript. Work on the manuscript was completed while I held a Doctoral Fellowship from the Social Sciences and Humanities Research Council of Canada and an Honorary Killam Scholarship from the University of Calgary.

Notes

1. See, for example, Perry Nodelman, "Children's Literature as Women's Writing," *ChLAQ* 13 (1988): 31-34; Jean Perrot's response to Nodelman, "Written From the International Androgynous!!: A Plea for Our Common Hide (and Seek?)," *ChLAQ* 14 (1989): 139-41; Julia Briggs, "Women Writers and Writing for Children: From Sarah Fielding to E. Nesbit," in *Children and Their Books: A Celebration of the Work of Iona and Peter Opie,* ed. Gillian Avery and Julia Briggs (Oxford: Clarendon, 1989) 221-50; and the special issue of *Children's Literature* 18 (1990), which deals with psychoanalytic criticism and children's literature. See, in particular, Michael Steig, "Why Bettleheim," 125-26; Jerry Phillips and Ian Wojcik-Andrews, "Notes Toward a Marxist Critical Practice," 127-30; U. C. Knoepflmacher, "The Doubtful Marriage: A Critical Fantasy," 131-34; Patrick Hogan, "What's Wrong with the Psychoanalysis of Liter-

ature?" 135-40; and Jack Zipes, "Negating History and Male Fantasies Through Psychoanalytic Criticism," 141-43.

Works Cited

Campbell, Norman, and Donald Harron. *Anne of Green Gables: A Musical*. New York: Samuel French, 1972.

Garvey, Maureen. *Morningside. CBC*. CBWT, Winnipeg, 18 Jan. 1988.

Hunter, Bernice Thurman. *As Ever, Booky*. Richmond Hill, ON: Scholastic-TAB, 1989.

McCullough, Colleen. *The Ladies of Missalonghi*. 1987. London: Arrow-Century Hutchinson, 1988.

Montgomery, L. M. *Anne of Green Gables*. 1908. Toronto: Seal-McClelland and Stewart-Bantam, 1981.

_____. *The Blue Castle*. 1926. Toronto: Seal-McClelland-Bantam, 1988.

Powell, Marilyn. "Unhappy Times." Rev. of *The Selected Journals of L. M. Montgomery, Volume II, 1910-1921*. Ed. Mary Rubio and Elizabeth Waterston. *Globe and Mail*, 9 Jan. 1988: C5.

Rubio, Mary, and Elizabeth Waterston. *The Selected Journals of L. M. Montgomery*. 2 vols. Toronto: Oxford UP, 1985-87.

"Queer Children"

L. M. Montgomery's Heroines

Muriel A. Whitaker

When I was a child, the novels of L. M. Montgomery occupied half a shelf in our glass-doored bookcase. First editions, mostly, they had been inscribed to my mother and aunt by various gift-giving relatives. I read them eagerly, supplementing our own holdings with others borrowed from the public library, until I had gone through the Anne books, the Emily books, *Kilmeny of the Orchard, The Story Girl* and the rest. My own daughters, at a time when they were reading almost nothing but horse stories, showed a similar enthusiasm for L. M. Montgomery. Evidently she is one of those perennial authors whom girls in their early teens cannot resist.

It was with some hesitation that I recently returned to *Anne of Green Gables, Emily of New Moon, The Blue Castle* and *Pat of Silver Bush;* a hesitation stemming partly from reluctance to burst the bubble of nostalgia, partly from an awareness of critical disapproval. In her study of Canadian children's literature, Sheila Egoff, while grudgingly accepting the original Anne as a national institution, condemns "the increasingly sentimental dishonesty of the succeeding books" (252). E. K. Brown is equally disparaging about an author "who was satisfied to truckle to mediocre taste" (41). On rereading, *Anne* seemed not at all bad and *Emily* interested me so much I wanted to read the rest of the series to see how things turned out. Admittedly, the charm was partly that of a period piece. Canadiana is "in" at the moment: though we no longer use gin jars for hot water bottles or keep up a parlor for serious occasions, hooked rugs, patchwork quilts, and butter churns are highly prized and highly priced. Is the appeal of L. M. Montgomery's novels simply a matter of nostalgia or do they contain something of lasting, if minor, literary value? In what context do her child heroines operate? What makes Anne and Emily particularly interesting, and Valancy and Pat less so?

When Mark Twain describes Anne as "the sweetest creation of child life yet written,"[1] he is implicitly setting her in the context of English children's literature, a genre that originated with the Puritans in the seventeenth century. Because the Puritan child was regarded as a "brand of hell,"[2] it was the duty of parents, teachers, and guardians to impress on him both the sinfulness of his fallen nature and the ideal which he should follow if he would escape the fires of hell. Gratitude, duty, reverence, sobriety, humility, industry, and above all obedience were the desired virtues; vanity, impertinence, impiety, and disobedience were the faults which, in the didactic literature that adults thought suitable for children, inevitably led to horrendous ends. Transported to New England by the Pilgrim Fathers and to the Maritimes and Ontario by the Presbyterians, the Puritan ethic continued to affect the life and literature of Canadian and American children for many generations.

Marilla Cuthbert, Rachel Lynde and Mrs. Barry in *Anne of Green Gables,* and Ellen Greene, Aunt Elizabeth and Miss Brownell in *Emily of New Moon* are purveyors of the moral and religious ethos which controls the lives of Montgomery's heroines. It is a highly ritualized society, supported on the twin pillars of church and work. Labor in the rural community is determined by the cycle of the seasons; social intercourse, by the round of Sunday church, midweek prayer meeting, Ladies' Aid, and school. Propriety and conformity, a regard for "decency and decorum," prevail. Explanations must be found for uncharacteristic behavior, a necessity that leads to the prying and gossiping that characterize any closely knit society. So Mrs. Rachel Lynde cannot rest until she finds out why Matthew Cuthbert, dressed in his best suit, is driving off in the middle of the afternoon when he should be sowing his late turnip seed in the big red brook field of Green Gables.

The odd and the out-of-place are immediately suspect. It is the queerness of Anne Shirley, both in physical appearance (bright red hair, with flowers on her hat) and character (garrulity, imagination) that catches the eye and ear of Avonlea and of the reader. The orphaned Emily Starr is told that her Murray relatives won't like her because "you're queer, and folks don't care for queer children." One mark of her queerness is pointed ears, indicating that she is "kin to tribes of elfland." (Calvinist orthodoxy combines with Celtic fantasy in the world of Prince Edward Island.) Even Anne's "bosom friend" Diana, an entirely conventional child in most respects, is set apart by the fact that she is named for a pagan goddess—"I'd ruther Jane or Mary or some sensible name like that," is Matthew's comment. Inevitably, Ilse Burnley's unconventional upbringing causes much head-shaking in the Blair Water Community.

Almost as suspect as the odd is the beautiful, utility being preferred when it comes to making value judgments. Thus the blossoming cherry tree to which Anne responds so ecstatically is dismissed by Marilla: "It's a big tree . . . and it blooms great but the fruit don't amount to much never—small and wormy." Girls' dresses should be "good sensible, serviceable dresses, without any frills or furbelows" rather than the prettily fashionable garments with extravagant puffed sleeves that Anne longs to wear. The high-buttoned shoes and "terrible" gingham sunbonnets and aprons in which Emily is dressed are models of utility and defences against vanity. The rigorous criteria regarding clothes extend also to reading material (novels are "wicked books and have ruined many souls"), to bangs, to whistling. In fact, "a great many jolly things" are, if not wicked, at least unladylike.

The Puritan view required that the child should be taught by exhortation, example, and punishment. "Correction in itself is not cruel," Dr. Samuel Johnson had proclaimed. "Children, being not reasonable, can be governed only by fear. To impress this fear is therefore one of the first duties of those who have the care of children" (487). Mrs. Lynde has no hesitation in impressing on Anne that she is full of original sin and in recommending to Marilla the use of a switch. The fearful Calvinistic doctrine of election is apparent in Anne's view of herself: "No matter how hard I try to be good I can never make such a success of it as those who are naturally good." Attendance at Sunday School and church, saying one's prayers, learning to cook, clean, and make patchwork squares are all part of a proper bringing up. The adults provide sustenance, direction, and good example; the children are to respond in the way that Aunt Elizabeth expects:

> Emily, you must understand right now that you are to be grateful
> and obedient and show your appreciation of what is being done
> for you. I won't have tears and repining. What would you have
> done if you had no friends to take you in? Answer me that.

In spite of genuine effort on the part of the children, the old Eve
will out. Vanity, disobedience, lying, anger, stubbornness, pride, a
regular Pandora's box of "viciousness," are illustrated by their
careers. Yet, unlike the children in the "horrendous example" school
of literature,[3] these heroines do not come to a bad end. Rather, in
the tradition of Rousseau's *Émile,* they learn by experience, as Anne
realizes:

> Ever since I came to Green Gables I've been making mistakes,
> and each mistake has helped to cure me of meddling with things
> that didn't belong to me. The Haunted Wood mistake cured me
> of letting my imagination run away with me. The liniment cake
> mistake cured me of carelessness in cooking. Dying my hair
> cured me of vanity. . . .

In the end, Anne conforms pretty closely to the adult view of
propriety, a fact that makes her a much less interesting character in
subsequent books. Writing to Ephraim Weber on September 10,
1908, Montgomery expressed her own awareness of the problem:
"Anne, grown-up, couldn't be made as quaint and unexpected as
the child Anne" (74).

The Puritan idea of the child is not the only determiner of
character in the novels of L. M. Montgomery. Combined with it is
the idea of the child as innocent victim, orphaned, abandoned, often
doomed to an early death. That this was a popular motif in Victorian
literature the novels of Dickens, MacDonald, and Kingsley, among
others, testify. The pathos of Anne and Emily depends to a considerable extent on the fact that they are orphans. (The germ of *Anne*
was a newspaper clipping about a couple who applied to an orphanage for a boy and were sent a girl instead.) The awareness of
deprivation is vividly illustrated by Emily's response to New Moon:

> She felt utterly alone and lonely—there in that darkness, with an
> alien, hostile world all around her—for it seemed hostile now.
> And there was such a strange, mysterious, mournful sound in the

air—far away, yet clear. It was the murmur of the sea, but Emily
did not know that and it frightened her. Oh, for her little bed at
home—oh, for Father's soft breathing in the room. . . .

At the same time, their dramatization of this awareness is psychologically convincing. Whenever Anne thinks it can benefit her, she
reminds the critical adults—Marilla, Mrs. Lynde, Mrs. Barry, Miss
Josephine Barry—that she is "a poor little orphan girl" whose
mistakes result from ignorance rather than intention. As a member
of the proud and successful Murray clan, Emily is not so rootless
as Anne; she has a sense of belonging to a family group even though
duty rather than love has motivated the Murrays' acceptance of her.
On the other hand, while Anne is immediately popular with her
classmates, Emily suffers at school for being a "proud" Murray and
a stranger. "Why don't you like me?" she asks. "Because you ain't
a bit like us" is the reply.

Isolation is the favorite punishment inflicted by Marilla and
Aunt Elizabeth—being banished to one's room, being forbidden to
attend parties and picnics, being ostracized. When Emily refuses to
kneel before the unjust teacher, Miss Brownell, and beg her pardon,
Aunt Elizabeth tells her

> . . . you will be outcast in this house until you do. No one will
> talk to you—play with you—eat with you—have anything to do
> with you until you have obeyed me.

The prospect is so horrifying to a sensitive child that she prefers the
shame of yielding.

Eventually, the qualities which in the beginning tended to
isolate them—Anne's rootlessness and active imagination, Emily's
pride and poetic gift—provide them with the motivation to overcome misfortune and win acceptance. Anne's severest critic, Rachel
Lynde, is forced to admit:

> . . . I did make a mistake in judging Anne, but it weren't no
> wonder, for an odder, unexpecteder witch of a child there never
> was in this world, that's what. There was no ciphering her out by
> the rules that worked with other children. It's nothing short of
> wonderful how she's improved these three years, but especially
> in looks. . . .

Although Valancy Stirling, the heroine of *The Blue Castle,* is a twenty-nine-year-old spinster, she also is a type of rejected child. Her father having died, she has been brought up by her mother, Mrs. Frederick Stirling, and Cousin Stickles with the advice of assorted relations. All of them are proponents of the Puritan view of child-raising and all of them persist in treating Valancy as a child. An awareness of her loveless condition stems from the time when, at the age of nine,

> she was standing alone on the school playground while the other girls of her class were playing a game in which you must be chosen by a boy as his partner before you could play. Nobody had chosen Valancy—little, pale, black-haired Valancy, with her prim, long-sleeved apron and odd, slanted eyes.

Valancy inhabits two homes: an ugly, red brick box on Elm Street and a Blue Castle in Spain where there are

> courts, marble-pillared where shimmering fountains fell and nightingales sang among the myrtles; halls of mirrors that re-flected only handsome knights and lovely women—herself the loveliest of all, for whose glance men died.

The likelihood that she will, in her state of sexual frustration, become completely unhinged, is aborted when she receives a doctor's letter informing her that she has a fatal heart disease that will carry her off within a year. Realizing that she cannot be worse off than she is now—"I'm poor—I'm ugly—I'm a failure—and I'm near death"—she ticks off her relations and leaves home to keep house for the village drunk and his betrayed daughter who, having lost her illegitimate child, is now about to die of consumption (the wages of sin motif neatly combining with that of innocent victim).

Unfortunately, we can neither sympathize with Valancy nor admire her. The Castle in Spain fantasy, realized as an island retreat in the wilds of Ontario, is pure corn, but not less so is the heroine's marriage to frog prince Snaith who turns out to be not only the famous nature writer, John Foster, but also the son of a multimil-lionaire Purple Pill producer (a fact that brings Valancy's disapprov-ing relatives round in a hurry). Nor are we surprised to learn, after a Perils-of-Paulinish episode involving a shoe heel caught in a railway track before an onrushing train, that Valancy's fatal heart condition really belonged to another Stirling and that violet-eyed Barney has married Valancy out of love, not pity. It is tempting to exculpate L. M. Montgomery by regarding *The Blue Castle* as a parody of romance rather than as a serious attempt at the genre, but I cannot quite convince myself that such is the case.

In the final book which I am to discuss, *Pat of Silver Bush,* the author returns to the female child as protagonist. Pat Gardiner is the fourth of five children. Because her mother is sickly and occupied with a new baby, Pat's upbringing, like that of Anne and Emily, is left to a surrogate parent. Judy Plum is a shanty Irish family retainer whose influence on the "quare child—touched wid a liddle green rose-thorn" by a leprechaun on the day she was born—is, from the modern point of view, deplorable. Judy can speak "English" when the Gardiners' fine relatives are present, but in the bosom of the family she affects an Irish brogue in which dialect she fills the child's head with fairy nonsense, assures her that babies are found in parsley beds, passes on malicious gossip, and instills in her a conviction that she is socially superior—"Remember the Binnies may sweat but the Gardiners perspire." That the lesson has been well learned is evident in a letter that Pat writes to her brother, Sid:

> Sylvia Copilla says that Fred Davidson and his sister Muriel used to be devoted to each other just like you and me but they quarreled and now they never speak.... Of course they are only Davidsons. Sylvia says May Binnie is your girl. She isn't, is she, Sid? You'd never have a Binnie for a girl. They are not in our class.

Pat of Silver Bush contains many of the ingredients found in *Anne* and *Emily*—the P.E.I. setting, the clan feeling, the visits to eccentric relatives, the bosom friend, the admiring boys, the education at Queen's—yet when I read *Pat* as a child I found it a disappointment. Pat seems a bore and a snob. Rereading has not changed my mind. Part of Pat's failure to interest us results from the lack of development in her character. Petted by the family and Judy, she is never placed in a position of real crisis where strength of character is required. Moreover, the love of nature which she shares with the other heroines is expressed in such tritely sentimental rhetoric that the character cannot help being diminished.

Whether running about in the garden to kiss the flowers or dancing naked under the impression that she is a bewitched princess, she comes across as a girl who is queer to the point of being dim-witted.

Why are Anne and Emily such memorable characters while Valancy and Pat are best forgotten? It is not a question of time bringing to slow fruition a writer's skill, for Anne, the first of Montgomery's creations, is also the best. The answer must be found in the fictional character's relationship to reality. Much of the interest in *Anne* and *Emily* results from the tension between the adults, with their rigid view of how a child should act, and the children, with their strong sense of justice and clear-eyed awareness of adult shortcomings. Though the heroines' characters may have been influenced by such fictional rebels against the establishment as Lewis Carroll's Alice[4] and Mark Twain's Huckleberry Finn, they must also represent the way in which real children reacted to the authoritarian adults who controlled their destinies. Even Kenneth Grahame in that sensitive recreation of happy childhood, *The Golden Age,* inveighs against the Olympians:

> This strange anaemic order of beings was further removed from us, in fact, than the kindly beasts who shared our natural existence. The estrangement was fortified by an abiding sense of injustice, arising from the refusal of the Olympians to defend, to retract, to admit themselves in the wrong, or to accept similar concessions on our part. (10)

When Anne shouts furiously at Mrs. Lynde, "How dare you call me skinny and ugly? How dare you say I'm freckled and red-headed? You are a rude, impolite, unfeeling woman!", she is expressing a justifiable sense of outrage at the insensitivity of adults. And when Emily confronts Aunt Elizabeth with "How dare you touch *my private papers?*" she is asserting her right to be treated as an individual.

Moreover, in *Anne* and *Emily* there is such genuine interaction between children and adults that the adults themselves are changed. Matthew and Cousin Jimmy, the weak but kindly father figures, are given an interest that lifts them out of the humdrum routine of their daily lives and enables them to stand up to formidable females. Aunt Elizabeth learns that she cannot treat children according to standards that differ from those applied to adults. And Marilla so far overcomes her distrust of emotion that after Matthew's death she confesses her true feelings about Anne:

> I know I've been kind of strict and harsh with you maybe—but you mustn't think I didn't love you as well as Matthew did, for all that. I want to tell you now when I can. It's never been easy for me to say things out of my heart, but at times like this it's easier. I love you as dear as if you were my own flesh and blood and you've been my joy and comfort ever since you came to Green Gables.

By the same token, what makes Valancy and Pat inadequate is their lack of influence. Valancy's pert putdown of the riddling uncle and boring aunts strikes us as rudeness rather than as a courageous expression of ego, while the self-dramatization which brings Anne so vividly to life seems, in Valancy, to be maudlin playacting. There is no better testimony to the adults' immobility in *The Blue Castle* than the fact that, regardless of how queerly Valancy behaves, her mother and Cousin Stickles continue to sit "drearily, grimly knitting. Baffling and inhuman as ever."

In *Pat of Silver Bush* there is no lack of incident—births, weddings, the departure of a brother, the death of a friend—but all is surface fussiness. Because the characters fail to interact with one another we remain uninterested. The lachrymose seems the dominant mood but there is no sense of proportion. Tears gush forth as profusely when Father shaves his beard as when the bosom friend dies. At the same time, there is no development of Pat's character. The woman who becomes "the Chatelaine of Silver Bush" is really no different from the seven-year-old listening to Judy's stories.

In the end, what contributes most of all to the sense of reality projected by Anne and Emily is the fact that the fabric of their lives is that of L. M. Montgomery's own experience.[5] Lucy Maud, too, was a motherless child brought up by relatives in a farmhouse at Cavendish, Prince Edward Island. She, too, struck callers as "queer" because she talked to objects, individually named apple trees, and imaginatively created child companions who were "kindred spirits." She suffered from the tension between Puritan expectations and the working of original sin. Years later, she wrote to Weber, "Some of the me's are good, some *not*" (25). Like Anne and

Pat, she had to stay at home to care for an elderly, ailing lady rather than embarking on travel or a career:

> You say you wonder why I didn't travel. It is simply because I cannot leave home. Grandma is 82 and I cannot leave her, for even a week's cruise. We live all alone and there is no one I can get to stay with her. I am very much tied down but it cannot be helped. (45-46)

The most nearly autobiographical of her child characters is Emily Starr. The jet black hair and deep blue eyes, the affection for cats, the stories of Scottish ancestors, the family pride, the strict Calvinistic upbringing, the sensitivity about being different from other children at school, the escape on the wings of imagination and the gift for the written word—"the best method of soul cultivation there is" (*The Green Gables Letters* 32)—belong to Lucy Maud. By using the epistolary device—Emily's letters to her dead father—the author projects an intimacy of experience that her other books lack:

> There has been a dark shadow over this day. I dropped my cent in church. . . . It made a dreadful noise. It felt as if everybody looked at me.
>
> My heart is very sore tonight. Mike died this morning. Cousin Jimmy says he must have been poisoned.
>
> I think maybe I'll write novels when I grow up as well as poetry. But Aunt Elizabeth won't let me read any novels so how can I find out how to write them?

The success with which Montgomery presents teenage boys—Jingles, the only believable character in *Pat*; Perry and Teddy in *Emily*; and Gilbert, who achieved immortality when he whispered "Carrots!"—results from her childhood association with Wellington and Dave, who boarded at her grandmother's, while the vivid pictures of uncles, aunts and cousins testify to the close observation of experienced clan life.

Because the author is so closely identified with Anne and Emily, she is able to present events, settings and other characters as they would be seen through the eyes of children. Anne's exuberant and exaggerated response to Green Gables is acceptable to the reader because it is appropriate to the character. Emily's appreciation of the Murray kitchen is what one might expect from a sharp-eyed eleven-year-old:

> The sanded floor was spotlessly white, but the boards had been scrubbed away through the years until the knots in them stuck up all over in funny little bosses. ... In one corner of the ceiling was a large square hole which looked black and spookish in the candlelight, and made her feel creepy. *Something* might pop down out of a hole like that if one hadn't behaved just right, you know.

In *Pat of Silver Bush* and *The Blue Castle* there is a confusion between the persona of the character and that of the author, with the cliché, cuteness and excessive romanticism which are evident in the author's own letters being imposed on the characters. For example, Valancy's rhapsodizing over the Blue Castle "drowned in sunset lilac light, incredibly delicate and elusive" seems inappropriate language for a thirty-year-old woman, even one who is considered queer.

In a letter to Weber of March 2, 1908, Montgomery somewhat deprecatingly describes *Anne* as "a story written more especially for girls and not pretending to be of any intrinsic interest to adults" (61). Whether an author is justified in placing limits of age and sex on a book is a questionable point; even more questionable is the implication that inferior writing is permissible in a book intended for children. That this kind of condescension mars many of L. M. Montgomery's books is unfortunately true. She wrote her "little yarns ... with an eye single to Sunday School scholars," as she told Weber in the last of the extant Cavendish letters (93-94). But Anne, the queer child, was approvingly received by the prestigious adult periodical, the *Spectator.* "I *did* feel flattered."

Notes

1. Cited in M. M. Mitchell's foreword to Hilda M. Ridley's *The Story of L. M. Montgomery* (London: Harrap, 1956). Montgomery gives another version of Mark Twain's views: "He wrote me that in *Anne* I had created

'the dearest and most lovable child in fiction since the immortal Alice'."
See *The Green Gables Letters from L. M. Montgomery to Ephraim Weber
1905-1909*, ed. Wilfrid Eggleston (Toronto: Ryerson, 1960) 80.

2. Cf. James Janeway's *A Token for Children: Being an Exact Account
of the Conversion, Holy and Exemplary Lives, and Joyful Deaths of
Several Young Children* (c. 1670).

3. See Leonard de Vries, ed., *Little Wide-Awake, an Anthology from
Victorian Children's Books and Periodicals in the Collection of Anne and
Fernand G. Renier* (London: Barker; Cleveland: World Publishing Company, 1967); *Young Wilfred or the Punishment of Falsehood* (London,
1821); Frederic Farrar's *Eric, or Little by Little* (London, 1858); and
Heinrich Hoffman's *Struwwelpeter* (trans. London, 1848) for examples
of the type.

4. That Montgomery admired Carroll is evident from her allusion to
Through the Looking Glass in a letter to Weber (10).

5. Biographical details are found in Ridley's *The Story of L. M.
Montgomery,* and in *The Green Gables Letters,* the general introduction
to which includes a brief biography of Montgomery (5-7).

Works Cited

Boswell's Life of Johnson. Oxford Standard Authors. London: Oxford
UP, 1953.

Brown, E. K. "The Problem of a Canadian Literature." *Masks of
Fiction.* Ed. A. J. M. Smith. Toronto: McClelland and Stewart, 1961.

Eggleston, Wilfrid, ed. *The Green Gables Letters from L. M. Montgomery to Ephraim Weber, 1905-1909.* Toronto: Ryerson, 1960.

Egoff, Sheila. *The Republic of Childhood.* Toronto: Oxford UP, 1967.

Grahame, Kenneth. *The Golden Age.* London, 1895.

Montgomery, L. M. *Anne of Green Gables.* Boston: Page, 1908.

_____. *The Blue Castle.* Toronto: McClelland and Stewart, 1926.

_____. *Emily of New Moon.* Toronto: McClelland and Stewart, 1923.

_____. *Pat of Silver Bush.* Toronto: McClelland and Steward, 1933.

The Decline of Anne

Matron vs. Child

Gillian Thomas

It is a cliché of popular literature that sequels tend to be disappointing, and students of children's literature are all too sadly familiar with the decline of writers who turn themselves into human factories on the basis of a successful first book. After the phenomenal success of *Anne of Green Gables* in 1908, L. M. Montgomery wrote well over a dozen more books with a similar setting, five of which concentrate on Anne herself as the central character. Although these five other Anne novels are by no means without interest, they lack many of the qualities that make the first book so appealing. Francis Bolger quotes Montgomery's own description of *Anne of Ingleside,* which records Anne's life as the matronly mother of five children, as "just a pot-boiler" (207), and one doubts if she would have taken Anne as the main character for another novel even if her writing career had been prolonged further.

The progressively unsatisfactory nature of the five Anne sequels reveals a good deal about why their forerunner was so successful. Several important factors are missing from the grown-up Anne. When we meet the young Anne, she is an orphan sitting alone in a railway station. As most children's librarians know, "books about orphans," evoking, as they do, a mixture of pity and envy, enjoy an immense popularity among child readers. However, far from being alienated and unwanted, Anne in the later books is totally absorbed in a dense social network of family and rural community. Similarly, much of the young Anne's appeal to female readers stems from the substance of the book's initial episode, in which Anne is almost sent away because Marilla and Matthew had wanted a boy but the orphanage has sent Anne by mistake. In a world in which most female children rapidly become aware that they would have enjoyed a higher status both within the family and in the outside world had they been born male, this episode is bound to have a powerful effect on its readers. By contrast, the grown-up Anne enjoys (at secondhand) the social status of her doctor husband and willingly accepts the social restrictions which result from that role.

If the Anne of the first book is often considered a spirited individualist, then the Anne of the final book seems a rather dreary conformist. A somewhat priggish tone is established at the very beginning of *Anne of Ingleside* where, when Anne remarks to her old friend Diana that Marilla still makes red-currant wine, "in spite of the minister and Mrs. Lynde . . . just to make us feel real devilish," Diana giggles at the piece of wickedness and thinks that she "did not mind 'devilish' as she would if anybody but Anne used it. Everybody knew Anne didn't really mean things like that. It was just her way" (7).

One of the episodes in *Anne of Ingleside* which is most reveal-ing of the adult Anne is the one in which her eight-year-old daughter, Di, becomes friendly with Jenny Penny, a new pupil at her school. Jenny's "background" is told to Anne by Susan, the Blythe family servant:

> They are a new family that have moved to the old Conway farm on the Base Line, Mrs. Dr. dear. Mr. Penny is said to be a carpenter who couldn't make a living carpentering . . . being too busy, as I understand, trying to prove there is no God . . . and has decided to try farming. From all I can make out they are a queer lot. The young ones do just as they like. He says he was bossed to death when he was a kid and his children are not going to be. (190)

Jenny, although a distinctly tougher character, has much of the storytelling ability of the young Anne and constantly fantasizes a more alluring family history for herself. Di is forbidden to go and stay overnight with Jenny because the Penny family are "unsuit-able" friends for the Doctor's children. When Di, at Jenny's insti-gation, sneaks away to the Pennys' house, she is appalled by its run-down appearance because she is "accustomed to the beauty and dignity of Ingleside." As the episode progresses, the Penny family fit more and more into the stereotype of the feckless working class, and the sequence culminates with the terrified Di playing dead and being dumped outside Ingleside by the equally terrified Penny children. Interestingly, however, there is no hint throughout this episode that Jenny's storytelling has a source similar to the fantasies of the young Anne in a lonely childhood or that her behavior merits any response short of condemnation.

The first few chapters of *Anne of Ingleside* are taken up with the deadening and interminable visit of Gilbert's Aunt Mary Maria. The old woman is an intolerable prude and bully, but Anne, out of loyalty to Gilbert, is unable to exert pressure to persuade her to leave, despite the fact that it is very clear that the situation is something of a nightmare for her:

> "I feel as you do in dreams when you're trying to run and can only drag your feet," said Anne drearily. "If it were only now and then . . . but it's every day. Meal times are perfect horrors now. . . ." (76)

This Anne, who seems the willing victim of social convention, is bound to disappoint the readers who so admired the spirited Anne of the first book. The child who stamped her foot at Mrs. Lynde and who walked the ridge-pole for a dare has vanished and left in her place a woman intent on observing the social proprieties and for whom "imagination" has come to mean something which very closely resembles sentimentality.

Curiously enough, in the midst of its flights of sentimentality, the final "pot-boiler," *Anne of Ingleside,* and its predecessor, *Anne's House of Dreams,* touch on much darker themes than the previous Anne novels. (Although it immediately precedes *Anne of Ingleside* in terms of the course of Anne's life, *Anne's House of Dreams* was actually published twenty-two years earlier in 1917. Another Anne novel, *Anne of Windy Poplars,* which takes up Anne's life as a teacher before her marriage, was published in 1936.) Anne's first baby dies. Her friend, Leslie Moore, lives out a death-in-life existence with her brain-damaged husband. Neither of these situations is permitted to become a permanent blight on the House of Dreams, however, for the stork (*sic*) brings Anne another child, and a highly contrived series of events, culminating in successful brain surgery, leads to the discovery that Leslie Moore's husband has been dead for many years and that "Dick Moore" is in fact her dead husband's amnesiac cousin. In *Anne of Ingleside* there is also the recurring theme of Anne's own death. Early in the novel, Anne's little son Walter, who is sent away in a state of mystification to stay with neighbors while his mother is due to give birth to another child, develops the obsession that she is dreadfully ill and likely to die. Naturally the episode ends cozily with hot milk, cookies, and comfort being dispensed, but the same theme recurs soon after when Anne almost dies of pneumonia.

Amid these reminders of death, the final Anne novel contains two other very odd episodes. In the first of these, Anne "remembers" what happened at Peter Kirk's funeral. Kirk had evidently treated both his wives quite brutally and was generally disliked in the community. His first wife's sister, Clara Wilson, attends the funeral and delivers a tirade against the dead man:

> "He smiled when he told her after her little baby was born dead that she might as well have died too, if she couldn't have anything but dead brats. She died after ten years of it . . . and I was glad she had escaped him. I told him then I'd never enter his house again till I came to his funeral. Some of you heard me. I've kept my word and now I've come and told the truth about him. It *is* the truth . . . *you* know it". . . . she pointed fiercely at Stephen Macdonald . . . "*you* know it". . . . the long finger darted at Camilla Blake . . . " *you* know it". . . . Olivia Kirk did not move a muscle . . . "*you* know it" . . . the poor minister himself felt as if that finger stabbed completely through him. (255-56)

The truth of Clara Wilson's tirade *is* confirmed by the action of Kirk's widow:

> Olivia Kirk rose before her and laid a hand on her arm. For a moment the two women looked at each other. The room was engulfed in silence that seemed like a personal presence.
>
> "Thank you, Clara Wilson," said Olivia Kirk. Her face was as inscrutable as ever but there was an undertone in her calm, even voice that made Anne shudder. She felt as if a pit had suddenly

opened before her eyes. Clara Wilson might hate Peter Kirk, alive and dead, but Anne felt that her hatred was a pale thing compared to Olivia Kirk's. (256)

This episode, the strangest and most powerful one in the novel, is immediately undercut by the "explanation" provided by Stephen Macdonald that Clara Wilson had been jilted in her youth by Peter Kirk. Thus the source of her hatred, which was originally shown as outrage at her sister's suffering, becomes instead the trivial vindictiveness of the jilted woman.

The novel, as a whole, ends on a muted note after an odd episode in which Anne believes that she is "losing" Gilbert to an old college acquaintance of theirs. They go to dinner with Christine Stuart, in whose company Gilbert is animated while having been quite remote and abstracted when with Anne. In the familiar Montgomery pattern, the darkness is quickly dispelled with the explanation that Gilbert's abstraction has been caused by his concern over a seriously ill patient who has now made a dramatic recovery. The book ends with a determined celebration of marriage and family which remains curiously unconvincing.

Marian Engel has remarked that Margaret Laurence's novels, "unlike the sentimental novels of . . . L. M. Montgomery . . . pull no punches about their community" (37). This remark, taken in relation to some of the elements in the later Anne novels discussed here, leads to some interesting conclusions about the nature of L. M. Montgomery's writing. If "serious" literature tends to explore individual consciousness and awareness, then popular literature tends more frequently to celebrate social bonding. The reunion with the long-lost relative and the cunningly engineered marriage of true minds make up the familiar fabric of nineteenth-century melodrama and "romantic" novels as well as of contemporary television soap opera.

If the young Anne's role is to transform Green Gables and its surroundings by the exercise of her "imagination," then the role of the grown-up Anne is more and more that of social engineer, bringing about the unions and reunions on which popular literature is so dependent. Once she is married, Anne becomes an indefatigable matchmaker:

"But they're all happy," protested Anne. "I'm really an adept.
Think of all the matches I've made ... or been accused of making
... Theodora Dix and Ludovic Speed ... Stephen Clark and
Prissie Gardner ... Janet Sweet and John Douglas ... Professor
Carter and Esme Taylor ... Nora and Jim ... Dovie and Jarvis.
..." (*Anne of Ingleside* 102)

Despite the incident at Peter Kirk's funeral, which raises the spectre
of sadism, and despite Anne's temporary apprehension that her own
marriage may be failing, all of Anne's matches are presented as
bringing about nothing short of perfect and permanent bliss for the
objects of her schemes. The only one of her matches which goes
awry does so because the couple she has marked out for one another
have already secretly planned to marry, and thus her scheming is
merely superfluous. The idea that some marriages can be unfulfill-
ing or destructive is scarcely allowed to intrude on Anne's world.
Similarly, while *Anne of Green Gables* and *Anne of Avonlea* incorporate and come to terms with some of the narrowness and petty
meanness which is a familiar component of life in a small community, this element is more and more firmly thrust aside in the later
Anne novels.

In part the shortcomings of the sequels to *Anne of Green Gables*
develop naturally from the genre of the sentimental novel to which
they belong. Their failings also spring from the social limitations
on Anne Blythe who must behave appropriately for her role as
"Mrs. Dr." It is a sad thought that, if the young Anne Shirley with
her sharp eye for social hypocrisy were to meet her own grown-up
self, she would probably not find that she was a "kindred spirit."

Works Cited

Bolger, Francis W. P. *The Years Before Anne*. Charlottetown, PE:
    Prince Edward Island Heritage Foundation, 1974.
Engel, Marian. *Globe and Mail*, 19 April 1975: 37.
Montgomery, L. M. *Anne of Ingleside*. 1939. Toronto: McClelland and
    Stewart, 1972.

Progressive Utopia

Or, How to Grow Up Without Growing Up

Perry Nodelman

A solitary young girl is traveling—in an old stage coach on a dusty road, or an open buggy on a pretty street, or another buggy on a road "fringed with blooming wild cherry-trees and slim white birches." Maybe she is in a railway carriage, or just on a footpath where "the air is fragrant with the scent of mountain flowers."[1] The girl may be five or nine but is most likely eleven. She probably has remarkable eyes—"big blue eyes" (Pollyanna), "big eyes . . . full of spirit and vivacity" (Anne), "eyes like faith" that "glowed like two stars" (Rebecca). Her other physical characteristics are less imposing. She is "a small dark-haired person in a glossy buff calico dress" (Rebecca) or "a slender little girl in . . . red-checked ging-ham" (Pollyanna) or in "a very short, very tight, very ugly dress of yellowish gray wincey" (Anne). Perhaps she is just "a plain little piece of goods" in a black dress (Mary), or perhaps she is "wearing two frocks, one on top of the other" (Heidi). Whatever she is wearing, the people she is traveling towards will probably not approve of it.

Those people will be old, or they will act as if they are old. They will be stiff and unfriendly, very strict about themselves and others. They will have suffered greatly in the past, probably because of thwarted love, and they will be unmarried or widowed. They will probably have a strong sense of duty. And the child who is about to descend on them will transform their lives and make them happy.

This is the warmhearted world of the traditional novel for girls. While such novels are no longer written, many of the ones produced decades ago are still widely read. The continuing popularity of these novels is surprising, given the great differences between ourselves and our grandparents; but even more surprising is their likeness to each other. Heidi, Anne of Green Gables, Pollyanna, Rebecca of Sunnybrook Farm, Mary of *The Secret Garden*—they live in widely separate countries, but their similarities outnumber their differences. They all live the same story, and they come to seem like variations of an ideal of female childhood that transcends national boundaries, and even the boundaries of time—for we still find the story enticing.

This is the story. The young girl, an orphan, arrives at her new home, which belongs to a relative, an aunt or a grandfather who has probably been living alone for a long time. Her sensible or faded clothing does not suit her character; she is a spontaneous and ebullient child, quite unaffected by her previous history of misfortune and deprivation. (Mary Lennox of *The Secret Garden* is an exception—her spontaneity and ebullience don't emerge until later in the novel.)

Luckily, our heroine's new home is a place of some physical comfort—a refuge from the deprivation she has suffered so far. There is enough food, and she will have a room of her own for the first time. The room is sparsely furnished, but it has a window. Through the window, she will see beautiful prospects of trees or flowers or mountains, and probably think of them as "delicious" (*Rebecca, Pollyanna*).

But as it turns out, the physical comfort of the new house is not matched by its emotional atmosphere. Its current inhabitants, who are old and solitary and unhappy, make it a bleak and sterile place. It is quite cut off from the beauty to be seen from its windows. There is little evidence of love, and there are many hard rules for a young child to learn.

Nevertheless, our heroine usually loves her new home. So she tries to love the people who live there, and to live by their rules. Sometimes she *does* love them, because she is too innocent to see how unlovable they are. Sometimes she finds them hard to love, but manages it anyway.

In fact, her almost magical qualities seem to triumph over every bad circumstance. She does not change much in the course of the events that follow—she manages somehow to age without becoming terribly different. But the wonderful qualities she starts with and

never loses have remarkable effects on other people, who change miraculously.

Bad ones become good ones; nasty people turn nice, uncharitable people give things away, potential divorcees decide to stay married. Or perhaps bad people are replaced by good ones; both the unsatisfactory minister and the unsatisfactory teacher Anne Shirley finds ensconced in Avonlea on her arrival are magically replaced by people she likes.

But most frequently, it turns out that the bad people were not really bad at all; while they have been soured by experience, they only need the presence of our remarkable heroine to rediscover their goodness. As Pollyanna tells an apparently nasty man, "I'm sure you're much nicer than you look," and he is, of course. Our heroine's major talent is the ability to restore the past—to return grown-ups to the happiness they felt in their youth. "That man is waking up after being asleep for over sixty years," says Rachel Lynde of Matthew Cuthbert.

Matthew is not the only grown-up awakened by the magic touch of youth; it happens to Aunt Jane and Aunt Miranda and Aunt Polly, to various friends and other people in the environs, to Heidi's grandfather, and so on. The process is carried to the extreme in *The Secret Garden*. Not only does the coming of spring and the resurrection of the garden change a desolate and decaying place into a lovely one; it also seems to cause human beings to spring up from nowhere, almost as if they had been hibernating. An apparently almost deserted house containing only a few unhappy people turns out to be a surprisingly populous one, and the people are all happy ones.

But despite, or perhaps because of, our heroine's magic ability to awaken dormant joyousness, this is a story without a plot. There is no suspense, no one action that gets more complicated as the novel progresses and is resolved at the end. In emotional terms, each episode merely repeats and amplifies the episodes preceding it; it causes an increase in the available amount of happiness, which gets larger as the novel gets longer.

In fact, there can be as many episodes as the novelist can think of, without much change to the texture or meaning of the whole. Entire chapters, like the one about Pollyanna's encounter with a minister in the woods, are quite separate from anything else that happens, and could easily be left out. Other chapters could be added, and perhaps that is why so many of these novels have sequels. The important thing is that each episode ends with someone feeling better about himself and the world he lives in. The same thing happens again and again; if we are entertained, it is not because we want to find out what will happen, but because we know what will happen, and like it happening, and want it to keep on happening.

What each episode consists of is this: our child heroine shocks, and then delights, repressed or unhappy grown-ups with her childish spontaneity and lack of artifice. In acting "naturally," she makes them more natural, and brings an end to the artificial repression of their overcivilized values. She restores them to what they once were. This is made particularly obvious in *Rebecca of Sunnybrook Farm*. Rebecca's Aunt Jane, who responds immediately to her, says, "I remember well enough how I felt at her age." Aunt Miranda, who is more rigid, and who never admits to the degree to which her contact with Rebecca has transformed her, says, "You was considerable of a fool at her age, Jane." Jane's answer reveals the heart of all these novels: "Yes I was, thank the Lord. I only wish I'd known how to take a little of my foolishness along with me, as some folks do, to brighten my declining years." Fortunately, she *has* brought it along, and Rebecca reveals it to her.

But there is some ambiguity about the "foolishness" of childhood. Our heroine does things that are meant to make us laugh. She dyes her hair green, or saves dinner rolls in her closet, or invites missionaries to dinner on the spur of the moment. Since she is too innocent to know what she ought not to do, her life is a series of comic disasters, in which her spontaneity and her ignorance of the ways of the world get her into trouble at the same time as they endear her to us. And while we are meant to find her actions delightful, we must also realize that spontaneity has its dangers.

Consequently, each time our heroine displays her innocence, she learns to be less innocent. As the grown-ups become more like children, the children become more like grown-ups. As the young Rebecca says to her friend Mr. Aladdin, "If you don't like me to grow old, why don't you grow young? Then we can meet at the halfway house and have nice times. Now that I think about it . . . that's just what you've been doing all along." In fact, that is what happens to the characters in all these novels. They start at opposite extremes, and gradually change until they are much like each other; old people find their sobriety balanced by joy, and young people have their spontaneity balanced by discretion; the old rediscover the pleasures of imagination, and the young discover the virtues of common sense.

Finally, because our heroine is learning something important, she is tested. We must see that she can apply her magic gifts of healing to herself—that she can act on her own teachings. So the even tenor of her life, the continuing ebb and flow of not particularly significant events, is interrupted. Something serious happens, usually in the second last chapter.

Not always, however—Heidi confronts her problem earlier, in her imprisonment in Frankfurt, and Mary Lennox's problems end as the novel begins. But in these two novels, the story is not complete; their heroines do not grow old enough to complete it. There is no test at the end, for the test seems to signify the end of childhood, and Heidi and Mary remain triumphantly young, triumphantly magical. This is not to say that the myth expressed by all these novels is not complete in *Heidi* and *The Secret Garden;* it is. Other people in these novels *do* pass the test and manage either to retain their youthful spirits or to rediscover them.

For a heroine who gets older, the test is hard indeed. She becomes seriously ill; perhaps, even, unable to walk. Will she have the strength to heal herself as she healed others? Or perhaps a loved one dies. Will she be able to accept death and still be joyful? Or her glorious plans for the future are thwarted. Will she be able to accept it? She will, of course. She will feel what L. M. Montgomery in *Anne of Green Gables* calls "the cold, sanctifying touch" of sorrow, and be sanctified by it. All ends happily; happiness has progressed to its point of perfect ripeness.

That is the story. The question is, why is it so consistent? Why are these novels so similar to each other, and so satisfying in their consistencies?

To begin with, the setting of these novels, a house in a pleasant rural location, is important. Such a place offers the pleasures of nature without its wild savagery, and the pleasures of civilization without its urban constrictions. It is a place to relax in, something like paradise. Clearly nothing very unpleasant will happen here.

In fact, nothing unpleasant does happen. The classic novels for boys always start with their heroes leaving home, and describe their exciting confrontations with hardship and evil in wild, uncomfortable places, until they finally come home again. These novels for girls start with their heroine's arrival at what is to be her home, *after* a series of unsettling adventures which are glossed over rather than described; once she gets home, she does nothing but grow up quietly. In boys' books, things start badly and get worse, almost until the very end. In these girls' books, things start well and get better, almost until the very end. The pleasure offered readers is something not usually considered desirable in fiction—lack of suspense, lack of excitement, lack of conflict; it is a pleasure we might associate more with our indulgence in utopian dreams than with our love of a good story.

But not quite; the place may be perfect, but the people who live there need working on. In fact, that is why these novels might best be called progressive utopias. They begin with a heroine's arrival at an almost perfect place; and after that, the heroine's action on the community makes it an even more perfect place. Sympathetic readers can partake in the creation of heaven on earth and be satisfied in realizing that heaven on earth is the world one already lives in—not a deserted island in the South Seas, not a lost corner of Africa, not the exciting past or the glorious future, but home. The growing happiness of the inhabitants of utopia is their growing understanding that home is in fact utopia.

The children who bring them to that satisfying awareness share some important characteristics. They are all girls, of course, and therefore ideally suited to the unexciting pleasures of home—or so these novels assume. And they are all orphans. Without parents (or in Rebecca's case, with only one parent) to guide them and restrain them, they have not been spoiled by grown-up attitudes—they are purely and essentially childlike. In fact, they are symbols of childhood and its virtues, pure manifestations of qualities that would be muddied in less detached children. These girls all transcend the specifics of their situations and develop almost mythic intensity. Their novelists adore them, and expect readers to adore them too. Rebecca is called "a little brown elf," and Anne "some wild divinity of the shadowy places." Such divinities clearly represent something of importance.

That thing is best expressed by the poet Wordsworth; as Kate Douglas Wiggin says in *Rebecca of Sunnybrook Farm*, "Blessed Wordsworth! How he makes us understand." What Wordsworth made the generations who followed him understand and take to heart is that childhood innocence is automatically sympathetic with the healing beauties of nature, which are themselves divine, and which we become blind to in maturity. "Heaven lies about us in our infancy," and as children, we perceive "splendour in the grass . . . glory in the flower." Grown-ups usually can't do that. But Anne says, "If I really wanted to pray I'll tell you what I'd do. I'd go out into a great big field all alone, or I'd look up into the sky—up—up—up—into that lovely blue sky that looks as if there was no end to its blueness. And then I'd just *feel* a prayer." Heidi feels the same way about mountains: "everything seemed more beautiful than she had expected. . . . It was so lovely, Heidi stood with tears pouring down her cheeks, and thanked God for letting her come home again." Both Rebecca and Pollyanna escape restrictive houses into "delicious" landscapes, and in *The Secret Garden,* the most symbolic of these novels, God's "Magic" expresses itself best in natural landscapes. Colin says, "Sometimes since I've been in the garden I've looked up through the trees at the sky and I have had a strange feeling of being happy, as if something were pushing and drawing in my chest and making me breathe fast. Magic is always pushing and drawing and making things out of nothing. . . . The magic in the garden has made me stand up and know I'm going to be a man." In fact, spontaneous feelings are prayer, and Nature is God's cathedral; L. M. Montgomery tells us how "a glimpse of painted sunset sky shone like a great rose window at the end of a cathedral aisle."

Children, being unrepressed by societal values, are naturally responsive to the divine joys of Nature. As Wordsworth said, a child is the

> . . . best Philosopher, who yet dost keep
> Thy heritage, thou Eye among the blind,
> . . . .
> Mighty Prophet! Seer blest!
> On whom these truths do rest,
> Which we are toiling all our lives to find,
> In darkness lost. . . .

Our orphans are all "seers blest." And because these novels give us, not the real world but an idealized one, all of them show the way to those older than themselves who are "in darkness lost."

They are lost in darkness because they feel a strong sense of "Duty"—a virtue Wordsworth called the "Stern Daughter of the Voice of God," and opposed to natural, childlike spontaneity, for it made him act against his own natural feelings. Wordsworth eventually got tired of "uncharted freedom" and "chance desires," and gave in to Duty; but as a poem by Rebecca suggests, that is not the case in these novels of child worship:

> When Joy and Duty clash
> Let Duty go to smash.

Not that Duty isn't important. Children do grow up and have to face responsibility, and in any case, natural spontaneity is not always a virtue, despite our wistful admiration of it; it is self-centered and antisocial. In fact, the authors of these novels even pretend to dislike it. Rebecca, we are told, "never stopped to think, more's the pity," and we are expected to see that our heroines get into trouble whenever they don't stop to think. But we cannot really take that seriously, for it is their spontaneity that makes these girls adorable. While our heroines do look Duty in the face, their spirits are not quenched by it. They age without losing their childlike qualities, grow up without actually growing up; that is the heart of the appeal of these novels.

Even from the beginning, our heroine's spontaneous joy in living has not been destroyed by circumstances that ought to have destroyed it. Only Mary Lennox begins depressed, and she soon regains her happiness and her innocence. So does her friend Colin; apparently one *can* go home again. The other girls have suffered before the novels begin, but show no signs of it; the message is that bitter experience does *not* quench true childish joy. In fact, Anne and Rebecca, who do eventually grow up physically, never lose their childlike qualities. That is why they are tested—tested and found to be unresponsive to experience, terminally incapable of not being, as Pollyanna insists, "glad" no matter what. They are only slightly restrained by the women's bodies and lives they inhabit. The mature Rebecca is still a "bewildering being, who gave wings to thoughts that had only crept before; who brought color and grace and harmony into the dun brown texture of existence." And as Anne tells us, "I'm not a bit changed—not really. I'm only just pruned down and branched out. The real me—back here—is just the same."

They are still childlike divinities of the shadowy places, just as Mary and Heidi and Pollyanna are.

Contemporary feminists might well find these novels objectionable. Their central message is that a comfortable home is heaven and that the perfect divinities to occupy that home are women who act much like children. The utopia these novels progress towards is actually a regressive world of perfect childlike innocence. But despite our revised ideals both of childhood and femininity, many readers are not revolted. In growing up, or merely in allowing people who have grown up to become children again, our heroines perform a miracle that readers apparently would still like to believe in.

One of the ugly things the philosophy of the Romantic movement accomplished for us in its admiration of childlike qualities was the divorce of childhood from maturity. Until the early nineteenth century, children weren't thought to be much different from grown-ups; they certainly weren't thought to be better than grown-ups. But Blake and Wordsworth changed all that, and we still believe that children think differently, see differently, and feel differently from the way we do. While this conviction helps us immeasurably in our dealings with children, it does create problems. It separates us from our own past selves, and it makes children into strangers in our midst. Worst of all, it makes childhood, which inevitably passes, agonizingly enticing to us—somehow better than, richer than, realer than the maturity we are stuck with. It forces us into a fruitless nostalgia—a lust for something we simply cannot have anymore.

But in the wish-fulfillment world of the novels of progressive utopia, we can have it again. Childhood never really ends; the most childlike children never really grow up, and even terminally mature people can become childlike again. It is the secret desire of grown-ups to be children again that makes these novels so appealing to grown-ups, and it may be the secret desire of children to never grow up that makes these novels appealing to them. Apparently these desires transcend both place and time.

Furthermore, these desires are just one version of a central concern of children's literature, no matter where or when it was written—how to grow up, as one inevitably must, without losing the virtues and delights of childhood. This is the subject of *Harriet the Spy* and *Tom's Midnight Garden* and *The Little Prince* just as much as it is the subject of *Treasure Island* and *Tom Sawyer* and *Swiss Family Robinson.* As long as we produce books especially for children because we are convinced that childhood is quite different from maturity, it may be the only thing a good children's book is ever about.

Notes

1. The novels the solitary young girl travels in are, respectively, *Rebecca of Sunnybrook Farm* by Kate Douglas Wiggin, *Pollyanna* by Eleanor H. Porter, *Anne of Green Gables* by L. M. Montgomery, *The Secret Garden* by Frances Hodgson Burnett, and *Heidi* by Johanna Spyri. The popularity of these books over the decades means that they have been available in many different editions. The translation of *Heidi* that I have used is by Eileen Hall (Penguin-Puffin, 1956).

Calling Back the Ghost of the Old-Time Heroine

Duncan, Montgomery, Atwood, Laurence, and Munro

Catherine Ross

Writing in *The Week* in 1886, Sara Jeanette Duncan pretends to regret the passing of the old-time romantic heroine, who has been pushed into oblivion by the new school of realists to which Duncan herself belongs:

> It would be strange indeed if we did not regret her, this daughter of the lively imagination of a bygone day. By long familiarity, how dear her features grew! Having heard of her blue eyes, with what zestful anticipation we foreknew the golden hair, the rose-bud mouth, the faintly-flushed, ethereal cheek . . . of the blond maiden! Wotting of her ebon locks, with what subtle prescience we guessed the dark and flashing optics, the alabaster forehead, the lips curved in fine scorn, the regal height, and the very unapproachable demeanour of the brunette! The fact that these startling differences were purely physical . . . never interfered with our joyous interest in them as we breathlessly followed their varying fortunes from an auspicious beginning, through harrowing vicissitudes, to a blissful close. . . . She was the painted pivot of the merry-go-round—it could not possibly revolve, with its exciting episodes, without her; yet her humble presence bore no striking relation to the mimic pageant that went on about her.

Thus directed by Duncan, we smile with nostalgia in memory of the old-time heroine and call to mind Canadian examples such as the fair Amélie in *The Golden Dog* (1877) or the fair Clara De Haldemar in *Wacousta* (1832). "To features which looked as if chiselled out of the purest Parian marble, just flushed with the glow of morn, and cut in those perfect lines of perfection . . ."—this passage describes Amélie although it might do equally well for Clara. As Duncan astutely observes, such a heroine is a compositional device, "the painted pivot of the merry-go-round." She is the passive but suffering center of an elaborately patterned design of incidents: "auspicious beginning . . . harrowing vicissitudes. . . a blissful close." Plot comes first; the heroine has no character to speak of to conflict with the plot or to make the unfolding incidents less likely to occur than any others. In *Wacousta,* for example, Clara I falls victim to De Haldemar's bride-snatching tactics in order to provide the motive for *Wacousta's* revenge plot. Clara II gets herself captured by Wacousta so that she can be taken to his grisly tent and told, along with the reader, Wacousta's secret history. In the "realistic" novel that Duncan herself champions, however, character comes first. "The woman of today," says Duncan in the same *Week* article, "bears a translatable relation to the world" and appears in novels that are "reflection[s] of our present social state." The realistic novel sacrifices the designing power belonging to romances like *Wacousta,* where apparent coincidences are there to clarify the moral relationships among events. Instead it chooses literary conventions that bear "a translatable relation to the world" or, more accurately, conventions that make the fictional world appear to correspond with something in the world outside.

A major one of these conventions is parody. The principle here is that the more the fiction departs from or inverts the conventions of romance, the more it appears to resemble life and therefore to be "realistic." This principle accounts for the continual reinvoking of the old-time heroine's shade from oblivion, chiefly as a contrast to the real heroine of the book. In *The Imperialist* (1904), Duncan herself parodies the old-time heroine in Miss Dora Milburn, a fallen divinity contrasting in every way with Advena, who is marked out by name and character as the heroine of the future.

Dora, when we first meet her, is "perform[ing] lightly at the piano" in the approved style for old-time heroines. The elements in her composition are all familiar, but Duncan subjects them to an unwonted scrutiny and passes judgment:

> She was a tall fair girl, with several kinds of cleverness. She did her hair quite beautifully, and she had a remarkable, effective, useful reticence.... [Her reflections] went on behind a faultless coiffure and an expression almost classical in its detachment; but if Miss Milburn could have thought on a level with her looks I, for one, would hesitate to take any liberty with her meditations. (53-54)

Dora can never recover from the devastating effect of Duncan's word "useful." Duncan's irony emphasizes the disparity between Dora's exterior loveliness and her poverty of character. Seeing the physical beauty, Lorne ascribes to Dora all those absent moral and spiritual qualities which the reader has always gladly supplied for the heroine of romance. Duncan's literary point here—that the old-time heroine represents a false ideal—comes to the aid of the social and political themes of the novel. In presenting Dora, Duncan parodies what she considers an outmoded literary convention to criticize the dying Colonial tradition—the "Filkin tradition"—that Dora represents. Lorne's misperception of Dora, moreover, parallels his misjudgment of the Imperial question, which misjudgment itself results from the same misplaced idealism.

Advena as heroine is another matter. She forms the greatest possible contrast to Dora, for Duncan, in presenting Advena according to the conventions of realism, systematically overturns most of the established conventions of romance. Dora is to be found sitting prettily at her piano; Advena always has her nose in a book. Dora accepts male adoration as her due; Advena's mother "would have been sorry for the man if he had arrived [to court Advena], but he had not arrived" (32). The plot involving Advena is a familiar one of comic romance, but Duncan gives it a new twist by parodying some of its central features. Frequently the low point for the romantic heroine is her exposure as a living sacrifice to some dreadful fate. In *The Imperialist,* drawn perhaps to mortification of the flesh because of her enthusiasm for Plato and for Yoga, Advena casts herself in this sacrificial role. In such a spirit, she offers herself up to Miss Cameron of Scotland, who has arrived in Elgin to marry Hugh Finlay, the man Advena loves:

she was there simply to offer herself up, and the impulse of
sacrifice seldom considers whether or not it may be understood.
. . . We know of Advena that she was prone to this form of
exaltation. (218)

This parody of the sacrifice of the virgin is used to criticize
Advena's and Hugh's immense idealism, which, like Lorne's idealism over Dora and Imperialism, must yield finally to the force of
social reality.

The solution to this plot is provided by Dr. Drummond, who,
attracted to Miss Cameron's mature charms and impressed by her
quick understanding of the points of church administration, decides
to marry her himself. This arrangement, "much more suitable in
every way" (254), represents in the novel the conquest of "realism"
over quixoticism. *The Imperialist* nevertheless conforms to the
conventions of comic romance in its final ritual pairings, leaving
only Lorne excluded from the general festivity; and it does not
escape the reader's attention that, however ironic the texture of the
book with its technique of parodying the old-time heroine, Advena
is in fact involved in a plot with exactly the same structure as that
which used to propel the old-time heroine from "an auspicious
beginning, through harrowing vicissitudes, to a blissful close." One
of the effects of the balance between Advena's plot with its happy
ending and Lorne's plot with its ironic ending is to draw attention
to the design of the book.

In *Anne of Green Gables* (1908), the old-time heroine, while
not a separate character like Dora, nevertheless exists in Anne's
imagination, embodied in the impossible Cordelias and Geraldines
of her reading. Red-headed and freckled, Anne herself seems
plausible, even "realistic," in comparison with those creatures with
golden locks and alabaster brows who cultivate "lifelong sorrow"
(18) and lead lives that are "a perfect graveyard of buried hopes"
(40). Anne tries to recreate Avonlea as a romantic setting, renaming
the Avenue as "the White Way of Delight," Barry's Pond as "the
Lake of Shining Waters," and herself as Cordelia. But the point
made repeatedly in incident after incident is the contrast between
the romantic Cordelia who inhabits a world completely bound by
convention and the "real-life" Anne who lives in Avonlea where
romance is sabotaged by "life." This contrast does not disguise the
fact that *Anne of Green Gables* itself follows an overall structure

that is pure comic romance. Anne's role is to be the "unprized precious maid" who, like Lear's Cordelia, "redeems nature from the general curse." The orphaned waif whom nobody wants or loves enters two unfulfilled lives and transforms them with her own love and imagination. Moreover, she starts off in yellowish-gray wincey and ends up in glorious puffed sleeves. But the technique of contrasting Anne with the old-time heroine is the justification for Anne's claim to a verisimilitude never possessed by the completely formulaic characters of romance—and this despite the very obvious structural similarities between Anne's own story of an orphan who finds happiness winning the hero and the fairytales and romances that Montgomery is parodying.

The chapter "An Unfortunate Lily Maid" shows clearly Montgomery's method of parody and the close connection between parody and what Northrop Frye calls "realistic displacement" (136-38). Anne and her friends dramatize Elaine's dolorous voyage on her death-barge by adjusting the details of Tennyson's "Lancelot and Elaine" to the capacities of Prince Edward Island school girls. Thus Anne, whose red hair has just been chopped off after she has dyed it a "queer dull bronzy green," becomes Elaine with "all her bright hair streaming down." An old black shawl is used to "pall the barge in all its length in blackest samite"; an old piano scarf becomes the "cloth of gold for coverlet"; a tall iris substitutes for Elaine's white lily. The outcome of this episode makes the point that the "real life" heroine has to contend with unruly incursions from the actual world that never disturb the conventions governing old-time heroines:

> For a few minutes Anne, drifting slowly down, enjoyed the romance of her situation to the full. Then something happened not at all romantic. The flat began to leak. In a very few moments it was necessary for Elaine to scramble to her feet, pick up her cloth of gold coverlet and pall of blackest samite and gaze blankly at a big crack in the bottom of her barge through which the water was literally pouring. (237)

Anne is forced to abandon her role as the doomed lily maid and clamber onto a slippery bridge pile to wait till Gilbert comes to the rescue "rowing under the bridge in Harmon Andrews' dory." This ending undercuts the romantic formulas by asserting the superior claims of reality that, with its sharp stakes, tears the bottoms out of barges. But while achieving this effect, Montgomery has also, one notes, shifted her pattern of literary parody from romantic elegy to romantic comedy; from Elaine's fatal unrequited love for Lancelot to the story of, as Anne puts it elsewhere, "an enchanted princess shut up in a lonely tower with a handsome knight riding to [her] rescue on a coal-black steed" (173). Thus Montgomery anticipates the happy outcome of Gilbert's role as patient suitor and princess-rescuer, while mocking the romance formula that she herself is using.

This episode of the unfortunate lily maid is the culmination of a series of earlier episodes that all follow—one might say too predictably—the same pattern and that all teach a similar lesson: adopting romance formulas as a basis for real life results in a mortifying comeuppance. Anne learns finally, so she says, to distinguish between romance, which is a convention of fiction, and "real life," which goes on in Avonlea: "I have come to the conclusion that it is no use trying to be romantic in Avonlea. It was probably easy enough in towered Camelot hundreds of years ago, but romance is not appreciated now" (242). This remark by a fictional character about a set of characters whom *she* considers fictional opens up a series of receding planes, like the girl on the Dutch Cleanser container who holds a Dutch Cleanser container which has another girl. . . . The effect for the reader resembles looking at a set of mirrors: a character at one remove from the reader's world uses parody to put at one remove from himself a romance world of recognized conventions and elaborate design.

Margaret Atwood's *Lady Oracle* (1976) also features a red-haired heroine who tries unsuccessfully to model her life according to fictional patterns. This book is deliberate in its use of receding mirrors to suggest the relation between what the heroine herself would call art and life but what we would perceive as the conventions of romance and of realism. *Lady Oracle* begins with Joan Foster on "the other side" in Terremoto, Italy, after a bungled fake suicide and a supposed rebirth to a new identity. (The opposition of "this side" and "the other side" is a recurrent metaphor used to distinguish between life and art.[1]) From this vantage point, she recalls her past life, from childhood to the present, while at the same time she tries to finish off her last Costume Gothic, *Stalked by Love*. This structure of juxtaposed episodes from her own life affords an opportunity for contrast between the conventionalized characters who belong in Costume Gothics and the multidimensional and shifting characters who belong in "realistic" fiction. According to the conventions of the Costume Gothic, the hero is always tall, aloof, and Byronic. The heroine is always a pale orphaned virgin who tracks down the hero to his Gothic manor, disposes of the unscrupulous rival female, and maneuvers the hero into marriage. According to the conventions that govern realism, characters can be both hero and villain simultaneously—like Joan's rescuer on the bridge who "was elusive, he melted and changed his shape" (61) or like her father "healer and killer" (295). Although the contrast here concerns the differing ways two literary conventions handle character and admit elements of design, Joan—herself a fictional character developed according to the conventions of realism—naturally sees the contrast as a difference between the art world of her Costume Gothics and the real world where she herself lives:

> I longed for the simplicity of the world, where happiness was possible and wounds were only ritual ones. Why had I been closed out from that impossible white paradise where love was as final as death, and banished to this other place where everything changed and shifted? (286)

Joan spends much of her time trying to escape from her own life by identifying herself with the heroines of romance who inhabit "that impossible white paradise" on the "Other Side" or on the "Far Shore." In one episode Joan, imagining herself to be Samantha Deane fleeing the illicit attentions of the hero Sir Edmund De Vere in *Escape from Love,* is approached by Arthur who is banning the bomb. In the Costume Gothic, Samantha rakes Sir Edmund's cheek with her handy crewelling needle; in the main narrative Joan is chagrined to find herself "lying on top of a skinny, confused-looking young man" (164) who has a cut cheek. This rhythm of romantic illusion and "realistic" accommodation, which in *Anne* is a repeated structuring principle of chapters and incidents, is in *Lady Oracle* more firmly tied to the main theme of the relation between art and life, romance and realism.

Curiously enough Montgomery and Atwood both have chosen Camelot and the Elaine-Lady of Shalott figure as their image for the shadowy world of romance. This world can be preserved only by being kept from contact with the real world, which sinks the barge, cracks the mirror, explodes the illusion. Joan remarks, "You could stay in the tower for years, weaving away, looking in the mirror, but one glance out the window at real life and that was that. The curse, the doom" (316). Like the mirror, the Lady of Shalott can create her gorgeous colored tapestries only at the expense of denying herself participation in the life she depicts. The outside world is admitted into her tower only as content for the artistic form she is weaving. Once it is allowed to provide the shape, the result is that collapse of order which "realistic" fiction tries to imitate by its technique of parody and inversion.

Both Anne and Joan use the image of the double in the mirror to suggest their sense of the difference between their own mixed and often painful lives and the simpler life of a romantic heroine in an Arcadian world. Anne's visual double Katie Maurice and her sound double Violet owe something to the myth of Narcissus and Echo:

> We used to pretend that the bookcase was enchanted and that if I only knew the spell I could open the door and step right into the room where Katie Maurice lived. . . . And then Katie Maurice would have taken me by the hand and led me into a wonderful place, all flowers and sunshine and fairies, and we would have lived there happy for ever after. . . . [Near Mrs. Hammond's] there was a long green little valley, and the loveliest echo lived there. . . . So I imagined that it was a little girl called Violetta. . . . (63)

Likewise Joan imagines that she has a "shadowy twin" living in the "never-never land" on the other side of the mirror (247) and enacting all the conventional wish-fulfillment plots of her Costume Gothics. The mirrors recede one plane further when Joan's heroine and romance double, Penelope in *Love, My Ransom,* herself enters the mirror world: "further into the mirror she went, and further, till she seemed to be walking on the other side of the glass, in a land of indistinct shadows" (220). And in the most obvious instance of mirror worlds, Atwood has written a book called *Lady Oracle* about Joan Foster who has written a book called *Lady Oracle.* The deeper one goes into this hall of mirrors behind mirrors, the less things seem to bear what Duncan calls a "translatable relation to the world" and the more they conform to the ritualized designs of plot, the elaborate patternings of characters, and the polarized oppositions of demonic and paradisal that are conventions of romance.

Both Anne and Joan write their mirror-double into plots whose very clear designs are stylized versions of their own less obviously shaped lives. In the chapter "The Story Club is Formed," Anne writes "The Jealous Rival; or, In Death Not Divided." Into the conventional opposition in romance of dark and fair heroine, Anne projects her own adolescent jealousy of Diana's future husband, a jealousy already admitted to at the end of chapter fifteen: "'It's about Diana,' sobbed Anne luxuriously.... 'Diana will get married and go away and leave me.... I hate her husband—I just hate him furiously'" (126). Here is how Anne describes "The Jealous Rival" to Diana:

> It's about two beautiful maidens called Cordelia Montmorency and Geraldine Seymour who lived in the same village and were devotedly attached to each other. Cordelia was a regal brunette with a coronet of midnight hair and duskly flashing eyes. Geraldine was a queenly blonde with hair like spun gold and velvety purple eyes. . . . Then Bertram De Vere came to their native village and fell in love with the fair Geraldine.... All [Cordelia's] affection for Geraldine turned to bitter hate and she vowed that [Geraldine] would never marry Bertram. . . . [After causing Geraldine's and Bertram's deaths by drowning, Cordelia] went insane with remorse and was shut up in a lunatic asylum. (223)

Wotting of these heroines' dark and fair hair, with what subtle prescience do we guess the rest. We know that the hero would have a name like Bertram De Vere, which clearly belongs in the same class as, say, Frederick De Haldemar in *Wacousta* or Edmund De Vere in Joan's *Escape from Love* and differs from names like Charlie Sloan or Chuck Brewer that identify characters of realism. The plot is a neat piece of design involving number patterns of two and one as well as the almost compulsory color pattern of dark and fair. Likewise Joan's fictional *alter ego* of her Costume Gothic participates in a ballet for three characters—the hero, heroine, and female rival—who go through conventional motifs of amnesia, madness, and ritual death before, in this case, the inevitable happy ending. Joan's comments on her writing of *Stalked by Love* indicate

her theoretical awareness of the conventional function of her characters as compositional devices in elaborate plots: "The heroines
of my books were mere stand-ins" (31) and "I knew what had to
happen. Felicia, of course, would have to die; such was the fate of
wives" (317).

Joan's difficulty in completing *Stalked by Love* is caused by her
inability, in practice, to keep separate these conventions of romance
and realism, a confusion which duplicates her tendency to confuse
romantic formulas with her own life. In defiance of the conventions
of romance, Felicia starts to develop the rounded character belonging to realistic heroines. She acquires most of Joan's own characteristics, she becomes sympathetic, and her qualities begin to
conflict with her role in the plot. Joan says, "It was all wrong.
Sympathy for Felicia was out of the question, it was against the
rules, it would foul up the plot completely" (321). While her heroine
is starting to behave as a character of realism, Joan herself still
yearns to be a romantic heroine in an "impossible white paradise."
Her flight to Italy, to the "Other Side," was of course intended as
an escape from her multiple and shifting identities. Realism is a
"snarl, a rat's nest of dangling threads and loose ends" (295), or at
least the shaped mimesis of such; Joan wants "happy endings. . . .
the feeling of release when everything turn[s] out right" (321).

The multiple endings provided by the double resolutions to
Felicia's Costume Gothic narrative and Joan's frame narrative bring
about the predicted implosion of the conventions of romance and
realism and a collapse into something approaching farce. Felicia
decides to stay safely in her tower of art behind the door, as a proper
romance character should. Joan decides to open the door to confront, presumably, the complexities of experience, as a realistic
character should. But a reversal occurs in the last chapter when we
realize that Joan, in opening the door to an unknown reporter,
imagines that she is Felicia opening the door to Redmond, just as
earlier she confused herself with Samantha Deane fleeing from Sir
Edmund De Vere. Joan's chagrin when she realizes she has as-
saulted a stranger with a Cinzano bottle resembles Anne's chagrin
at the outcome of the lily maid episode and results from the same
painful process of being disabused of romantic illusions. Where
Duncan's double ending in *The Imperialist*—comic upbeat for
Advena and ironic downbeat for Lorne—clarifies the possible
shape of plots, Atwood goes further by distinguishing between, and

then playing with, the proper endings for realism and romance. In a concise statement of the endings available for romances, Anne remarks that it is "so much more romantic to end up a story with a funeral than a wedding" (223). *Lady Oracle,* about a character modeled according to the conventions of realism (however unsatisfying Joan herself may find these conventions), denies its central character the consoling neatness of either of these endings of funeral or wedding. The botched fake suicide, whose tidiness was supposed to contrast with the disorder of Joan's actual life, is a parody of the death as ending, but not itself the ending of the book. *Lady Oracle* has to make do instead with the circular ending which is really a beginning. The book closes with Joan's returning to her old patterns as she observes that "a man in a bandage" can be as romantic as a man in a red-lined opera cloak. Unlike either Advena or Anne, Joan never relinquishes her secret idea of herself as an old-time heroine.

"Jericho's Brick Battlements," the concluding story of Margaret Laurence's *A Bird in the House* (1970), is another work that counterpoints the different plots of romance and realism and contrasts different versions of the heroine. There are in fact three plots: one, the romance that the narrator Vanessa is writing is regarded within the story itself as fiction; the other two, involving Vanessa and her Aunt Edna, form the frame narrative and are presented as the "real world." All three are concerned with the theme of getting out. The parallels as well as the contrasts among the three plots form a design within which Laurence can investigate the developing role of her new-time heroine Vanessa.

Vanessa's romance, which corresponds to Anne's storyclub narratives and to Joan's Costume Gothics, is about Marie who lives "in Quebec in the early days of the fur trade" (177) and who is, of course, an orphan. Vanessa's difficulty in completing this story comes from her sense of the resistance that literary conventions encounter from some intractable thing outside, which we can call life:

> The problem was now plain. How to get Marie out of her imprisoning life at the inn and onto the ship which would carry her to France?... Neither Radisson nor Groseilliers would marry her. ... They were both too busy. ... and besides, they were too old for her.

> I lay on the seat of the MacLaughlin Buick feeling disenchant-
> ment begin to set in. Marie would not get out of the grey stone
> inn. She would stay there all her life. The only thing that would
> ever happen to her was that she would get older.... I felt I could
> not bear it. I no longer wanted to finish the story. What was the
> use, if she couldn't get out except by ruses which clearly
> wouldn't happen in real life? (178)

Vanessa's distinctions are by now familiar: there is the enchantment
of romance where the ruses work and the miraculous escapes are
executed; and then there is the "disenchantment" of "real life" (what
we have been calling the conventions of realism) where the ruses
fail and escapes, if they work at all, turn into other forms of
bondage. The two endings to Marie's story—she gets out in the
romance; she doesn't get out when the romance darkens into
realism—are parallelled by the contrasting endings to Aunt Edna's
and Vanessa's stories in the frame narrative. The story of Aunt Edna
and Wes Griggs is very clearly a realistic displacement of the
romantic convention of entrapment and heroic rescue, with the
conventional "ruses" being given plausibility. In contrast, the story
of Michael's failure to rescue Vanessa from the Brick House calls
into question the ruses and suggests that some new convention must
be discovered to mirror the needs of the new-time heroine who is,
as Duncan put it, an intelligent agent in the "reflection of our present
social state."

In Aunt Edna's story, diction like "old dungeon" (186), "dragon
throat" (189), and "magic powder" (191) reminds us that beneath
this plausible story of Aunt Edna and the train man lies the story of
the hero on the coal-black steed who rescues the imprisoned princess.[2] The dragon who guards the dungeon is Grandfather Connor,
who is forever stoking the furnace in "his territory"—the basement
of the Brick House. In the crucial struggle, Grandfather goes into
his firebreathing dragon act, and the furnace pipes catch fire:

> In my grandfather's room the pipe was a bright light crimson.
> From inside its dragon throat came a low but impressive rumble.
> ...The pipes were beginning to chortle evilly. The light crimson
> was getting lighter and presumably hotter. The stench was terri-
> ble. (189-91)

Wes Griggs conquers with a magic weapon, "a small boxful of blackish powder." "For an instant," says Vanessa, "I half expected the whole house to go up in a last mad explosion. But no. The magic powder acted swiftly. . . . The flame-roaring subsided" (191). To conclude, there are the usual flourishes—escape from the Brick House, wedding bells, and the honeymoon trip to Montreal using a free pass on the Canadian National Railway.

"Jericho's Brick Battlements" thus provides a comic ending for Aunt Edna's plot which the companion story "The Mask of the Bear" has left unresolved. In that story, Vanessa is writing a romance, "The Silver Sphinx," about a heroine who is like "some barbaric queen, beautiful and terrible . . . wearing a long robe of leopard skin and one or two heavy gold bracelets, pacing an alabaster courtyard and keening her unrequited love" (64). Like Anne who laments the lack of romance in Avonlea, Vanessa is convinced that both "death and love" seem "regrettably far from Manawaka and the snow" (65). In the frame story about Jimmy Lorrimer's failure to release Aunt Edna from the Brick House prison, however, Vanessa begins to see structural similarities between what to her is romance and "real life." After Jimmy Lorrimer has left for good, Vanessa hears Aunt Edna crying: "There arose in my mind, mysteriously, the picture of a barbaric queen, someone who had lived a long time ago. I could not reconcile the image of the known face, nor could I disconnect it" (78). The counterpointing of Marie and the barbaric queen from Vanessa's romance with the "real life" Aunt Edna establishes Aunt Edna, by contrast, as a character of realism. It also shows how works of realism can, by displacing patterns of romance, acquire access to mythic levels of human experience.

The third plot in "Jericho's Brick Battlements," concerning Michael's failure to rescue Vanessa, to some extent resembles the revised ending of Marie's story where the prince doesn't come and Marie stays in the grey stone inn and grows older. But the differences are perhaps more instructive. Whereas the old-time heroine of romance was the passive focus for episodes of self-sacrifice, battle intrigue, and heroic rescue, the new heroine, in the absence of a likely rescuer, packs her suitcase and boards a Greyhound bus. Michael has promised to fly Vanessa to the "ferned forests" of British Columbia, but he actually takes her "home to the Brick House instead" (195)—back to the prison. Like Morag in *The*

Diviners who discovers that Brooke is no prince to rescue her from Hill Street and transport her to the "Halls of Sion," (253) so here Vanessa eventually realizes that any rescuing to be done she will have to do herself. The Stephen Spender poem that Vanessa and Michael read together, "I Think Continually of Those Who Were Truly Great," expresses the false tone of their whole relationship and hints at the coming collapse of romantic expectations. Michael turns out to have a wife, just as Raddison and Groseilliers turn out to be too old and too busy to marry orphans. But the clash with Grandfather Connor over Michael makes Vanessa into her own Joshua who trumpets down Jericho's battlements: "I shouted at him, as though if I sounded all my trumpets loudly enough, his walls would quake and crumble" (199). Soon after this incident, she goes away to university in Winnipeg. Release for the new heroine does not come with wedding bells, it seems, but with self-discovery in the city. Like Duncan, Montgomery, and Atwood, Laurence exploits the device of parallel plots and multiple endings to contrast the proper roles for the old-time and the new heroine. The ending to Vanessa's story is tentative, of course, since in realism there can be no decisive battles and no once-and-for-all releases. We could compare with this Joan's sense of her role as Houdini, repeatedly "entering the embrace of bondage, slithering out again" (335). When Vanessa gets on the bus for Winnipeg she says, "Now I was really going. And yet in some way which I could not define or understand, I did not feel nearly as free as I had expected to feel" (203).

It is the nature of a work of realism that it should claim to be asserting something about society and the realities by which we actually live. Duncan concludes her article in *The Week* by saying:

> The novel of to-day is a reflection of our present social state. The women who enter into its composition are but intelligent agents in this reflection, and show themselves as they are, not as a false ideal would have them.

This "false ideal," as we by this time know, is Dora at her piano, Elaine on her death-barge, the Lady of Shalott in her tower, and the princess in her lonely prison. The new heroine is Advena, Anne, Joan, and Vanessa who, we are invited to believe, reflect in a documentary way the changing conditions of our "social state." As

Del Jordan's mother in Alice Munro's *Lives of Girls and Women* (1971) says, "There is a change coming I think in the lives of girls and women" (146), and it is the job of the realistic novel to reflect this change. Still, Vanessa's boarding the bus begins to look like another literary convention when we compare her departure from Manawaka with Del's departure from Jubilee, after very similar failures in romance. In the last chapter "Baptizing," when Garnet French does not show up as he has promised, Del looks soulfully into her mirror and in despair recites a line from Tennyson's "Mariana": "He cometh not, she said" (200). Once again, here as in *Anne of Green Gables* and *Lady Oracle,* the Tennysonian figure is a romantic heroine from the mirror world whose insubstantial presence shadows forth, we are expected to realize, a false ideal. Del enjoys the tears of her mirror self and the ecstasy of self-torture, but eventually, like Advena and like Anne, she firmly puts from her these romantic fantasies as self-indulgent:

> I opened the city paper up at the want ads, and got a pencil. . . .
> Cities existed; telephone operators were wanted; the future could
> be furnished without love or scholarships. Now at last without
> fantasies or self-deception, cut off from the mistakes and confu-
> sion of the past, grave and simple, carrying a small suitcase,
> getting on a bus, like girls in movies leaving home, convents,
> lovers, I supposed I would get started on my real life.
>
> Garnet French, Garnet French, Garnet French.
> Real life. (200-01)

Just so—"real life." Yet whenever we think we are being told something about real life, the question keeps doubling back into matters of form, as we puzzle over how it can be said that real life is Avonlea, not Camelot; Jubilee, not Mariana's moated grange. The epilogue of *Lives of Girls and Women* is chiefly interesting for its confrontation with these questions, for its self-consciousness and its awareness of its own forms. In "Epilogue: The Photographer," Alice Munro mirrors the process of her own choosing between literary conventions to create Del. She does this by showing her own fictional heroine Del choosing between conventions to create *her* heroine Caroline-Marion. Del tells us how she had planned to turn the Sherriff house and family in Jubilee into material for a

Gothic romance of Southern aristocratic degeneracy. The pudgy tennis-playing daughter Marion was to become the romance heroine Caroline, "taunting and secretive," "a sacrifice, spread for sex on moldy uncomfortable tombstones" (204). But when Del actually enters the Sherriff's house, talks to Bobby Sherriff, and observes the "ordinariness of everything," she is brought up short and wonders:

> And what happened, I asked myself, to Marion? Not to Caroline.
> What happened to Marion? What happened to Bobby Sherriff
> when he had to stop baking cakes and go back to the asylum?
> Such questions persist, in spite of novels. (209)

Del decides for "real life" here as she does at the end of the chapter "Baptizing." But the mirroring device of the book invites us to step outside Del's view and to see Del's decision as the writer's—Alice Munro's own—choice between the old-time heroine, mysterious Caroline, and the pudgy, ordinary heroine of realism, Marion. Alice Munro, as she has said in interviews, began young by writing Gothic tales of decay and madness, doubtless very like Del's story of Caroline. Later she wrote stories of realism which resemble comedies of manners in their faithful recording of the texture of life at a particular time and place. Yet organizing the realistic surface are the underlying designs of the stories taken from myth and fairytales. And faintly shadowing the Marions that she has chosen to write about are the ghosts of the Carolines.

So the Carolines and the Cordelias will not be allowed to disappear altogether from our fiction. We seem to be discovering that the new heroine usually has her shadowy romantic double somewhere close by. After consigning the old-time heroine's ghost to oblivion, our writers seem unable to do without her. Just as she was "the painted pivot of the merry-go-round" in the old romances, she returns again as a compositional device in works of realism. In *The Imperialist* she appears as an actual character Dora, the debunked love goddess, whose role is to contrast with the new heroine Advena. In *Anne of Green Gables* and *Lady Oracle* she has existence only in the imaginations of Anne and Joan. Her function in these books is to enhance the distinction between, on the one hand, romantic Camelot and the "impossible white paradise" where old-time heroines live and, on the other hand, "real life" Avonlea and

Terremoto. *A Bird in the House* and *Lives of Girls and Women* win plausibility for their own realistic heroines by parodying the romantic heroine's conventional role of passive suffering as she waits for rescue by the magnificent hero. The old-time heroine, then, establishes the superiority of her rival, the realistic heroine, in achieving a "translatable relation to the world." But by her own contrived presence she reminds readers interested in literary conventions that the worlds in which all heroines have residence are fictional.

Notes

1. See, for example, pages 5, 33, 105, 109, 135, 205, and 311.
2. An acknowledgment is due to Professor Donald Hair, who first drew my attention to this pattern.

Works Cited

Atwood, Margaret. *Lady Oracle.* 1976. Toronto: Bantam-Seal, 1977.
Duncan, Sara Jeanette. *The Imperialist.* 1904. New Canadian Library. Toronto: McClelland and Stewart, 1971.
_____. "Saunterings." *The Week* (8 Oct. 1886): 771-72.
Frye, Northrop. *Anatomy of Criticism: Four Essays.* New York: Atheneum, 1966.
Kirby, William. *The Golden Dog.* 1877. New Canadian Library. Toronto: McClelland and Stewart, 1971.
Laurence, Margaret. *A Bird in the House.* 1970. New Canadian Library. Toronto: McClelland and Stewart, 1971.
_____. *The Diviners.* Toronto: Bantam, 1975.
Montgomery, Lucy Maud. *Anne of Green Gables.* 1908. Toronto: McGraw-Hill, 1968.
Munro, Alice. *Lives of Girls and Women.* 1971. New York: Signet, 1974.

The Uses of Setting
in *Anne of Green Gables*

Marilyn Solt

Anne of Green Gables, the first book Canadian author Lucy Maud Montgomery wrote about Anne Shirley, was published by the L. C. Page Company of Boston in 1908. The book has been continuously in print since that time, and more than a million copies have been sold. The red-haired, eleven-year-old orphan girl with the lively imagination that Marilla and Matthew Cuthbert of Green Gables Farm, Avonlea, Prince Edward Island, Canada, received from a mainland orphan asylum—even though they had sent specifically for a boy—is, according to John Robert Sorfleet, "probably Canada's best-known fictional export."

How can we account for the fact that *Anne of Green Gables* is still read and loved, while most children's books of this vintage have been long out of print, and long ago vanished from library bookshelves? I won't conjecture why books that were popular contemporaries of *Anne of Green Gables*—the Pollyanna books by Eleanor H. Porter, for example—have not lasted, but I will suggest one reason that *Anne of Green Gables* has. And that reason is Montgomery's superb use of setting.

I came to this conclusion after rereading the book with Eudora Welty's essay "Place in Fiction" at hand. Welty says that excellence in writing is closely related to place:

[When] we consider what good writing may be, place can be seen, in her own way, to have a great deal to do with that goodness, if not to be responsible for it. (116)

Having linked the goodness of a novel to place, Welty suggests what the setting must do:

The good novel should be steadily alight, revealing. Before it can be that it must of course be steadily visible from its outside, presenting a continuous, shapely, pleasing and finished surface to the eyes. (120)

Although the components of setting in *Anne of Green Gables,* as in any fine novel, never exist isolated from but always in conjunction with the other elements of fiction, removing them from the story lets us see that the world of the novel is "steadily visible from the outside."

This world is a small turn-of-the-century Prince Edward Island community, very like the one in which Lucy Maud Montgomery grew up and was living at the time she wrote the book. The village of Avonlea occupies "a little triangular peninsula jutting out into the Gulf of St. Lawrence, with water on two sides of it" (5). Mrs. Rachel Lynde lives "just where the Avonlea main road" dips "down into a little hollow" (1). Green Gables is "a scant quarter of a mile up the road from Lynde's Hollow" (4) and back a long lane. To get to Diana Barry's home, Orchard Slope, one crosses the log bridge that spans the brook running right below Green Gables and goes up through a little spruce grove. The Avonlea church, school, and post office are all within easy walking distance. The young people often walk to Carmody, a village a little larger than Avonlea, but their elders usually go there by horse and buggy. It's four miles to Newbridge and five miles to White Sands (take the shore road to get there) where the large hotel is located, to which "heaps of Americans" come in the summer. It's thirty miles into "town," which is Charlottetown, the provincial capital. A trip there once or twice a year is an event to be looked forward to eagerly. Given even this much information, the reader begins to form a picture in his mind.

Concrete details about Green Gables and its environs make the picture, in Welty's words, more "shapely" and "pleasing." Green

Gables is a "big rambling orchard-embowered house" (3) (there's an apple orchard on one side and a cherry orchard on the other) with a "very green and neat and precise backyard set about on one side with great patriarchal willows and on the other with prim Lombardies" (4). The large Green Gables kitchen has windows facing both east and west and contains a sofa and a rocking chair, for most of the time it is used as a sitting room as well as a kitchen. Anne's little room in the east gable is described in detail; each piece of furniture is named and its location given. By the time Anne has been at Green Gables for four years "a dainty apple-blossom paper" and a "few good pictures" (282) cover the walls, which were "whitewashed" and "painfully bare" (29) when she first went there. From her window she can see the orchards, the garden, a tree-covered hill and beyond the big barns "away down over green, low-sloping fields . . . a sparkling blue glimpse of the sea" (33), a scene on which Anne's beauty-loving eyes often linger.

The picture becomes more "finished" as we acquire broader knowledge of the way of life. Even though located within sight and sound of the sea, Avonlea is an agricultural community. Matthew, like most of the men of Avonlea, has a hired boy (a French boy, "little Jerry Buote from the Creek" [39]) to help him in the fields, with the livestock, and to haul and split wood. The women of Avonlea cook the meals, keep their houses clean, do the laundry, sew, garden, and can and preserve. They take pride, as did Lucy Maud Montgomery, in their beautiful flower gardens. In the evening Matthew drowses by the fire on the kitchen sofa, reading the *Farmer's Advocate*. When women sit down, they occupy themselves with some kind of handiwork. Mrs. Lynde knits cotton warp quilts—she has knitted sixteen at the time the story opens. Community activities revolve around church and school functions. The Sunday school picnic in the summer is long anticipated with pleasure. Having the new minister and his wife to tea is an event to be planned for with care. The pace of life is slow. Everyone knows everyone and everything that goes on. Few people are wealthy, but few are extremely poor, either. There is a great deal of visiting back and forth, for Avonlea does not yet have a telephone system.

Because the story extends over a period of five years, the author needs many settings to supply continuity and to keep the reader in constant touch with the world through which the characters move. Montgomery marks the years with annual events such as birthdays and the starting and closing of school, but her chief means to show the passage of time is by descriptions of the outside world in the various seasons. This is suitable because Avonlea is a community that lives close to nature, and because Anne, through whose eyes most events are seen, is intensely aware of the natural beauty surrounding her.

Sensory images, so closely interwoven into the story that the reader is scarcely aware of description as such, bring to life the physical world. In early June, after Mayflowers and violets in May, the orchards are "pink-blossomed," the frogs sing "silvery sweet in the marshes," and the air is filled with the "savour of clover fields and balsamic fir woods" (172). A little later, gardens are a "bowery wilderness of flowers" (91) and fireflies flit "over in Lovers' Lane, in and out among the ferns and rustling boughs" (191). One October Anne revels in the "world of color around her": birches "as golden as sunshine," "royal crimson" maples, and wild cherry-trees "the loveliest shades of dark red and bronzy green" (127). In another October, as Anne and Diana walk to school by the Birch Path which is "a canopy of yellow," "valleys . . . filled with delicate mists," "heavy dews," and "heaps of rustling leaves" are noted (202).

The above and dozens of other images provide Anne's world with the total and continuous visibility which Welty says is essential to carry along the sense of story believably. And, because Montgomery so successfully brings "place to life in the round" (121), setting in her novel has "the most delicate control over character, too: by confining character, it defines it" (122). In other words, these characters, given these circumstances, in this time and place, behave as they do.

This relationship between setting and character is demonstrated in the clashes that develop between Anne and Marilla in the course of Anne's "bringing-up." Reared in a strict Presbyterian environment, Marilla read only religious and "moral" literature in her childhood and never imagines things different from the way they are. In contrast to Marilla's stern realism is Anne's extravagant daydreaming. Nourished by fairy tales and romantic fiction, Anne's wonderful imagination—which made the pre-Green Gables life of drudgery, poverty, and neglect bearable—sometimes takes over when she should be thinking of her work. This happens on the day she starches Matthew's handkerchiefs and lets a pie in the oven burn to a crisp while she is imagining that she is "an enchanted princess shut up in a lonely tower with a handsome knight riding to [her] rescue on a coal-black steed" (173). Anne likes pretty clothes, but Marilla considers it "sinful" to even think of them. She says that the important thing is that clothes are "neat and clean and service-able," so she makes Anne's dresses with plain sleeves rather than the fashionable puffed ones that Anne's friends wear and for which Anne longs. When Anne wishes that she were less homely, Marilla tells her that being good is "better than being pretty" (62). In Marilla's estimation, children should be seen and not heard, and talkative Anne's "got too much to say" (45). When Anne dyes her long red hair, hoping to turn it "a beautiful raven black" (240), it comes out a horrible green. Marilla says that dyeing her hair was a "wicked thing to do" (229) and hopes that Anne realizes that this is where her vanity has led her. It is fortunate for Anne that Marilla's basic kindness more often governs her words and actions than does the austere moral code of Marilla's youth.

In addition to illuminating character, setting is closely related to point of view in *Anne of Green Gables*. In the following quota-tions, the same stretch of countryside is seen first as Matthew sees it and then as it appears to Anne.

> Matthew Cuthbert and the sorrel mare jogged comfortably over the eight miles to Bright River. It was a pretty road, running along between snug farmsteads, with now and again a bit of balsamy fir woods to drive through or a hollow where wild plums hung out their filmy blooms. The air was sweet with the breath of many apple orchards and the meadows sloped away in the distance to horizon mists of pearl and purple; while
> > "The little birds sang as if it were
> > The one day of summer in the year,"
> Matthew enjoyed the drive after his own fashion. (10)

Except for the two lines of poetry, which are out of character for him, the details recorded are those that Matthew, a farmer who has lived in the area all his life and takes the scenery for granted, might observe.

The return trip, with Anne making the observations, is entirely different. Even before they start back, the reader is prepared for the idea that Anne will pay more attention to the "pretty" road than Matthew had. She tells him that if he hadn't come for her that evening she had planned to spend the night in a big wild cherry tree a little way down the railroad track because "it would be lovely to sleep in a wild cherry tree all white with bloom in the moonshine" (13).

During the two-hour drive over the tree-shaded red dirt road, Anne becomes convinced that what she had heard is true: Prince Edward Island is the prettiest place in the world. It's also the "bloomiest" (15) place. They've passed many blooming wild cherry trees before a wild plum leaning out from the bank "all white and lacy" (14) reminds Anne of "a bride all in white with a lovely misty veil" (15). But all past beauties are merely prelude to the "Avenue":

> The "Avenue," so called by the Newbridge people, was a stretch of road four or five hundred yards long, completely arched over with huge, widespreading apple trees, planted years ago by an eccentric old farmer. Overhead was one long canopy of snowy fragrant bloom. Below the boughs the air was full of a purple twilight and far ahead a glimpse of painted sunset sky shone like a great rose window at the end of a cathedral aisle. (19-20)

Anne is so overcome by this beauty that at first she cannot speak. Finally she asks Matthew in a whisper: "Oh, Mr. Cuthbert . . . that place we came through—that white place—what was it?" (20). Matthew says it's called the "Avenue" and comments "it is a kind of pretty place" (20). Considering that name too prosaic for such a wonderful place, Anne renames it the White Way of Delight.

In retrospect, this particular scene seems to operate on two levels of meaning. It becomes symbolic in that it anticipates Anne's life on the island, where she will blossom physically and emotionally. Further, it suggests that Matthew, her companion in her initial encounter with loveliness, will contribute to her blossoming as much as the beautiful world in which she finds herself.

The experience of driving through the White Way of Delight could also serve as an example of setting affecting mood, with each accentuating the other. A second notable example occurs on the night Anne comes dancing home in the "purple winter twilight" after Mrs. Barry has forgiven her for mistakenly giving Diana currant wine instead of raspberry cordial. The song in Anne's heart is as sweet as the "tinkles of sleigh-bells" that come to her ears "like elfin chimes" across the snowy hills through the frosty air (155). And the Christmas morning on which Anne receives her first party dress—"a lovely soft brown gloria" with puffed sleeves, a gift from Matthew—is as lovely a day as the dress (213).

Welty says that there is some magic in the name of a place and that by naming a place "we have put a kind of poetic charm on its existence" (119). Anne expresses a similar idea in her own words: "When I hit on a name that suits exactly it gives me a thrill" (21). The White Way of Delight is the first of many fanciful names invented by Anne. Even before they are at Green Gables she has said that she is going to call Barry's Pond, a much too ordinary name for such a beautiful body of water, the "Lake of Shining Waters" (21). She names the spring down by the log bridge the "Dryad's Bubble" (93) and a round pool in Mr. Barry's field "Willowmere" (98). And she calls the huge, bloom-filled, "radiantly lovely" cherry tree just outside her bedroom window "Snow Queen" (35).

"The truth is," wrote Welty, "fiction depends for its life on place" (118), a truth Montgomery realized intuitively and practiced in *Anne of Green Gables*. She created, as Welty says the author must, "a chink-proof world of appearance" (125) that the reader accepts as actuality. The characters that inhabit that world are confined and defined by it. This is perceived in point of view which shows the characters as products of their own personal experience and time. Mood is frequently connected to setting, and names are inseparable from it. Because of all this, it does not seem an exaggeration to claim that Montgomery's setting is responsible for *Anne of Green Gables* still seeming fresh and alive to contemporary readers even though the time portrayed is now far in the past.

Works Cited

Montgomery, Lucy Maud. *Anne of Green Gables*. 1908. Toronto: Mc-Graw-Hill Ryerson, 1942.

Sorfleet, John S., ed. *L. M. Montgomery: An Assessment*. Guelph, ON: Canadian Children's Press, 1976.

Welty, Eudora. "Place in Fiction." *The Eye of Story: Selected Essays and Reviews*. New York: Random, 1977.

Anne of Green Gables

The Architect of Adolescence

Mary Rubio

When *Anne of Green Gables* was first published in 1908, the terms "teenage" and "adolescent" were not in common use. Yet *Anne* caught—and continues to catch—the salient elements in teenage experience: yearning, rebellion, intense response to beauty, difficulty in accepting community standards, desire for an identity, friends, clothes, and popularity—all parts of an often difficult transition from childhood to maturity.

Anne of Green Gables was written by thirty-year-old Lucy Maud Montgomery, a woman living in a small rural community in Prince Edward Island, Canada's smallest province. Before 1908, L. M. Montgomery had published many short stories and poems, but *Anne* was her first full-length novel. She was to become a prolific writer: twenty-two books of fiction, a book of poetry, a serialized version of her life, 494 individual poems, and 497 short stories are listed in the Russell and Wilmshurst bibliography. At the time of her death in 1942, Robertson Davies, then a newspaper editor and now a don of Canadian letters, wrote:

> Nations grow in the eyes of the world less by the work of their statesmen than by their artists. Thousands of people all over the globe are hazy about the exact nature of Canada's government. . . .but they have clear recollections of *Anne of Green Gables.* (4)

This statement was true in 1942, and it is even truer now. *Anne of Green Gables* has become one of the immortals of children's literature. The appeal of L. M. Montgomery seems to be universal, going beyond the confines of the English language and the Western hemisphere.

Today, the island that L. M. Montgomery made famous is a summer mecca for tourists, who come from all over the world to see the landscapes that Montgomery used as the settings for that novel and its seven sequels, as well as for other works. *Anne* has been translated into numerous languages. There have been two movies: the first a silent film in 1919 and the second a "talkie" in 1934; and a third, a television movie produced by Sullivan Films, now has been made. In Canada, a very successful musical version of *Anne* has been playing since 1965 in Charlottetown, P.E.I., and it has toured across Canada and abroad. In Poland, according to Barbara Wachowicz, Montgomery was selected as the second most popular author for young readers of the magazine *Plomyk;* Krystyna Sobkowska reports that a Polish stage play based on *Anne of Green Gables* has been seen by over a quarter-million people since 1963. The Canadian Broadcasting Corporation has made a documentary drama of L. M. Montgomery's life, and "Anne" is big business in P.E.I., as well as in Japan, where innumerable dolls, businesses, and other spinoffs capitalize on her name. As Yuko Katsura reports, the Japanese publishers even arrange air tours to P.E.I. for Anne aficionados to visit the island in the summers. They can see the real town of Cavendish, on which the mythical "Avonlea" is based, the house upon which Green Gables is modeled, and the haunts that Montgomery loved and named. Seeing Anne's island, readers can connect with their own first experience of *Anne.*

Anne of Green Gables has been an unusually enduring novel. Few books listed in Frank Mott's *Golden Multitudes,* an early study of American best-sellers, are still popular as *Anne* is over seventy-five years after publication.[1] Some of the classics like *Huckleberry Finn* still enjoy large sales, but these are assisted by their being staples in literature courses. *Anne*'s popularity is based on no such extraneous factors—it sells well because generation after generation relates to the age-old conflicts that it embodies.

Statistics underline what a phenomenon *Anne* really is. In the ten years between its publication and 1919, when L. M. Montgomery sold her rights to it, *Anne of Green Gables* sold 311,273 copies. By the time that Montgomery sold the copyright to the Page Company (after a bitter lawsuit), she calculated in her "Book Sales Book" that *Anne of Green Gables,* as a single title exclusive of its sequels, had brought her $22,119.38. In a time and a place where, according to the Canadian census book for 1921, a woman could expect to earn around $300 a year from gainful employment—in fact, Montgomery notes in her journal entry of September 15, 1895, that she had earned a salary of $180 from her first year of school teaching in 1894—*Anne* did very well indeed. And of course her other books, including sequels to *Anne,* sold very well also: by 1921, according to her "Book Sales Book," she had made a total of $97,552.56 from her writing, and that was only at mid-career.

L. M. Montgomery's *Anne of Green Gables* has enchanted other writers as well as the general public. Mark Twain was one of the first to praise the novel: "In 'Anne of Green Gables' you will find the dearest and most moving and delightful child since the immortal Alice." Writers as far afield as Astrid Lindgren, the Swedish author of the immensely popular stories about the little red-haired Pippi Longstocking, also tell of their affection for "Anne." Lindgren says,

> And then, of course *Anne of Green Gables*—oh, my unforgettable one, forever you will be riding the cart with Matthew Cuthbert beneath the flowering apple trees of Avonlea! How I lived with that girl! A whole summer my sisters and I played at Anne of Green Gables in the big sawdust heaps at the sawmill. I was Diana Barry, and the pond at the manure heap was the Dark Reflecting Waves. (Cott 46)

Jean Little, the well-known contemporary Canadian author of children's books, says,

> L. M. Montgomery was a major influence on me—I read and reread her books. During my childhood Anne Shirley was more than a beloved character in a book; she was a member of our family. . . . Whenever I was told I had a great imagination I was proud because it linked me with Anne.

That writers and children who have loved *Anne of Green Gables* never outgrow their love for the book is perhaps explained by Jane Cowan Fredeman, who sees in the "fairyland" that Montgomery's characters speak of "a metaphor both for the golden days of childhood and the font from which creative artists, separated from the common run, continue to draw their imaginative powers." Montgomery speaks of this fairyland both in her journals and in the following quotation from *The Story Girl:*

> There is such a place as fairyland—but only children can find the way to it. And they do not know that it is fairyland until they have grown so old that they forget the way. One bitter day, when they seek it and cannot find it, they realize what they have lost and that is the tragedy of life. On that day the gates of Eden are shut behind them and the age of gold is over. Henceforth they must dwell in the common light of common day. Only a few, who remain children at heart, can ever find that fair, lost path again, and blessed are they above mortals. They, and only they, can bring us tidings from that dear country where once we sojourned and from which we must evermore be exiles. The world calls them its singers and poets and artists and storytellers; but they are just people who have never forgotten the way to fairyland. (165-66)

If writers of the last seventy-seven years have read and appreciated Montgomery, she herself was a writer steeped in the works of authors who came before her. Montgomery knew her Shakespeare very well—indeed, there are allusions to at least four of his plays in *Anne*—and she follows a pattern in *Anne* that Shakespeare uses in his plays: the novel begins with a situation of order, moves to disorder, and concludes with a superior new order. This is a traditional, simple, and perennially satisfying structure.

Avonlea, an invented name suggesting both Shakespeare's River Avon as well as King Arthur's Avalon, is Montgomery's mythical and peaceful little village in rural Prince Edward Island, in the early 1890s when the book begins.[2] It is a village filled with Scots-Presbyterians—staid, hard-working, emotionally suppressed and judgmental, but eminently good folk. Their lives are spent in the orderly transactions of the day and they have no interruptions from the outside world—until little Anne Shirley arrives. The entrance of an alien force into a settled community is a classic way to upset the *status quo.*

Little red-haired, freckle-faced, skinny Anne is an eleven-year-old waif from an orphanage. Sent by mistake to an elderly brother and sister, Matthew and Marilla Cuthbert, who ordered a boy to help them on the farm, Anne displays every surface quality from which the community shrinks: in a place where children should be seen and not heard, she is a child with a never-ceasing tongue and a boundless imagination to keep it going; in a community that suppresses all signs of emotion or feeling, she is passionate and given to emotional outbursts. She comes from an unsettled past and longs to find a permanent home. As soon as she sets eyes on Avonlea she thinks her dreams have been answered—but then she discovers that the good folk of Avonlea do not want *her.*

L. M. Montgomery uses the "prepared entrance," a typically Shakespearean technique, in order to arouse the reader's curiosity and to heighten the drama before Anne arrives. Other characters discuss what "the orphan" will be like before Anne arrives, and the dialogue, as well as the imagery and symbols, makes the readers anticipate that something threatening to the stability of the community is going to present itself when she appears.

The Cuthberts have a neighbor, the inestimable Mrs. Rachel Lynde, whose house overlooks the road that all must pass who enter or leave Avonlea. Mrs. Lynde is the watchdog and the conscience of Avonlea, as well as the prime mover of most of its religious-cum-social events. As the novel begins, Mrs. Lynde sits making a patchwork quilt (a symbol of order). Symbolically, even the natural landscape succumbs to order around Mrs. Lynde. A small brook which begins in "dark secrets of pool and cascade" becomes a quiet, well-conducted little stream by the time that it flows past the house and judgmental eyes of Mrs. Lynde. Even the names of the vegetation around her house suggest her overriding influence on the environment: "alders" and "ladies' eardrops" grow nearby whereas cherry trees and wild roses grow elsewhere in Avonlea. This Mrs. Lynde looks out of the window (a symbol of her restricted vision) to see the departing old Matthew Cuthbert, dressed in his best suit (a sign to her that something is wrong), rattling out of town in a buggy—an extraordinary event, for Matthew never goes anywhere. Mrs. Lynde, her solid two hundred pounds buttressed by the full weight of her prejudices and opinions, flies up the road to Marilla's house for an explanation about Matthew's journey. Her all-seeing eye refracts the entire small Scots-Presbyterian community: religion, order, and decorum prevail in all aspects of the residents' lives, and they all resist change.

Mrs. Lynde tells Marilla that taking in orphans is both foolish and dangerous. Images of disorder are connected with Anne, of course. Red hair has a long association with witchcraft and fairies in medieval literature. Anne's greenish-gray eyes and little pointed chin suggest kinship with Celtic fairies, and Marilla soon becomes suspicious of Anne's power to enchant. Anne seems partly magical because she uses her imagination as a passport to fairyland; and the fairyland provides either a haven from or a visionary vantage point from which to view the real world. Mrs. Lynde's forecast that she may become a demonic force—like other orphans she has heard about who have burned houses and put strychnine in wells—supports this imagery. Thus, it seems a foregone conclusion that Anne will be incorrigible when she has a temper outburst. During the rest of the book Anne gets into one scrape after another, but she also learns to conform to the social and behavioral expectations of Avonlea, and she slowly matures, taming down her passion and imagination, until she is a beloved member of the community at the end. In the process of growing up, she in turn exerts a strong humanizing influence on the whole community. Most important, she gives Matthew and Marilla Cuthbert a much fuller and happier life than they had before.

Montgomery carefully takes Anne through three stages of growth to maturity. First, she must win the affection of those in her immediate environment—Matthew, Marilla, and Mrs. Lynde. (Mrs. Lynde becomes Anne's advocate once she is won over.) Second, she must win the acceptance of the wider Avonlea community, including other children, parents, and visiting relatives. Third, Anne must mature and change enough that she will be capable of taking on the world outside Avonlea and of developing a mature love relationship with a young man. Her own needs for love and a home are so well met as a child that she in turn is able to give love not only to her surrogate parents, Matthew and Marilla, but also to the community, as a teacher. The unpromising little waif of chapter one, who was given to all kinds of excesses, grows into a balanced young woman whose imaginative inner life is guided by acceptable social values.

In the process of teaching the Avonlea folk to feel joy in living, to appreciate beauty in nature, and to express love to those held dear, Anne enlarges not only their experience of life, but also their philosophical concept of duty. When she enters Avonlea, the women enact their narrow concept of duty by keeping spotless houses, by sweeping their lawns until they are immaculate, by ensuring that their children are well catechized and do not play with undesirables, and by watching their husbands and neighbors to make sure that everyone does the proper thing. In her outspoken innocence, Anne debunks their sacred cows. Her comments serve as social commentary which gives the adults new perspectives, and, even more unstabilizing, makes them laugh. L. M. Montgomery liked laughter and disliked the attitude that found fun and laughter inimicable to religion. She was also very skeptical of the narrow way in which many people practiced religion, and she gives to the shy inarticulate Matthew one of the most important lines in the book. It at once sets events into motion and articulates a broad sense of duty that shames the others who call themselves religious. When Marilla asks what good a little girl would be to them, Matthew replies: "We might be some good to her" (31).

The collision between the child perspective and the adult one makes *Anne of Green Gables* a perennial favorite with children. There are few children who do not at some point feel thwarted by adult conservatism and restraints. The resolution appeals at a deep level to boys as well as to girls. They, too, need to move from excesses of rebellion and nonconformity towards acceptance of societal expectations. While *Anne* is primarily a book read by girls, both girls and boys can respond to Montgomery's representation of this, even though it is set in another time or place.

Or perhaps it is precisely because *Anne* is so firmly rooted in another time and place that it is so successful. If *Anne* rings true as an idyll of childhood, it may be because it comes right out of L. M. Montgomery's own world and childhood, replete with authentic emotions, attitudes, and social practices. L. M. Montgomery left ten volumes of personal journals which cover the entirety of her life, and these show how many elements in *Anne* have their origin in the psyche and actual experience of the child, Maud Montgomery.

First, L. M. Montgomery knew exactly what it was to *feel* like an orphan. Her own mother had died when Maud was twenty-one months old, and her father had gone West to remarry and to establish a new life. The baby Maud was left to be raised by her maternal grandparents, Alexander and Lucy Macneill. They had already raised six children of their own, and clearly found their granddaughter's liveliness and precociousness a taxing proposition. They were austere in their manner, inflexible in their beliefs, and harsh in their judgments. By contrast, little Maud was volatile, imaginative and independent-minded. They cared for her physical needs dutifully, but she grew up without any real emotional closeness or psychological support. Later in her life, L. M. Montgomery says that, although she knew that her grandparents had loved her, she regretted that they had been so poor at showing their love; she says that their words often bruised her childish feelings. They did not remember what it was like to be a child, nor did they have the flexibility to comprehend her sensitive nature. They simply demanded the behavior they wanted, and if she protested, they reminded her that she owed them obedience, since they were giving her a good home when her father wasn't.

Their method of discipline predictably made her feel abandoned and unwanted, like an orphan. She could therefore write with great feeling about how Anne wanted a place where she belonged, a place that was her own, one where she would be loved and valued. It is significant that the Matthew and Marilla of the novel are the age of Maud's own grandparents and that at the beginning of the book they obviously share with her grandparents the quality of being emotionally remote. In real life, Maud's grandparents grew more rigid with age, but in *Anne* Matthew and Marilla grow younger and more human as the result of their contact with Anne. The adult Montgomery also wrote in her journal on January 2, 1905, that her aunts and uncles arrogated to themselves the right to chastise her—a right that she thought belonged only to her grandparents—and that her lack of parents to protect her against the detailing of her faults in family conclave left her with a permanent sense of insecurity.

L. M. Montgomery lived in a time and a community where people believed that children should be seen and not heard. Children's feelings were simply not considered important. Montgomery knew well what it was like to have adults discuss her as if she were not present, and the well-known scene in which Mrs. Lynde tells Marilla that Anne is ugly and has "hair as red as carrots"

(69), while Anne stands listening under her disapproving gaze, is written with such force because Montgomery had experienced similar situations. In real life, Maud would never have dared stamp her foot like Anne and shout "I hate you—I hate you—I hate you!" It must have given her an enormous emotional release to do so in fiction.

Montgomery also knew what it was like to be forced to apologize to someone without feeling the remorse attendant upon the apology. Many children have been in the same situation—if they don't apologize there will be no dessert, no overnight friends, no trip to the park—and thus insincere apologies are wrung from them. Anne wins friends among young readers because she turns the table on adults with her apology to Mrs. Lynde: her apology is supposed to be a humiliation, but she transforms it into a joy. She so loves stringing together impressive sounding words that she gets caught up in her own rhetoric and gives an apology which is, in fact, a splendid dramatic performance. Marilla is left in the impossibly awkward position of feeling that she should scold Anne because Anne has apologized too well.

Such are the types of psychological situations around which L. M. Montgomery builds *Anne*. Like Anne and all children, whether orphans or not, Maud wanted to be taken seriously and loved for what she was, not for what she should have been. In real life Maud Montgomery was close to what Anne is—a very bright and temperamental child who reads on the sly and loves big words and purple passages. Thus, bookish, bright children usually recognize themselves in Anne. And like Anne, Maud was also uncommonly sensitive to the beauty of the landscape, and she gave things names just as Anne does: "The White Way of Delight," "The Lake of Shining Waters," and "Lovers Lane" were real places in Maud's personal landscape that have embedded themselves in the psychic landscape of countless children the world over.

Maud looked out on the same landscape that her grandparents did, but she saw a different world. Their world was a practical place where one got on with the serious business of living. Like Anne, the little Maud in the journals sees a world covered with romance, and peopled with fairies, nymphs, and beautiful heroines. The emotional isolation forced on her by her grandparents' remoteness drove her into herself, into whatever books she could get hold of, and into creating her own imaginative world. By the time she was writing *Anne* in 1905, she was thirty and living a very lonely life caring for an eighty-one-year-old grandmother who was becoming senile. She knew, as Matthew warns Anne, that people must not give up all their "romance": to deny one's imaginative faculties and batten down to a totally practical existence is to kill one's soul. Montgomery believed that the words one puts on the world to some extent create the reality or, to be more precise, the world that people *perceive* as reality. Anne says that she has read that "A rose by any other name would smell as sweet" but that she has never been able to believe "a rose *would* be as nice if it was called a thistle or a skunk cabbage." This theme runs throughout the book, as well as in Montgomery's journals. It is only through Anne's imagination that she introduces a new vitality to all of Avonlea. She looks at its landscape and people through fresh eyes, finds new words to describe it, and creates a new reality for the people who live there. Though only a child, Anne plays the role of an artist in a culture: she gives people a new vision of themselves and a myth through which to live. Her purple passages and mellifluous phrases make them smile at first, but they eventually adjust their flat colorless vision until they see some of the color and glory that she showers over things.

In addition to its themes, many of the actual incidents in *Anne* also have their origin in fact. For instance, Anne wants fashionable puffy sleeves to be like the other girls; in real life, little Maud wanted to go barefoot to school like the other children, but had to wear proper button-shoes. Anne develops a fierce hatred for a boy who called her "Carrots"; Maud wrote a poem about a boy, entitling it "The Boy with the Auburn Hair," and this classmate was angry at her for weeks. Anne pours liniment into a cake instead of flavoring; a friend of Maud's did the same. And the list goes on and on. When Montgomery herself talks about the relationship between fact and fiction in her journals, she points out many of the superficial similarities between events and places in her own life and those in *Anne of Green Gables*. What she does not talk about, and perhaps did not even see, is that she bears so many psychological similarities to Anne. Yet, it is the fictional capturing of her own tensions—those between age and youth and between personal freedom and the restrictions of society—that fuel the fire that makes Anne still glow.

It took a child of great sensitivity, a woman with a near total recall of childhood (but helped, of course, by journals kept since she was young), and a mature writer with unusual narrative skill to make *Anne of Green Gables* the classic that it is. Had L. M. Montgomery lived a happier, fuller life, the tensions which created the book might not have surfaced. And had she had less sense of the comedy that occurs when human beings take themselves too seriously, or lose sight of the fitness of things, the book would be less charming.

Humor is one of the features of *Anne of Green Gables* which helps endear it to generation after generation. The particular skill of Montgomery lies in the fact that no person or age group is diminished either through her humor or her satire. The two chief characters, Anne and Marilla, represent extremes in both cases. Anne is an uncommonly impulsive child, and Marilla is an unusually strict and practical adult. Children can always identify with Anne because they see some of their own characteristics and feelings in her many faceted character; they can likewise identify traits in Marilla that they have seen in other adults. Likewise, adults find part of their lost childhood in Anne, and they can sympathize with Marilla's position. What Montgomery does *not* do is to play off either the child's or the adult's views against each other to the point that either is made to look ridiculous. She instead lets them co-exist in a humorous counterpoint, until each wears the other down and the two points of view begin to coalesce. As this happens, the comedy in the book lessens and a more serious mood takes over.

When the novel begins, Anne's extremes are those of a child who acts primarily by impulse and feelings. Marilla's are those of an adult who has extremely rigid beliefs about how a child should act—beliefs which she probably derived from her own childhood and which have been reinforced by the strict community in which she lives. Anne is a hyper-excitable child and her tongue has no trouble keeping up with her brain. But her overblown diction sounds ridiculous in plain old Avonlea, in Marilla's spare and well-swept kitchen. Anne prattles on, to Marilla, paragraph after paragraph, in this vein:

> The world doesn't seem such a howling wilderness as it did last night. I'm so glad it's a sunshiny morning. But I like rainy mornings real well, too. All sorts of mornings are interesting, don't you think? You don't know what's going to happen through the day, and there's so much scope for the imagination. But I'm

glad it's not rainy today because it's easier to be cheerful and to bear up under affliction on a sunshiny day. I feel that I have a good deal to bear up under. It's all very well to read about sorrows and imagine yourself living through them heroically, but it's not so nice when you really come to have them, is it?

Marilla retorts, "For pity's sake hold your tongue. You talk entirely too much for a little girl" (36). But Anne does *not* hold her tongue—she is irrepressible. She goes on talking about trees and flowers. She christens a geranium "Bonny" so that it won't have its feelings hurt by being nameless (like an orphan), and she names the blooming cherry tree outside her window the "Snow Queen." Marilla can only mutter, "I never in all my life saw or heard anything equal to her," as she beats a retreat down to the cellar after potatoes.

Anne's language is derived from the same sources as the youthful Maud Montgomery's: from nineteenth-century sermons, from "Bible literature," from the King James Bible itself, from women's magazines, from popular novels and poetry, and from classical writers like Shakespeare. Montgomery had a liking for epigrammatic phrases and mellifluous passages. She memorized with great ease and let echoes of her wide reading flow as allusions into her writing. Furthermore, she lived in an age and a culture where the memorization of set pieces was encouraged. Not only did children recite them at school concerts, but literate and well-read adults, such as Montgomery's relatives, recited them to each other in social gatherings. Anne had no trouble speaking endlessly and glibly out the pastiche of phrases, images and cadences from the religious and popular literature reverberating in her creator's memory bank. The result is comic—Anne's verbal excesses, so inappropriate to her everyday life, are clearly traumatic for the ears of practical, plain Marilla, who is a woman of limited experience and narrow sensibilities.

Many of the elements of human nature and religious practice that L. M. Montgomery satirizes are those which were also satirized by Mark Twain. But there are notable differences. Twain had a much more romanticized view of childhood than did Montgomery. He depicted childhood as a time of innocence which was in contrast with the rigid and often corrupt adult society. Twain did not attempt to reconcile the two: Huck merely "lit out" for new territory at the end of *Huckleberry Finn*. By contrast, Montgomery's adult society has its share of selfish, nosey, and hypocritical people, but her children are not "noble savages": they are filled with imperfections. But faults that she has notwithstanding, a child like Anne infuses her community with warmth and life. There is accommodation operating between the child's and the adult's world: Anne has too much imagination and the town has too little. But in the process of bridling her imagination, her warmth and fanciful flights revitalize all she associates with. This gives *Anne of Green Gables* a realistic element that *Huckleberry Finn* does not have.

Like Mark Twain in *Huckleberry Finn* and *Tom Sawyer*, Montgomery satirizes the way that religion is interpreted and practiced in a small Presbyterian community. One of Marilla's initial shocks is in the discovery that Anne doesn't pray regularly. Anne's explanation horrifies Marilla: "Mrs. Thomas told me that God made my hair red *on purpose,* and I've never cared about Him since" (54). Prompted to pray "properly," Anne declaims her prayer with rhetorical flourishes and concludes with a sincere if inappropriate closing to God: "Please let me be good-looking when I grow up. I remain. Yours respectfully, Anne Shirley" (55). She immediately asks Marilla if she did the prayer right and adds: "I could have made it more flowery if I'd had a little time to think it over" (56). Marilla concludes, indeed, that this child is "next door to a perfect heathen," and she resolves to begin Anne's religious education. This consists of teaching Anne always to tell the truth and to go to Sunday School. Later, when Marilla asks Anne how she has liked Sunday School, Anne is only too truthful: "I didn't like it a bit. It was horrid." She goes on to explain that she has nevertheless behaved very well through it all, imagining all sorts of splendid things instead of actually listening to the minister's sermon, which droned on and on. When Marilla tells her that she should have been *listening* to the prayer, Anne protests, "But he [the minister] wasn't talking to me. He was talking to God and he didn't seem to be much interested in it, either. I think he thought God was too far off to make it worthwhile" (86). This is satire as deft as Twain's on the same subject. Montgomery has already shown how a child's sincere prayer, delivered with rhetorical flourishes, seems insincere to an adult; next she shows how a highly ritualized adult prayer seems insincere to a perceptive child. In her journals, Montgomery speaks of her dislike of the institution of public prayer, and in *Anne of Green Gables* she clearly satirizes it with enjoyment. It is interesting to reflect that at the very moment she is writing *Anne,* she is being courted by the minister whom she will later marry in spite of considerable misgivings.

On a deeper level, Montgomery gently satirizes the incongruity between religious teaching and practice. Avonlea is full of good religious folk. We learn in chapter one that the worthy Mrs. Rachel Lynde, conscience of all the community and capable manager of her own and others' affairs, is the "strongest prop of the . . . Foreign Missions Auxiliary" (2). In the latter function, Mrs. Lynde may devote tremendous energy to helping send missionaries to save the heathen in China, but her charity does not reach to saving the "heathen" at home. She cautions Marilla not to take in an orphan once she finds out that they have decided to: "You don't know a single thing about him nor what his disposition is like nor what sort of parents he had nor how he's likely to turn out" (18). The community is not only uncharitable towards orphans, but it is deeply prejudiced against the French and a lot of other groups, including those who don't come from "good families." Americans, Germans, and Irish are all objects of prejudice in Avonlea. Montgomery herself shared some of the prejudices in real life, but she also saw their innate hypocrisy, and hence their potential for satire in literature.

Likewise, Montgomery enjoys poking fun at the Presbyterian tendency to see the black side of everything and to forecast doom and gloom. For instance, when Anne first looks out the bedroom window at a beautiful world which includes a tree in bloom, her eyes sweep over the whole scene and she exclaims: "Oh, isn't it wonderful?" Marilla, seeing only the tree and its blooms, but not its beauty, replies: "It's a big tree and it blooms great, but the fruit don't amount to much never—small and wormy" (34). According to Montgomery's diaries, taking a dim and negative view of things was a widespread trait in her Cavendish community.

Other elements of small town behavior also come under attack. Montgomery is skillful at showing how people watch each other and sit in judgment on others' actions. The opening scene with Mrs. Lynde showing her curiosity over Matthew's departure is a *tour de force* in caricaturing a busybody. Mrs. Lynde's forceful personality, and her disapproval of any actions taken without her advice, create much of the tension and the comedy in the first part of the book.

There is subtle satire on the ways in which Rachel and Marilla dominate their respective menfolk, Thomas Lynde and Matthew Cuthbert. Thomas is merely known as "Rachel Lynde's husband" (2), but Matthew, the shyest and most inarticulate man in Avonlea, manages to hold his own and get his way: he just *won't* argue or talk. Marilla finds this exasperating: "I wish he was like other men and would talk things out. A body could answer back then and argue him into reason. But what's to be done with a man who just *looks*?" (39). The internal ironies in such speeches probably escape most children, but they give the novel a depth that adults enjoy. Nor would many children note how the characters manipulate and interact with each other, but adults can appreciate that too. The richness of the novel is responsible for the fact that so many children who loved *Anne* reread it again as adults and say that they enjoy it each time.

Some adults who reread *Anne* feel that Anne's decision to stay with Marilla and accept her "duty" at the end of the novel presents a poor role model for contemporary girls. Without debating the question of whether society is richer or poorer for our changing attitudes towards the care of the elderly, or determining whether any evaluation of literature on the basis of the role models that it provides is another form of didacticism, one can still justify the conclusion of *Anne of Green Gables* for many reasons.

First, Anne must choose to stay with Marilla at Green Gables because the themes developed throughout the novel as well as its overall structure demand it. If Matthew did not die, and if Anne did not have to make the choice between duty to Marilla and self-fulfillment in an outside career, the novel would lack the power that comes from its thematic resolution. Montgomery builds the novel around Anne's human needs and her sense of place: when young, she needs a home and she needs love. Matthew and Marilla's gift of love to her as a child makes her into a whole person as an adult, and her maturity can only be illustrated by showing that she can reciprocate, giving the gift of love to them, and a home to Marilla. This ending may appear sentimental to some people, but it is both thematically and structurally consistent.

Second, Anne's choice is realistic because the novel is a period piece and her decision was inevitable in the context of the 1890s in rural P.E.I. Life sometimes forces choices on people which put them in "damned-if-you-do-and-damned-if-you-don't" situations, and when Montgomery herself (just like Anne) gave up the possibility of a career to keep house for her aging grandmother, she did it knowing that she really had no choice: if she abandoned her grandmother, her own conscience would give her no peace. But if she stayed with her grandmother, life might indeed pass her by.[3]

It is worth emphasizing, however, that L. M. Montgomery does not make Anne's choice final: it does not limit her future. In the final page of the novel, Anne sits at her bedroom window, just as Mrs. Lynde sat at her window as the novel opened. Whereas Mrs. Lynde saw an image of disorder on the road beyond, Anne sees "the bend in the road," an image representing the unknown elements in the future. She does not feel alarm, as did Mrs. Lynde, because Anne knows she is equal to whatever the future may hold. "The bend in the road" is a powerful and poetic symbol and those concerned with role-modeling might well argue that Anne provides the model for delaying gratification in the interests of duty and responsibility.

At any rate, it is not fitting that we censure historical novels (or domestic novels with a definite historical setting) for accurately reflecting the time in which they are set. Instead, classroom teachers and parents can discuss with young people how attitudes and social practices have changed. Left to their own devices, young people reading a novel like *Anne of Green Gables* today are likely to find the stable family life and caring community that it presents a consoling alternative to the descriptions in many contemporary adolescent novels of lonely children who live in single parent or nuclear family situations and who face life in a disorderly society. Like the child Maud Montgomery, as well as later writers like Astrid Lindgren and Jean Little, some contemporary children may anchor themselves in life through their imaginative friends in books.

Whatever readers in the past and readers in the future will make of *Anne of Green Gables,* the novel has proved to be a classic in the fullest sense: it operates on many levels simultaneously. It is a simple story about a child's most basic needs for a home, love, friendship, and acceptance. It is a complex psychological study of the way adults and children think, act, and interact. It is a period study about a rural Canadian community in the 1890s, and, as such, is filled with sociological and cultural realism. Last, it is a novel utilizing acute observation, high comedy, gentle satire, and some of the conventions of romance. *Anne of Green Gables* operates successfully on many levels from the simple narrative to the mythic, and provides a rich literary experience for readers of all ages. It is not a novel that people outgrow.

Notes

1. *Anne of Green Gables* is classed with the "overall best-sellers." Mott states that *Anne of Green Gables* had sold between 800,000 and 900,000 copies by 1947. To be a best-seller, a book had to sell in numbers equal to 1 percent of the population of the continental U.S.A. in the decade in which it was published.

2. Using references to clothing, furniture, and social and political events, Virginia Careless, a social historian with the British Columbia Provincial Museum, has established the dates of the Anne stories.

3. At his death, L. M. Montgomery's grandfather left the house that he and his wife had lived in all their lives (where they raised Lucy Maud) to his son, John, with the provision that his wife be allowed to live out her natural life there. John did not get on well with his mother, and he tried to force her out of the house so that his own grown son could live there. Because of the constant pressure to oust her grandmother from the house, L. M. Montgomery could not consider hiring someone to live with and care for her grandmother.

Works Cited

Cott, Jonathan. "The Astonishment of Being." *New Yorker* (28 Feb. 1983): 46+.

Davies, Robertson. "The Creator of Anne." *Peterborough* [Ontario, Canada] *Examiner,* 2 May 1942: 4.

Fredeman, Jane Cowan. "The Land of Lost Content: The Use of Fantasy in L. M. Montgomery's Novels." *L. M. Montgomery: An Assessment.* Ed. John R. Sorfleet. Guelph, ON: Canadian Children's Press, 1976. 60-70.

Katsura, Yuko. "Red-haired Anne in Japan." *Canadian Children's Literature* 34 (1984): 57-60.

Little, Jean. Personal Interview. 1 June 1985.

Montgomery, L. M. *Anne of Green Gables.* 1908. Toronto: McGraw-Hill Ryerson, 1968.

_____. "Book Sales Book." L. M. Montgomery Collection. U of Guelph, Guelph, ON. (A bound ledger in which Montgomery kept records of all her sales statistics from book titles until her death.)

_____. *The Selected Journals of L. M. Montgomery, Volume I: 1889-1910.* Ed. Mary Rubio and Elizabeth Waterston. Toronto: Oxford UP, 1985.

_____. *The Story Girl.* 1910. Toronto: McGraw-Hill Ryerson, 1966.

Mott, Frank. *Golden Multitudes.* New York: Bowker, 1947.

Rubio, Mary. "Satire, Realism, and Imagination in *Anne of Green Gables.*" *L. M. Montgomery: An Assessment.* Ed. John R. Sorfleet. Guelph, ON: Canadian Children's Press, 1976. 27-36.

Russell, Ruth Weber, D. W. Russell, and Rea Wilmshurst. *Lucy Maud Montgomery: A Preliminary Bibliography.* Waterloo, ON: U of Waterloo, 1986.

Sobkowska, Krystyna. "The Reception of the *Anne of Green Gables* Series by Lucy Maud Montgomery in Poland." Diss. U of Lodz (Poland), 1982-83.

Twain, Mark. Letter to L. M. Montgomery. 3 Oct. 1908. L. M. Montgomery Collection. U of Guelph, Guelph, ON.

Wachowicz, Barbara. "L. M. Montgomery: At Home in Poland." *Canadian Children's Literature* 46 (1987): 7-36.

L. M. Montgomery's Portraits of the Artist

Realism, Idealism, and the Domestic Imagination

T. D. MacLulich

Anne of Green Gables and *Emily of New Moon* are generally accepted as L. M. Montgomery's best books. These two novels tell the stories of spirited and imaginative girls who struggle towards maturity in societies that attach little value to the imagination or to individual self-fulfillment. In fact, *Emily of New Moon* and, to some extent, *Anne of Green Gables* are worthy anticipations of the portraits of young female artists that are given in the works of later writers such as Margaret Laurence and Alice Munro. I mention Montgomery in conjunction with Laurence and Munro in all seriousness. Like them, she had the ambition to write "serious" fiction, and she took as a major theme of her work a subject that Laurence and Munro have now made familiar to all readers of our fiction: the development of a young female artist. Montgomery's best work, then, announces the beginning of a struggle for self-expression by Canadian women writers that has continued virtually to the present day. In both her work and her life, however, Montgomery drew back from claiming the full personal autonomy that later writers have demanded.

Some critics grow visibly exasperated when they are forced to deal with Montgomery's work. Their patronizing comments make it plain that they see Montgomery as a writer of sentimental fiction who once had the luck to stumble on a formula that touched a universal nerve.[1] But Montgomery was, in intention at least, a more committed and a more serious writer than is generally recognized. I must be careful, however, in stating my thesis. I do not want to make an absurdly inflated claim for Montgomery as an instance of neglected greatness, though I do feel that *Anne of Green Gables* and *Emily of New Moon* deserve a more thoughtful consideration than they are usually given. Rather, my claim is that Montgomery's career reveals a good deal about the literary and social climate shaping—and sometimes retarding—the development of Canadian fiction during the turn-of-the-century era. In particular, an examination of both Montgomery's fiction and her ideas about literature highlights several of the forces that hindered her from consistently attaining the level of excellence she exhibits in her best work.

Throughout her life, Montgomery told stories. As a young girl, she invented tales of sentiment or piety, modeled on popular romantic fiction such as that she read in *Godey's Lady's Book,* in which, she says, "villains and villainesses were all neatly labeled and you were sure of your ground" (*The Alpine Path* 48). One of her most striking early efforts, recounted in Mollie Gillen's biography of Montgomery, was a lugubrious saga titled "My Graves," which detailed the sufferings of a Methodist minister's wife who buried a child in every one of her husband's postings, on a journey that took her from Newfoundland to British Columbia (18). As she grew older, however, Montgomery learned that fiction could be built around the ordinary doings of the people of her native Island. Eventually, in her twenty novels and several books of stories, Montgomery created a pastoral image of Prince Edward Island that endures to the present day.

Montgomery thought of her fiction as realistic, in that it presented characters and situations resembling the people and events she had observed during her own childhood. Moreover, her best fiction contains dialogue that is lively and colloquial, and she displays an alert eye for those personal foibles that make literary characters amusing and endearing. Yet, on the whole, Montgomery's fiction presents what to modern eyes appears to be a highly distorted and selective image of the world. The Prince Edward Island of her fiction is an unblemished bucolic paradise; her novels are populated mainly by figures who are either picturesque caricatures or romantic idealizations. But literary realism lies very much in the eyes of the beholder. What seems implausibly rose-tinted to modern readers may have seemed considerably more realistic to many readers of Montgomery's own day, especially when they compared her fiction to the stories that were common in the popular ladies' periodicals.

It may take an effort of the historical imagination to see Montgomery as one of the pioneers of realism in Canadian fiction. But we must remember that she did not write out of a sophisticated literary milieu. Montgomery was born in 1874, and came to maturity in a provincial culture dominated by values that were already old-fashioned in the metropolitan centres of Europe and the United States. Therefore, to understand the literary climate in which Montgomery's ideas were formed, we should not turn to the writings of the leading Victorian critics, but rather to the pages of the general periodicals published in Canada during the last decades of the nineteenth century.

In these publications, literary contributors often allude to a controversy that was widespread in Victorian Britain and in post-Civil War America, the debate over "realism" and "idealism" in fiction. One Canadian writer, in an article on the then-popular Norwegian writer Bjornstjerne Bjornston, explained the "ordinary and well-understood meanings" of the terms in this way:

> I take it that . . . realism, as applied to fiction, is the doctrine of the superior importance of the real facts of life; that is, the reproduction of actual life utterly devoid of any striving for romance, poetry, or uncommon incidents and situations. Idealism, I take it, is the doctrine of the superiority of ideal creations over the facts of life. (Livingston 98)

Like most Canadian critics, this writer favored idealism because it was "filled with a great purpose to benefit mankind," whereas realism only resulted in morally reprehensible works such as those of Zola and the French school of fiction.

A vigorous expression of the idealists' position is found in this lament by Graeme Mercer Adam:

> The good old romantic and imaginative novel of our grandmothers' time seems a creation wholly of the past. What we have in its place is the English melodrama of such books as "Called Back": the intellectual vivisection methods of the Amer-

ican schools of James and Howells; or, worse still, the loathsome
realism and putridity of the school of Zola and France. (103)

As these comments suggest, the principal aversions of the idealists
were found among American and French writers, though British
novelists whose works hinted at naturalistic doctrines, such as
Hardy, were not exempt from criticism. For example, Louisa Murray, in the title of her polemic against "Democracy in Literature,"
made a commonly accepted equation between dangerous republi-
can political ideas and immoral literary doctrines. She cited with
approval the imprisonment of the London bookseller Vizetelly for
selling Zola's novels, and she said that Howells' novels "if accepted
as true pictures of the best that life can give, could scarcely fail to
check all aspirations after the higher possibilities of existence,
without which life would certainly not be worth living" (550).

Sara Jeanette Duncan was one of the few Canadian writers who
welcomed the new fiction with anything approaching an open mind.
Above all, she appointed herself the Canadian champion of the
fiction of Howells and James, whom she often defended against the
attacks of those she viewed as censorious Philistines. She approvingly described Howells and James as "engaged in developing a
school of fiction most closely and subtly related to the conditions
and progress of our time, of which we all should know something"
("Literary Pablum" 831). Yet even Duncan could write: "The
modern school of fiction, if it is fairly subject to any reproach, may
bear the blame of dealing too exclusively in the corporealities of
human life, to the utter and scornful neglect of its idealities" ("The
Art Gallery of the English Language" 533). Apologists for both
realism and idealism, then, based their arguments on moral
grounds. At bottom, they simply disagreed over whether literature
could best impart its messages by portraying the world as it was, or
by portraying the world as it ought to be.

Montgomery showed little of Duncan's receptivity to the new
modes of fiction. Instead, she steadfastly hewed to the idealist
position, long after it had dropped from favor almost everywhere
else. As a result, when Montgomery read twentieth-century American and Canadian fiction, she seldom liked what she found there.
In a letter to Ephraim Weber, she said of Upton Sinclair's *The
Jungle*: "It is *hideous,* morally as well as physically!" (47). Morley
Callaghan's *Strange Fugitive* she found "'the deadliest dull thing'"

she had ever read. She objected to Callaghan's insistence on presenting characters and events that she found repellent. Callaghan's aim, she wrote, "seems to [b]e to photograph a latrine or pig-sty meticulously and leave nothing else in the picture" (qtd. in Gillen 160). Even Mazo de la Roche's *Jalna* could not earn her complete approval. She conceded that *Jalna* was "clever and 'modern.'" Nonetheless, even as she sent a copy to her friend G. B. MacMillan, she wondered in the accompanying letter if he would like it. "I can hardly say I did," she told him (128).

An early short story, "Each in his Own Tongue," from *Chronicles of Avonlea* (1912), illustrates Montgomery's conception of art. In the story the strict minister Mr. Leonard has forbidden his musically gifted son Felix to play the violin, for Mr. Leonard associates this instrument with the dissolute musician who ruined his older daughter's life. Felix sadly but dutifully obeys his father— that is, until Montgomery arranges a happy ending. The dying sinner Naomi Clark, whom Reverend Leonard cannot move to repentance with his prayers, asks that Felix play the violin for her. Mr. Leonard is unable to refuse a dying request, and he allows Felix to play. Felix's music touches Naomi's heart and brings her to repentance. Mr. Leonard, naturally enough, then drops his opposition to Felix's musical career.

Montgomery explains the story's message in these terms: "Mr. Leonard thought rightly that the highest work to which any could be called was a life of service to his fellows; but he made the mistake of supposing the field of service much narrower than it is—of failing to see that a man may minister to the needs of humanity in many different but equally effective ways" (80). This explanation of art's social function allows Montgomery to support the claims of the artist to autonomy, while simultaneously she can insist on the morality of the artist's endeavour.

Throughout her career, then, Montgomery predictably rejected the sort of realism that dominated the serious fiction of her day. Instead, she modeled her own stories on the efforts of the American local colorists, and above all on the domestic stories for girls that followed in the wake of Louisa May Alcott's *Little Women*. Her use of rural Prince Edward Island settings and characters, together with her occasional flashes of ironic wit, provide a measure of realism in her work. But her adherence to the idea that fiction should provide its readers with inspiration and uplift makes her work seem implausibly sentimental to most modern readers. In other words, Montgomery's version of realism has very narrow limits.

Montgomery's penchant for sentimentality in her fiction was also encouraged by her belief in a vulgarized Romantic view of the artist as someone who lives in a sort of perpetual childhood. Some of the child-protagonists of her fiction, such as Sara Stanley in *The Story Girl,* embody Montgomery's rather simplistic conception of the artist. In that book, Montgomery's narrator directly tells us that artists are people

> who remain children at heart. . . . They, and only they, can bring
> us tidings from that dear country where we once sojourned and
> from which we must evermore be exiles. The world calls them
> its singers and poets and artists and storytellers; but they are just
> people who have never forgotten the way to fairyland. (111)

The rudimentary theory of art sketched here fits Montgomery's work very well. Her own youthful stories and poems were the literary continuation of a childhood fantasy world, and to the end of her life her fiction retained a quality of escapism.

In *The Alpine Path,* a short autobiographical memoir first published in 1917, Montgomery calls *The Story Girl* "my own favourite among my books, the one that gave me the greatest pleasure to write, and the one whose characters and landscape seem to me most real" (78). At first glance, this preference may seem unaccountable, for *The Story Girl* is certainly one of Montgomery's weakest efforts. But the explanation for her preference may lie in the themes she chooses to explore in the book. *The Story Girl* presents a version of one of Montgomery's favorite themes. Namely, it deals with a sensitive and imaginative child who, even though she does not have literary ambitions in the usual sense, is nonetheless a projection of the artist-in-embryo that Montgomery herself once was.

On the surface, *The Story Girl* is a lovingly imagined account of an idyllic Prince Edward Island summer spent by several farm children and their guests from the city. The book is best understood, however, as an examination of the value of the imagination. Indeed, *The Story Girl* has little plot in any conventional sense. The emphasis falls instead on the tales that are told by one of the children, Sara Stanley, who is better known as "the Story Girl." Sara Stanley has an apparently inexhaustible fund of anecdote, family history, local gossip, and legends. She can produce a story to suit any occasion and uses her storytelling skills both to entertain and to influence her hearers. In short, Sara Stanley's tales captivate her youthful audience—and some adult listeners as well—just as Montgomery wants to captivate her readers.

Montgomery's fiction was also strongly influenced by her acceptance of restrictive standards that were prevalent in her society. There is an enormous range of events she would not have dreamed of mentioning in a novel or a story. Moreover, the plots of her fiction lean heavily on sentimental formulas adopted from the popular fiction of her youth. Often these self-chosen limitations— for such I think they are—reveal Montgomery's acquiescence to the secondary and largely domestic role her society traditionally assigned women.

Montgomery's life and art were both shaped by an outlook that exalted the household and the local community as the embodiment of the highest good to which women could aspire. From her family and from her childhood community, Montgomery acquired what can only be called a thoroughly domestic imagination. In her own life she repeatedly adopted traditional women's roles, ministering to others rather than striving after her own personal fulfillment. Montgomery was raised by her maternal grandparents, with whom her father left her after her mother's death. Later, when her grandfather died, she left her teaching position and returned to her childhood home to assume responsibility for her aging grandmother. She kept her engagement to the Presbyterian minister Ewan Macdonald a secret, delaying their marriage until her grandmother died. After her marriage, Montgomery conscientiously added the onerous social duties of a minister's wife to her household tasks and her literary pursuits.

In her fiction, Montgomery demonstrates a strong awareness of the limitations that hedge a woman's life, but she seems unable to imagine any escape for her characters from a conventional role. For example, in her only two "adult" novels, Montgomery portrays young women who face a highly restrictive choice: they may marry, or they may become old maids. For a woman to think of taking up a career is not considered respectable. As Margaret Penhallow grimly reflects in *A Tangled Web:* "There was only one career for women in her clan. Of course you could be a nurse or a teacher or dressmaker, or something like that, to fill in the time before marriage, but the Darks and Penhallows did not take you seriously" (93-94). And in *The Blue Castle* Montgomery comments, concerning the unmarried state of her heroine Valancy Stirling: "One does not sleep well, sometimes, when one is twenty-nine on the morrow, and unmarried, in a community and connection where the unmarried are simply those who have failed to get a man" (1). Despite her awareness of this female dilemma, Montgomery can imagine in her fiction only one resolution of this situation: the unhappy woman must finally acquire a man of her own.

Montgomery's restricted view of woman's role is also clearly apparent in *Courageous Women,* a collection of short biographical sketches of famous women she prepared in collaboration with "Marian Keith" (Mary Esther MacGregor) and Mabel Burns McKinley. The women described in this book all fulfill an ideal of service to humanity; even the artists and performers are applauded for the pleasure they give to others rather than for the fulfillment they gain for themselves. Moreover, the authors never portray a woman's struggle as painful or destructive to her personality. The book demonstrates no real awareness of the extent to which social institutions can impose virtually unbreakable limitations on a woman's horizons. There is an implicit faith that all a woman's legitimate desires can be accomplished by means of genteel persistence.

Montgomery claimed that writing was an essential part of her life. In *The Alpine Path,* she reports: "I cannot remember the time when I was not writing, or when I did not mean to be an author. To write has always been my central purpose around which every effort and hope and ambition of my life has grouped itself" (52). But in Montgomery's own life, the conception of a woman's proper role that she acquired from her childhood milieu threatened to clash with her devotion to her art. Therefore, in spite of her commercial success and in spite of her very real talents, Montgomery remained uneasy in her chosen role as a writer. She needed to justify her writing to herself by viewing it as an extension of her woman's mission to comfort, uplift, and improve the world. This understanding of her art is evident not only in the self-censorship she willingly imposed on her fiction, but also in the fates she arranged for her two best-known heroines.

I have already remarked that Montgomery liked to tell stories. But there was only one story that she *needed* to tell: the story of an imaginative and emotional girl who loses her beloved parents, enters the forbidding world of her stern and old-fashioned new guardians, eventually earns the affection of her surrogate parents, yet does so without effacing her own personality to meet their expectations or demands. This was, of course, her own story, altered just enough to excise much of the pain and resentment she felt over what was, in effect, her desertion by her father. In much of her fiction, then, Montgomery drew on her own experiences to depict the lot of an emotional and articulate young person set down amid people who are taciturn and undemonstrative.

There is, therefore, an element of wishful self-portraiture in Montgomery's portrayals of most of her young heroines. Above all, she projects her artistic aptitude and her imagination onto the protagonists of *Anne of Green Gables, The Story Girl, Emily of New Moon,* and *Magic for Marigold.* She also casts creative children as important characters in several of the novels that continue Anne's story into adulthood and marriage. But Montgomery's presentation of these characters shows her reservations about the propriety of a woman pursuing an artistic career to the exclusion of conventional societal concerns. Even Anne and Emily, Montgomery's most talented and self-willed young artists, lose much of their rebelliousness as they grow into womanhood. In the end, they meekly agree to marry the mate that Montgomery has created specially for them. Montgomery, then, cannot let her heroine's literary career interfere with the course of true love. This outcome is disappointing. It seems to represent a failure on Montgomery's part of both the literary and social imagination.

A revealing example of Montgomery's cautious treatment of the imaginative child is provided by the protagonist of *Magic for Marigold.* Marigold arouses her stern grandmother's anger by inventing an imaginary playmate, but the psychologist Dr. Adam Penhallow comes to her rescue when he explains that Marigold's imaginings are not lies, but have their own kind of truth:

> They are not falsehoods. They are truths to her. She sees things invisible to us. She is a queen in the lovely Kingdom of Make-Believe. She is not trying to deceive anybody. She has the wonderful gift of creation in an unusual degree. It is such a pity

that she will lose it as she grows older—that she will have to
forego its wonder and live, like us, in the light of common day.
(116)

And at the novel's end Marigold readily, if a little sadly, gives up
her fantasy world in favor of a precocious acceptance of her
domestic vocation.

Montgomery's first extended study of the imaginative child,
however, is found in *Anne of Green Gables*. Although the disciplin-
ing of Anne's too-active imagination is a central theme of the novel,
Anne's flights of fancy are nonetheless an important source of the
renewed life she brings to Green Gables. At one point Anne is
astonished by Marilla's resolutely down-to-earth outlook:

"Do you never imagine things different from what they really
are?" asked Anne wide-eyed.
"No."
"Oh!" Anne drew a long breath. "Oh, Miss—Marilla, how much
you miss!" (59)

At such moments Anne reveals the vision of a potential artist, and
throughout the novel many of her difficulties resemble the problems
encountered by an artistic child facing a materialistic and unimag-
inative society.

One of the traits that most clearly identifies Anne as having a
creative temperament is her fondness for the overblown rhetoric
she has learned from her reading of sentimental fiction. Anne learns
many things in the course of Montgomery's novel, but perhaps her
hardest lesson involves curbing her fondness for the flowery language and melodramatic plotting common in her favorite sort of
fiction. Anne tells Marilla that her teacher, Miss Stacy, "won't let
us write anything but what might happen in Avonlea in our own
lives" (271). Moreover, Miss Stacy "makes us write all our essays
as simply as possible. It was hard at first. I was so used to crowding
in all the fine big words I could think of—and I thought of any
number of them. But I've got used to it now and I see it's so much
better" (271). Here, expressed very briefly, is the kernel of a theme
that Montgomery returns to several times in her later works. In *Anne
of the Island,* for example, the eccentric but shrewd Mr. Harrison
tells Anne that she should set her stories in Avonlea; she should use

ordinary people as her characters, not just rich people; and she should write in the language of ordinary speech, not in a high-flown imitation of literary diction.

Montgomery casts creative children as important supporting characters in several of the novels that continue the Anne series, but she obviously has reservations about the propriety of allowing Anne to pursue her literary ambitions to the exclusion of all else. In fact, she cannot allow Anne to put her literary ambitions ahead of her domestic vocation as helpmate to Dr. Gilbert Blythe. For example, in *Anne's House of Dreams,* Montgomery makes Anne tell a visiting writer: "Oh, I do little things for children. I haven't done much since I was married. And I have no designs on a great Canadian novel" (176). It is the visitor, Owen Ford, who eventually uses Captain Jim's "life-book" (a sort of diary) as the basis for a novel that is well received by the critical press. Anne, being a woman, cannot be allowed to define herself primarily in terms of her public career. She must remain above all a wife and mother. Only a male child, such as Paul Irving, whom Anne teaches in *Anne of Avonlea,* can be allowed to develop into a full-fledged professional writer.

In the later Anne books, the plots still revolve around the private emotional difficulties of the individual characters. There is little recognition of larger social or political issues, and little acknowledgment that society may impose a severe burden on the individual. Only in *Rilla of Ingleside* does the outside world, in the form of the First World War, impinge seriously on the private lives of Montgomery's characters. With *Rilla of Ingleside* Montgomery called, as she thought, a permanent halt to the Anne books. She wanted to end the series in part because she refused to confront the transformation time had wrought on the golden world of her childhood. Although she had left the Island when she married, she was extremely reluctant to move her fiction out of her idyllic childhood world. Instead, she plunged back into the past once again by creating another aspiring young writer, Emily Byrd Starr.

In the Emily series, especially in *Emily of New Moon,* Montgomery again drew on her own early years. She told one of her correspondents: "People were never right in saying I was Anne, but *in some respects,* they will be right if they write me down as Emily" (qtd. in Gillen 134). Montgomery's biographers, especially Hilda M. Riley (114-21), have industriously compiled traits and experiences that are shared by Emily and her creator. But the single most important trait Montgomery projected onto Emily was the determination to become a writer, a determination she makes Emily cling to in the face of strong opposition from her relatives and guardians, the Murrays. "It is *in me*," Emily insists (317). In building the Emily series around Emily's artistic development, Montgomery drew on virtually all of her thoughts about writers and writing, so that Emily's story contains the most complete exposition she ever provided of her own ideas about literature.

Many of Emily's traits resemble characteristics Montgomery ascribes to herself in *The Alpine Path*. Like Montgomery, Emily has moments of intense awareness, when she experiences what she calls "the flash." This sensation seems to bring her close to "a world of wonderful beauty" (7) that lies just beneath the surface of the everyday world: "Between it and herself hung only a thin curtain; she could never draw the curtain aside—but sometimes, just for a moment, a wind fluttered it and then it was as if she caught a glimpse of the enchanting realm beyond—only a glimpse—and heard a note of unearthly music" (7). These moments when Emily experiences "the flash" are closely linked with her need to write, for even as a child she feels compelled to describe her moments of intense feeling. She says of one such experience, "it would hurt her with its beauty until she wrote it down" (7). Initially, then, Emily's writing is linked with her hunger for contact with an ideal world. Her earliest attempts at formal literary composition are modeled on popular romantic fiction, in which the characters and settings are far removed from her own daily experience. As she grows up, however, she learns—as did Montgomery—that fiction can be built around stories and characters encountered in her own immediate environment.

Emily's writing plays an integral role in her emotional development, as she struggles to accept her father's death and to make a place for herself with the relatives who have grudgingly adopted her. Emily first uses her writing as a channel to vent her feelings when she is publicly humiliated as her relatives bicker about who should take charge of the unwelcome new orphan. "Yes," she tells herself, "she *would* write them all out in the account book—describe every last one of them—sweet Aunt Laura, nice Cousin Jimmy, grim old Uncle Wallace, and moonfaced Uncle Oliver, stately Aunt Elizabeth and detestable Aunt Ruth" (30). Later she finds that writing about her painful experiences does relieve her feelings: "As her fingers flew over the faded lines her cheeks flushed and her eyes shone. She forgot the Murrays although she was writing about them—she forgot her humiliation—although she was describing what had happened" (43).

Later on, Emily pours out her innermost feelings in a series of letters addressed to her dead father, whom she salutes as *"Mr. Douglas Starr, On the Road to Heaven"* (97). In these letters she gives voice to the feelings she is unable to express to her new guardians. Not until she learns that she is loved by stern Aunt Elizabeth, the dominant figure at New Moon (as her aunts' house is called) does she stop writing these letters. But by then her letters have given her a kind of literary training that her attempts at more formal kinds of literature do not provide. By writing about her own life and feelings, Emily has learned to speak simply and directly of the people and things immediately around her. As a result, she has also compiled a series of character vignettes describing local people. These sketches are not flattering to their subjects, for they often express Emily's resentment over some injury she has received. But they have a freshness and life that are lacking in her attempts at polite literature.

Emily's informal character sketches play a significant role in the final scene of *Emily of New Moon*. When Emily's teacher, Mr. Carpenter, offers to read some of her literary efforts and give her some advice, she prepares both a selection of her best poems and a notebook containing

> three or four of her latest stories—*The Butterfly Queen*, a little fairy tale; *The Disappointed House*, wherein she had woven a pretty dream of hopes come true after long years; *The Secret of the Glen*, which, in spite of its title, was a fanciful little dialogue between the Spirit of the Snow, the Spirit of the Grey Rain, the Spirit of Mist, and the Spirit of Moonshine. (348-49)

Mr. Carpenter first reads her poetry, in which he finds "[t]en good lines out of four hundred" (347), and on that basis urges her to continue. Then Mr. Carpenter turns to the notebook containing Emily's stories.

When Mr. Carpenter starts to chuckle over her literary efforts, Emily suddenly realizes that she has given him the wrong notebook.

Instead of a few romantic and fanciful tales, the notebook her
teacher holds contains

> [s]ketches of everyone in Blair Water—and a full—a very full—
> description of Mr. Carpenter himself. Intent on describing him
> exactly, she had been as mercilessly lucid as she always was,
> especially in regard to the odd faces he made on mornings when
> he opened the school day with a prayer. (349)

To Emily's surprise, Mr. Carpenter is not offended by her uncom-
promising description of his habits and appearance: "Thanks to her
dramatic knack of word painting, Mr. Carpenter *lived* in that sketch.
Emily did not know it but *he* did—he saw himself as in a glass and
the artistry of it pleased him so that he cared for nothing else.
Besides, she had drawn his good points quite as clearly as his bad
ones" (349). Emily tries to apologize, but gets an unexpected
reaction. Mr. Carpenter exclaims: "Why, I wouldn't have missed
this for all the poetry you've written or ever will write! By gad, it's
literature—*literature*—and you're only thirteen" (349).

Montgomery intends to have Mr. Carpenter endorse the sort of
realism she practices in her own work, almost all of which depicts
farm and village life in Prince Edward Island. But there is a
discrepancy between Mr. Carpenter's words in this passage and
Montgomery's own practice in her work. Here Mr. Carpenter is, in
effect, enjoining Emily to produce realism rather than idealism. His
comments support the view that the best literature presents a true
image of the world, warts and all. Certainly Emily's strength as a
writer—like Montgomery's strength—lies in creating a picture of
her own local world. But we are told that Emily's best writing often
expresses the hostility she feels towards her subjects, or rests on her
ability to tell the unpleasant truth about other people. Montgomery
severely curbed this aspect of her own writing. Her satirical gifts
were considerable, but she never allowed her talent for satire to
have its way unchecked. Her version of literary realism would not
offend the strictest apostle of idealism.

In *Emily Climbs* and *Emily's Quest* Mr. Carpenter reverts to
being a spokesman for Montgomery's idealistic view of art. He
warns Emily away from satire in *Emily Climbs* by telling her:
"There is a place for satire—there are gangrenes that can only be
burned out—but leave the burning to the great geniuses. It's better

to heal than hurt" (21). In other words, most art should uplift its audience, or at least give pleasure. Emily endorses Mr. Carpenter's attitude when she confides in her journal:

> I read a story tonight. It ended unhappily. I was wretched until I had invented a happy ending for it. I shall always end *my* stories happily. I don't care whether it's "true to life" or not. It's true to life as it *should be* and that's a better truth than the other. (214)

In all likelihood, this passage also represents Montgomery's own viewpoint. With his dying breath, Mr. Carpenter gasps out a renewed statement of Montgomery's allegiance to idealism. He warns Emily:

> Don't be—led away—by those howls about realism. Remember—pine woods are just as real as—pigsties—and a darn sight pleasanter to be in. . . . And don't—tell the world—everything. That's what's the matter—with our—literature. Lost the charm of mystery—and reserve. (*Emily's Quest* 29)

As fiction, the two additional Emily books are a disappointment. The central focus shifts away from Emily's struggle to become a writer, and instead we get a rather dreary succession of unsatisfactory suitors for Emily's hand. Interest revives only the first one-third or so of *Emily's Quest,* when she carries on a strange love affair with the older and more sophisticated Dean Priest, who in effect becomes jealous of Emily's devotion to her work, which he correctly perceives will prevent her from belonging wholly to him. After this romantic episode ends, Emily is annoyingly slow in realizing what Montgomery makes glaringly obvious to the reader—that Emily's youthful companion Teddy Kent is her destined soul-mate. Eventually, however, Emily goes the way of all Montgomery's postadolescent heroines, and acknowledges her attachment to her fated mate.

In her subsequent fiction, Montgomery moves away from the direct concern with literature that is so conspicuous in the Emily series. Instead, her later fiction seems to express an increasingly strong sense of regret that she ever left her childhood home. The two books about Pat Gardner, *Pat of Silver Bush* (1933) and *Mistress Pat* (1935), portray a heroine whose attachment to the family home borders on a morbid resistance to all change. In *Jane of Lantern Hill* (1937), she takes her heroine on a reviving journey to Prince Edward Island that expresses Montgomery's own wish to recapture the idealized world of her childhood. And in the two additions to the Anne series that she composed in her last years, Montgomery engaged in narcissistic nostalgia when she reinserted herself into the world of her first major fictional success. "At first," she wrote to G. B. MacMillan, "I thought I could never 'get back' into that series. It seemed to belong to another world. But after the plunge I began to find it possible—nay to enjoy it—as if I really had found my way back to those golden years before the world went mad" (177). By this stage in her career, however, Montgomery had forgotten Anne's rebellious side. In *Anne of Windy Poplars* (1936) and *Anne of Ingleside* (1939), Anne is busy contriving marriages rather than promoting her own personal development.

It should be clear by now that Montgomery's lifelong commitment to the imagination was tempered by an alternative commitment that grew stronger throughout her career, a commitment to the moral and social norms she had learned during her childhood. Montgomery's strongest fiction portrays apostles of the imagination who rebel against the standards of a conservative community. But Mrs. Grundy always seems to be looking over Montgomery's shoulder as she writes, so that Montgomery never dares to let her protagonists put themselves deeply and permanently at odds with their society. Unlike most twentieth-century writers—men or women—Montgomery does not endorse the priority of the artist's needs over the needs of society. In her fiction she habitually resolves the conflict between society and the imaginative individual in favor of conformity to social expectations.

Whenever Montgomery's fiction lost touch with childhood, her writing lost much of its sparkle. Apparently, when she dealt with adults, the literary convention that made marriage the conclusion of so much popular fiction reinforced a social convention so pervasive in Montgomery's milieu that she could not imagine an alternative way of ending a story. As a result, when she followed her heroines past their childhoods, she succumbed to formulas of popular sentimental fiction, and filled her pages with variations on the theme of courtship, using marriage as the happy ending that makes up for any amount of prior suffering. In her life and her art, then, Montgomery was consistent, always adhering to the conventional pattern. In her own life, despite her awareness of the difficulties society placed in the path of a woman who tried to make her own way in the world, Montgomery was reluctant to adopt a radical feminist outlook. In her fiction, she softens and domesticates the unruly emotions that underlie all her best work, and makes her writing espouse standards of decency and decorum that would please even Mrs. Rachel Lynde, the vigilant arbiter of Avonlea society.

Notes

1. Desmond Pacey remarks, "it would be silly to apply adult critical standards" to *Anne of Green Gables,* and he says the book "achieves a quaint, naive perfection" *(Creative Writing in Canada,* rev. ed. [Toronto: McGraw-Hill Ryerson, 1961] 106). Sheila Egoff querulously writes: "To denigrate the literary qualities of *Anne of Green Gables* is as useless an exercise as carping about the architecture of the National War Memorial. Anne arrived and she has stayed" *(The Republic of Childhood,* 2nd ed. [Toronto: Oxford UP, 1975] 304.)

Works Cited

Adam, Graeme Mercer. "Some Books of the Past Year—II." *The Week* 14 Jan. 1885.

Bolger, Frances W. P., and Elizabeth R. Epperley, eds. *My Dear Mr. M: Letters to G. B. MacMillan.* Toronto: McGraw-Hill Ryerson, 1980.

Duncan, Sara Jeanette. "The Art Gallery of the English Language." *The Week* 15 July 1886.

_____. "Literary Pablum." *The Week* 24 Nov. 1887.

Eggleston, Wilfrid, ed. *The Green Gables Letters: From L. M. Montgomery to Ephraim Weber, 1905-1909.* Toronto: Ryerson, 1960.

Gillen, Mollie. *The Wheel of Things: A Biography of L. M. Montgomery.* Toronto: Fitzhenry and Whiteside, 1975.

Livingston, Stuart. "Bjornstjerne Bjornston." *Canadian Magazine* April 1893: 93-100.

Montgomery, L. M. *The Alpine Path: The Story of My Career.* 1917. Toronto: Fitzhenry and Whiteside, 1974.

_____. *Anne of Green Gables.* 1908. Toronto: McGraw-Hill Ryerson, 1968.

_____. *Anne's House of Dreams.* 1917. Toronto: McClelland and Stewart, 1922.

_____. *The Blue Castle.* Toronto: McClelland and Stewart, 1926.

_____. *Chronicles of Avonlea.* 1912. London: Harrap, 1925.

_____. *Emily Climbs.* Toronto: McClelland and Stewart, 1925.

_____. *Emily of New Moon.* Toronto: McClelland and Stewart, 1923.

_____. *Emily's Quest.* Toronto: McClelland and Stewart, 1927.

_____. *Magic for Marigold.* Toronto: McClelland and Stewart, 1929.

_____. *The Story Girl.* 1911. London: Harrap, 1925.

_____. *A Tangled Web.* Toronto: McClelland and Stewart, 1931.

_____. Marian Keith, and Mable Burns McKinley. *Courageous Women.* Toronto: McClelland and Stewart, 1934.

Murray, Louisa. "Democracy in Literature." *The Week* 2 Aug. 1889.

Ridley, Hilda M. *The Story of L. M. Montgomery.* Toronto: Ryerson, 1956.

"Kindred Spirits" All

Green Gables Revisited

Carol Gay

Lucy Maud Montgomery's Anne series represents a common problem in children's literature, the problem of the enduring classic that retains its popularity through the years without much evidence of what is usually defined as literary merit. Almost as much as *Little Women*, Montgomery's Avonlea books are a common bond shared by women of our century; but there is no gainsaying that Montgomery is sometimes sentimental, frequently cliché-ridden in plot and style, and often given to excessively flowery descriptive passages. What explains her enduring appeal and gives her a place in the history of literature, a history that continues to ignore her in spite of her impact on millions of readers in the past seventy-five years?

One explanation is that those readers were mostly women and girls, and thus invisible. Gerda Lerner called attention to their invisibility in her *The Female Experience: An American Documentary* in 1977, and in 1979 gave us a new way to look at history in her seminal *The Majority Finds Its Past: Placing Women in History*. "Women have been left out of history," Lerner tells us in the latter,

> not because of the evil conspiracies of men in general or male historians in particular, but because we have considered history only in male-centered terms. We have missed women and their activities, because we have asked questions of history which are inappropriate to women. To rectify this, and to light up areas of historical darkness we must, for a time, focus on a woman-centered inquiry, considering the possibility of the existence of a

female culture *within* the general culture shared by men and
women. History must include an account of the female experience over time and should include the development of feminist
consciousness as an essential aspect of women's past. This is the
primary task of women's history. What would history be like if
it were seen through the eyes of women and ordered by values
they define?

What Lerner suggests for historians is a legitimate task of the
literary critic as well. Pursuing it will not only help elucidate the
"development of feminist consciousness," but should place in a new
perspective the role and impact of a large number of books for
children and young adults written by women, *Anne of Green Gables*
among them.

There are six books in the Avonlea series by one count, eight
by another, and the count could go up to ten if all Montgomery's
books with the Avonlea setting and some connection with Anne
were included. Mollie Gillen, Montgomery's most reliable biographer and bibliographer, cites eight and lists them chronologically
in sequence of Anne's life. *Anne of Green Gables* appeared first in
1908, and introduced to Marilla and Matthew Cuthbert and the
world the red-headed orphan "without a pick on her bones." They
were expecting a boy. On that slight donnée depend all the books
that follow: *Anne of Avonlea* in 1909, about Anne's experiences as
a teacher; *Anne of the Island,* 1915, about her college days; *Anne
of Windy Poplars,* 1936, about her engagement to Gilbert Blythe
and her term as school principal; *Anne's House of Dreams,* 1917,
about her marriage and the death of her first-born child; *Anne of
Ingleside,* 1939, about the raising of her six children; *Rainbow
Valley,* 1919, more about the children; and finally, *Rilla of Ingleside,*
1921,* about Anne's daughter and her reaction to the war.

These capsule summaries and Montgomery's chapter titles
mirror Lerner's feminist categorization of history, in which she
discards such familiar headings as "The Age of Revolution" and
"The Age of Jackson" for such categories as "Childhood," "Marriage, Motherhood, and the Single State," and "Just a Housewife."

---

* *Rilla of Ingleside* was first published in Canada in 1920; 1921 is the date
of the first American edition.

In Montgomery's books we have "Anne Is Invited to Tea," "Gilbert and Anne Disagree," "Just a Happy Day." Not much happens, but only if one defines the action against *Moby Dick*. And why should we? Especially since, as Lerner points out in *The Majority Finds Its Past,*

> women's culture is not and should not be seen as a subculture. It is hardly possible for the majority to live in a subculture. . . . Women live their social existence within the general culture and, whenever they are confined by patriarchal restraint or segregation into separateness (which always has subordination as its purpose), they transform this restraint into complementarity (asserting the importance of woman's function, even its 'superiority') and redefine it.

In Lerner's words, then, "What would history be like if it were seen through the eyes of women and ordered by values they define?" Very much like life in Avonlea. When *Anne of Green Gables* was first published in 1908, there had been nothing like it in children's literature since Alcott's *Little Women*. *Little Women* spawned the so-called "family story"—*Five Little Peppers* and such—but no one until Montgomery took the female protagonist and, with the realism that Alcott had pioneered, created a worthy successor to Jo March. It had been a long time for readers to wait, and perhaps this is one reason why the response to *Anne of Green Gables* was so immediately strong and, to Montgomery, so unexpected.

But it is not Alcott who comes to mind when one is reading *Anne*. It is Sarah Orne Jewett and her superb *The Country of the Pointed Firs,* written in the tradition of the New England local colorists with its depiction of "a rural realm that existed on the margins of patriarchal society, a world that nourished strong, free women" and which "created a counter-tradition to the sentimental/domestic convention that dominated American women's writing through most of the nineteenth century," according to Josephine Donovan's recent *New England Local Color Literature.* Unlike Jewett's women, Alcott's Jo is clearly constrained within a patriarchal world. She doesn't succumb, but she doesn't overcome it either. This is the paradox (and tragedy) of Alcott and Jo. Jo remains the perennial tomboy. But not Anne; she's always a girl.

Anne's sorrows are not those that come from chafing against her womanhood and the deprivation this entails in a man's world; her sorrows are those of womankind: the death of a child, the loneliness of old age, separation from a child, the loss of a beloved. For Anne lives in a woman's world. Not that men disappear. There are a few, Matthew, for instance, and Gilbert, of course, and Mr. J. A. Harrison, and Captain Jim and Owen Ford and a few others, but they, most of them, are "kindred spirits" who share traditionally women's values and who, without becoming emasculated, share with Anne the world she inhabits.

That world is a very real one, situated squarely on Prince Edward Island's rocky coast with its fruit trees and farms and woods that still thrill with their beauty. Here, in a realistic credible world, the reader is introduced to an extraordinarily rich ménage of female characters.

Few writers can characterize so adeptly, so quickly, and frequently, so poignantly, as Montgomery. She does it as well as Jewett and better than Harriet Beecher Stowe. And she has a sense of humor. There are always the shifting groups of girls, and, later, women, which Anne draws around her wherever she settles. And there are the memorable individuals that stand out so clearly. There is Rachel Lynde, who appears on the first page of *Anne of Green Gables,* "notable housewife," "one of those capable creatures who can manage their own concerns and those of other folks into the bargain." There are also Janet Sweet, in *Anne of Avonlea,* who waited twenty years for John Douglas to propose; Miss Lavender, whose pride let her lover leave her over a petty quarrel and who then retires to a life of solitude; Leslie Moore of *House of Dreams,* the gorgeous beauty married to a husband with the mind of a five-year-old; Mrs. Allan, of *Green Gables,* the minister's young wife, whose joy of following her husband to his next parish is marred by the grief of abandoning the grave of her first-born. Or Miss Patty, age seventy, and Miss Maria, age fifty, in *Anne of the Island,* who live together contentedly and quietly in a house called "Patty's Place" until one day they up and go to Europe. As Miss Patty declares, "I daresay I'd have gone to Europe before if the idea had occurred to me." When they hear of Anne's approaching marriage they write in *House of Dreams:* "We send you our best wishes. Maria and I have never married, but we have no objection to other people doing so." And there is Miss Cornelia Bryant who knows everyone around Four Winds Harbor in *House of Dreams* and who hates all men.

The life stories of these women, joyful and tragic, do not disturb the plot line of the novels. They are, indeed, the fabric of Montgomery's work, for the novels depend not on plot, but on the even flow of life, women's life. They revolve around a steady pattern of breakfast, dinner, and supper, and the intricate relationships between neighbors, mothers and sons, mothers and daughters, and the problems of growing up and raising children.

We need to look more closely at the lives of Marilla and Matthew Cuthbert as they are lived out within the narrow boundaries of Green Gables farm, for they reveal much. Through them, we catch glimpses of a harsh and rigid upbringing that stressed endurance, duty, and righteousness. We catch glimpses of marriage or a life beyond the farm passed by because of duty and obedience to family. Marilla and Matthew have survived the rigor of their upbringing and their harsh farm life and cling to the values that give it substance, just enough unsure of the methods that had produced them to bend a bit in the raising of Anne. Their lives have been lived mostly in silence. They are unused to expressing their feelings; the deeper emotions—love, sorrow, a sense of loss—remain deeply buried in their hearts, and the softer emotions—exuberance, mirth, joy—have disappeared. Matthew had looked as grim at twenty as he does at sixty. The silent strength, the repressed emotions, the deep goodness, and the lack of an imagination are common characteristics that Marilla and Matthew share with the older inhabitants of Avonlea. Marilla is the strongest of the two, and although Matthew does the outside work at the farm, it is Marilla who manages and runs the farm and takes care of him. The deep love that they share for each other is unexpressed; in fact, what they are most appalled by and yet most fascinated by are Anne's exuberant, imaginative outpourings and her direct and unconventional way of seeing and saying things.

Matthew does not represent an intrusion of the values of a patriarchal culture. If anything, he and the other members of the older generation in Avonlea are victims of that which Donovan (and of course others) define as "the masculine tyranny" of Calvinism. His humanity has survived because of the "feminine values" that predominate in his makeup. He is gentle, forgiving, soft. Indeed it is he who first recognizes (intuitively, for Matthew is not logical)

the saving grace that Anne offers. At key points in Anne's upbringing, he insists on the softer act. At one point, when Anne has shone
forth at a concert, Marilla concedes, "Anyhow, I was proud of Anne
tonight, although I'm not going to tell her so," fearful of encourag-
ing the sin of pride. "Well now," says Matthew, "I was proud of her
and I did tell her so 'fore she went upstairs." His simple statement
represents an enormous concession on the part of Matthew, who
has not in sixty years made himself so vulnerable.

While the dimmed patriarchal shadows cast by Calvinism are
an element in Avonlea's culture, they operate as something that the
women have overcome. They seem to have seized the strength that
the harshness and rigidity can instill; those softer ones who didn't
survive or who became totally twisted never surface, for Montgomery peoples her landscape with the survivors. And their lives are
based on what society defines as traditionally women's values.
Their strength is fostered by a strong sense of sisterhood, and the
"networking" that is everywhere expressed either implicitly or
explicitly; and a large part of this "networking" is based on an
intuitive recognition of imaginative insight. Perhaps the strongest
example of it is expressed in a scene between Anne and her best
friend Diana, in *Anne of Avonlea:*

> "Do you remember that evening when we first met, Diana, and
> 'swore' eternal friendship in your garden? We've kept that 'oath,'
> I think . . . we've never had a quarrel nor even a coolness. I shall
> never forget the thrill that went over me the day you told me you
> loved me. I had had such a lonely starved heart all through my
> childhood. I'm just beginning to realize how starved and lonely
> it really was . . . I should have been miserable if it hadn't been
> for that strange little dream-life of mine, wherein I imagined all
> the friends and love I craved. . . . And then I met you. You don't
> know what your friendship meant to me. I want to thank you here
> and now, dear, for the warm and true affection you've always
> given me."
> "And always, always will," sobbed Diana. "I shall *never* love
> anybody . . . any *girl* . . . half as well as I love you."

The close bond evidenced here is given expression in the
catch-phrase of the series—"kindred spirit"—by which Anne identifies those who have the power of the imagination and whose

values, like hers, are predominantly feminine. It serves as a common motif that appears throughout the series.

Although Maud Montgomery created in her fiction a landscape dominated by "woman's culture," she herself lived in a man's world. It was a world that brought her pain, confusion, and ultimately, like many other women writers, tragedy. In order to accommodate it, she lived an almost schizophrenic life as a minister's dutiful full-time wife, while maintaining at the same time an active, full-time career as a professional writer in which she consciously and unconsciously gave free rein to the intellectual and imaginative world she was afraid to reveal as a wife and mother. Montgomery reveals her "strange little dream-life" through her writings; Anne is one of the characters who expresses it. Anne, with her talkative ways, makes Marilla and Matthew and all her friends see things from a new perspective: the road leading to Green Gables becomes "The White Way of Delight," the small pond near the farm becomes "The Lake of Shining Waters." Marilla never manages to train her out of having too much to say; in fact it is her ability to communicate her feminine "romantic" way of looking at things, her "ladylikeness" and her strong "womanliness" that helps to illuminate the Avonlea landscape and every life she touches. Anne offers to her children and those around her, as well as to her readers, a romanticized and passionate way of viewing life and nature that will wrest happiness from it in spite of everything.

This romanticized, often sentimentalized, viewpoint is the major flaw of the Avonlea books just as it is one of their major strengths. Romance and sentiment are not strong enough weapons to win with. They merely offer escape. However Montgomery may not have realized, or wanted to accept, that you cannot substitute imagination for reality, her books show that a life lived without imagination is not worth living. She created through her Avonlea series a world where the traditional women's values of love, warmth, sensitivity, imagination, and quiet endurance survive and overcome, a world where kindred spirits are intuitively identified and cherished. It is a world that has enough reality for women and girls of the past seventy-five years to respond to with deep recognition, and thus, it serves as an important document in "the development of feminist consciousness." This helps explain Montgomery's lasting appeal, perhaps even more than her sense of humor, her descriptive skill, and her talent for creating lively, authentic characters.

Works Cited

Donovan, Josephine. *New England Local Color Literature: A Women's Tradition*. New York: Ungar, 1983.

Lerner, Gerda. *The Female Experience: An American Documentary*. Indianapolis, IN: Bobbs-Merrill, 1977.

_____. *The Majority Finds Its Past: Placing Women in History*. New York: Oxford UP, 1979.

Sexism Down on the Farm?

Anne of Green Gables

Janet Weiss-Townsend

A municipal draftsperson by trade, an interior designer by education, and a student of children's literature by interest and inclination, I am quite honestly impressed by the essays of educators and literary scholars such as Perry Nodelman and Carol Gay, and the ideas of writers such as Alan Garner and Virginia Hamilton. I learn a great deal from them. But sometimes I learn more from the articles and opinions that impress me less than they annoy me. It is in disagreeing with an idea that I'm forced to think about it in greater depth, particularly when the idea comes from a respected source and I can't just dismiss it as foolishness. This essay is about that sort of idea—a comment made by Perry Nodelman during a class in the children's literature course I took from him which provided such a mental catalyst.

We were studying L. M. Montgomery's *Anne of Green Gables* as an example of a "girls' book." Apparently it had evolved amidst a history of series books about wonderful girls, such as the Pansy books, the Elsie Dinsmore books, and *Heidi,* that were intended to confirm certain ideals of feminine behavior. They were written at a time when it was generally believed that women were different from men and that women should ideally be impractical and imaginative, loving and not gruff, and so on. "*Anne of Green Gables* is one of the most definitively sexist books I know of," Nodelman said, "because Anne becomes an ideal woman at the end of the book: she never stops being a child."

Well, I don't claim to be a feminist. But I am a woman, working in a traditionally male environment and, like most women in the eighties, I do have a feminist conscience of sorts. I had enjoyed *Anne of Green Gables* both as a child and again as an adult. My feminist conscience was livid! How could Nodelman say that the book I took such pleasure from was sexist?

In fact, I was convinced that *Anne of Green Gables* is *not* a sexist book. Anne herself is not stereotypically female, with stock female weaknesses and sex-linked characteristics. She undoubtedly acts within a female framework, but many of her character traits, were they classified stereotypically, would be decidedly unfeminine.

Anne is aggressive. The things she wants and dreams of most in life, she goes after. She gives of herself to become and get a "best friend." She works hard for her academic achievements. She even goes to great lengths to create an elaborate confession for Marilla, in order to be allowed to go to the church picnic and taste her first ice cream. This is not a passive child. She dreams, but she also tries very hard to make those dreams come true.

Anne is independent. She still acts within the inherent, day-to-day restrictions of dependency, as all children must, but beyond that she has a certain independence of spirit. Her thoughts on such significant topics as religion, life, and her ways of viewing the world are her own, coming from her own life experiences, and she will not easily give them up unless *she* is ready: "Other people may call that place the Avenue, but I shall always call it the White Way of Delight" (18).

Anne is practical. If imagination is stereotypically female and action is stereotypically male, then Anne's response seems to me ultimately more practical than a "male" reaction might be. Anne is an orphan, with no home, no means of support. A male protagonist would presumably react to a life with which he was dissatisfied by action, by running away and creating a new and better life. But practically, the life available to an eleven- or twelve-year-old boy on his own in the Maritimes would be limited. Employment opportunities in a conservative, rural setting distrustful of outsiders (Marilla doesn't even trust the local French boys) would be slim at best. Given the parameters of her existence and the unlikelihood of surviving on her own, Anne does the practical thing. She accepts the world as it is, seeing and being aware of its imperfections, and at the same time tackling the problems of life with a profound optimism.

And when her optimistic outlook is not enough, Anne has another very real resource for personal strength. Paradoxically, that resource is her imagination:

> "I did hope there would be a white one with puffed sleeves," she whispered disconsolately. "I prayed for one, but I didn't much expect it on that account. I didn't suppose God would have time to bother about a little orphan girl's dress. I knew I'd just have to depend on Marilla for it. Well, fortunately I can imagine that one of them is snow-white muslin with lovely lace frills and three-puffed sleeves." (79)

Therein lies Anne's power. Her use of her imagination to make her world a better one may be described quite literally as wish-fulfillment fantasy, but it is a real power, precisely because Anne controls it. She knows her imaginings are just that—imaginings; but they help her to cope with the world as it is given to her. It is a peculiar power, a power for the powerless, if you like, but it works for Anne.

Anne's power comes from within. Hers is a strong personality. She doesn't become immersed in finding her perfect boyfriend as the protagonists in some more recent "girls" stories do. The currently popular Silhouette Romances are an extreme example. Anne knows that, although men are important, they don't define who she is; she does that for herself: "Ruby Gillis thinks of nothing but young men, and the older she gets the worse she is. Young men are all very well in their place, but it doesn't do to drag them into everything, does it?" (239). Anne's reaction to Gilbert Blythe is not romantic adoration, although it does become a romantic attraction in later books, nor is it a sense of personal inferiority. Her feelings for Gilbert find their outlet in an intense academic rivalry. She meets and competes with Gilbert on an equal footing.

During our class on *Anne,* another student suggested that the book's setting, a dominantly female atmosphere in which Gilbert and Matthew could be described as the only important male figures (and both are sympathetic to Anne), gives a slanted, female bias to the story, a bias which might itself be considered sexist. But if it is true, as some feminist literary critics assert, that there is a "female" way to read a story, outside or different from the "male" way of reading which a predominately male-oriented society teaches most of us, then perhaps the female atmosphere in *Anne of Green Gables* is merely a vehicle for steering the reader towards a "female" reading of the story. In searching for a feminist viewpoint that might help me clarify my own impressions, I came across Carol Gay's article in a 1982 *ChLA Quarterly* which suggested, "a re-reading of *Anne of Green Gables* in light of Lerner and Showalter, for instance, will, surprisingly, perhaps, reveal a quite distinct woman's world existing within a dominant patriarchal society" (33). So I went to Lerner and Showalter to explore the possibilities.

Showalter, I discovered, broke feminist criticism into two modes, one concerned with the feminist as reader, the other with the feminist as writer. The feminist reading, or feminist critique, as Showalter terms it, offers readings

> which consider the images and stereotypes of women in litera-
> ture, the omissions and misconceptions about women in criti-
> cism and women-as-sign in semiotic systems. . . . But in a free
> play of the interpretative field, the feminist critique can only
> compete with alternative readings, all of which have the built in
> obsolescence of Buicks, cast away as newer readings take their
> place. (182)

It struck me that my attempts to describe Anne as beyond the stereotypes of the female had that same "built in obsolescence." Nodelman's reading of the book, which may include female stereo-types, was just as valid as my own reading negating those stereo-types. I would, I supposed, have to explore further, using Showalter's second feminist mode, that of woman as writer. But a passage further on in her discussion sent me in a different direction entirely:

> Many forms of American radical feminism also romantically
> assert that women are closer to nature, to the environment, to a
> matriarchal principle at once biological and ecological. Mary
> Daly's *Gyn/Ecology* and Margaret Atwood's novel *Surfacing* are
> texts which create this feminist mythology. (201)

Anne has much to do with the idea of people being romantically close to nature but the people are children, not women. It began to dawn on me that *Anne of Green Gables* probably had more in common with *Treasure Island,* a boys' book, than with *Surfacing,* a women's book; and I will get back to that thought later.

My examination of Lerner similarly sent me in an unexpected direction. I was drawn, not to Lerner's analysis of the female historical perspective, but to this entry in Louisa May Alcott's diary:

Fruitlands
March, 1846

I have at last got the little room I have wanted so long, and I am very happy with it. . . . My work-booklet and desk are by the window and my closet is full of dried herbs that smell very nice. The door that opens into the garden will be very pretty in summer, and I can run off to the woods when I like.

I have made a plan for my life, as I am in my teens, and no more a child. I am old for my age, and I don't care much for girl's things. People think I'm wild and queer; but mother understands and helps me. I have not told anyone about my resolutions, and written sad notes, and cried over my sins, and it doesn't seem to do any good. Now I'm going to *work really* for I feel a true desire to improve, and be a help and comfort, not a care and sorrow to my dear mother. (qtd. in Lerner 10)

This excerpt from Louisa's diary at age 13 struck me as a very Anne-like passage. Anne's vision of life was not as unique as I had first thought. Alcott and Montgomery, raised as children during roughly the same time period, shared a similar viewpoint. Lerner says of Louisa's father, "Bronson Alcott believed in treating children kindly and respecting their reason, considering them to be not damned, but blessed . . . but the direction of their education was the same: girls were to acquire patience, self-discipline, and the virtues of obedience" (6). Surely these are some of the same virtues Anne struggles to acquire.

Nodelman was probably correct to suggest that I should realize how much Anne was a cliché, that I should be aware of nineteenth-century concepts of childhood. Presumably, Bronson Alcott shared in the view that children were somehow closer to nature, to God and to Truth; that they were somehow blessed and therefore their viewpoint was to be respected, even envied. Perhaps L. M. Alcott and Montgomery did too:

> Heaven lies about us in our infancy!
> Shades of the prison-house begin to close
> Upon the growing Boy. . . .
> (Wordsworth 5.66-68)

Life is certainly not common from Anne's viewpoint. And it is very easy to envy Anne her carefree, ecstatic view of the world, where everything is still alive with hope and endless possibilities. It is easy to envy her innocence.

But, having understood that, I suddenly realized that, for all my reading, research and contemplation of feminist analyses, I had been missing out on the key issue entirely. I had let my own feminist defenses lead me down the proverbial garden path.

When I try to argue that Anne is not like a child but like a woman, and a nonstereotypical woman at that, I give more credence to Nodelman's statement about her than it deserves. "Anne becomes an ideal woman at the end of the book: she never stops being a child." I've been arguing in a manner that accepts the very premise that upsets my feminist conscience most: the premise that eternal childhood is a valid, desired feminine state. Obviously it is not.

Upon reflection, I believe that Nodelman's controversial statement was intended purely as a catalyst for classroom discussion and exploration. In my case, obviously, it worked, but it also threw me a little off track. I had been looking for sexist evidence from an adult perspective, forgetting that this is not an adult book.

Anne of Green Gables moves to a close with Mrs. Lynde observing that "[t]here's a good deal of the child about her yet in some ways." "There's a good deal more of the woman about her in others," retorts Marilla (307). Anne, of course, is not a child at the end of the book, though many of her childhood traits are still with her. But she is not entirely an adult either, because this is not a women's novel; it is a children's novel. As Nodelman himself said to my class, "One of the key elements of children's literature is that it is written from a position of innocence. There is usually no real character growth until the end of the book. That is not what the book is about. The book is about that period of innocence before you start to become an adult"—or words to that effect. *Anne of Green Gables* is not a sexist book. But it *is* a girls' book; at least L. M. Montgomery saw it as a girls' book. "'I thought girls in their teens might like it but that was the only audience I hoped to reach,' she wrote, astounded at the book's instant success when it was published in June 1908" (Gillen 26).

In fact, *Anne* has the sort of plot usually found in girls' books, a plot quite different from a boys' book like *Treasure Island.* The girls' book occurs, basically, in a safe, domestic setting; the boys' book is an adventure, set against a backdrop of action and violence. But despite this gender difference, they both operate as wish-fulfillment fantasy for children. The child in each book has the capability or power to change the lives of the adults he or she touches.

Anne can't help but affect those she touches for the better. Her ecstatic buoyancy and nature-loving spirit melt the heart even of Marilla, a person, we are told, "always slightly distrustful of sunshine, which seemed to her too dancing and irresponsible a thing for a world which was meant to be taken seriously" (4). Anne's imagination not only enriches her own life, but helps others to see the world in a new and better light. Anne is a nurturer. She enriches the lives of those around her emotionally and spiritually. The nurturing role is traditionally an adult female role.

If Anne's role is that of the nurturer, Jim Hawkins of *Treasure Island* acts as a protector and provider for the adults in his life. You would expect that, as the only child in *Treasure Island* amidst cutthroats and pirates, Jim would require the protection, but this is not so. It is Jim who overhears the pirates' mutinous plans. He is the one who finds Ben Gunn, without whom the treasure would never have been found; and in the end it is Jim who singlehandedly recaptures the ship. All that Jim does seems somehow to point him and their tiny group away from trouble. Most often his actions are instinctive, with little or no thought beforehand:

> I had scarce time to think—scarce time to act and save myself. I was on the summit of one swell when the schooner came stooping over the next. The bowsprit was over my head. I sprang to my feet and leaped, stamping the coracle under water. With one hand I caught the jib-boom, while my foot was lodged between the stay and the brace; and as I still clung there panting, a dull blow told me that the schooner had charged down upon and

struck the coracle and that I was left without retreat on the
Hispaniola. (148)

Jim is responsible, because of his actions, for the safety and
well-being of the captain, the squire and the doctor. He is, in a sense,
their protector. He is also responsible, more than anyone perhaps,
for their finding the treasure which provides each of them with a
handsome financial reward. He is, therefore, their provider. The
adult male member of the household is traditionally the protector
and provider.

In a peculiar way, both Anne's and Jim's innocence and youth
are precisely the characteristics that allow them to obtain these adult
roles. Were Anne an adult she would be considered a frivolous
scatterbrain. Those same characteristics which are so endearing in
the young Anne appear quite foolish in an adult. Were Jim an adult,
he would never have been able to abandon the group, helping
himself to food and pistols, to steal over the wall and eventually
recapture the ship. As a child he can get away with it: "But as I was
certain I should not be allowed to leave the enclosure, my only plan
was to take French leave and slip out when nobody was watching.
And that was so bad a way of doing it as made the thing itself wrong.
But I was only a boy, and I had made my mind up" (134).

Anne and Jim, as children, share a common, innocent and
romantic way of viewing their respective adventures. Though both
are touched by death, neither is ultimately damaged by it. In fact
they see death quite romantically. When Jim discovers that the
pirates have taken over the block house with no sign of his friends,
"I could only judge that all had perished, and my heart smote me
sorely that I had not been there to perish with them" (168). There's
a certain romance in dying bravely with your friends. Or in Anne's
case, dying bravely *for* your friends:

> I was thinking the loveliest story about you and me, Diana. I
> thought you were desperately ill with smallpox and everybody
> deserted you, but I went boldly to your bedside and nursed you
> back to life; and then I took the smallpox and died and I was
> buried under those poplar trees in the graveyard and you planted
> a rosebush by my grave and watered it with your tears; and you
> never, never forgot the friend of your youth who sacrificed her
> life for you. (309)

Anne and Jim each represent a delicate balance: they are both children with the power of adults and the security of being children. Anne can be a nurturer; Jim can be a protector and provider. But when the story is over, they both go back home, as all children do, because home is, after all, where security lies for most children. They do go home changed, but there is no real sense that their childlike innocence of the world has entirely vanished.

Anne of Green Gables is not, then, a sexist book. It is merely a typical children's book. As with most children's storybook heroes and heroines, there may be some sense of Jim and Anne having reached maturity at the end of the story; but we are still left with that ambiguous mixture of part child and part adult. When Anne returns to Green Gables to care for Marilla, she accepts her adult responsibilities, but "nothing could rob her of her birthright of fancy or her ideal world of dreams" (309). *Anne of Green Gables* is a "girls' book," as *Treasure Island* is a "boys' book." But surely, to the reader willing to ignore those "sexist" classifications, there are elements in both books to be enjoyed and understood by the androgynous aspects of all our characters, young or old.

Works Cited

Gay, Carol. "From the 'Other' to 'Us.'" Rev. of *The Female Experience: An American Documentary,* by Gerda Lerner. *Children's Literature Association Quarterly* 7.4 (1982): 20-22.

Gillen, Mollie. *The Wheel of Things: A Biography of L. M. Montgomery.* Don Mills, ON: Fitzhenry and Whiteside, 1975.

Lerner, Gerda. *The Female Experience: An American Documentary.* Indianapolis, IN: Bobbs-Merrill, 1977.

Montgomery, L. M. *Anne of Green Gables.* 1908. Toronto: McClelland and Stewart-Bantam, 1983.

Showalter, Elaine. "Feminist Criticism in the Wilderness." *Critical Inquiry* (Winter 1981): 179-205.

Stevenson, Robert Louis. *Treasure Island.* 1883. New York: Signet, 1981.

Wordsworth, William. "Ode: Intimations of Immortality From Recollections of Early Childhood." *The Complete Poetical Works of Wordsworth.* Ed. Andrew J. George. Boston: Houghton Mifflin, 1932.

Community and the Individual
in *Anne of Green Gables*
The Meaning of Belonging

Susan Drain

Finding one's rightful place in the social fabric is part of the challenge of growing up, and as such, it is an important focus of many books for and about children. An entire tradition of nine-teenth- and early twentieth-century "orphan tales" is explicitly concerned with the problem of identifying and occupying that rightful place. In books like *The Wide, Wide World* (1850), *Elsie Dinsmore* (1867), and *Pollyanna* (1913), an orphaned or motherless heroine finds herself in a new and strange situation; the novel traces the course of events and adjustments which are made to ensure that the heroine takes her proper place at last. These adjustments usually work in one of two ways: either the child is subdued to the pattern of the adults, as in *The Wide, Wide World* (a book which is in this way not much more than a Sunday school tract), or like Elsie and Pollyanna, the child manages by the sweetness of her character and the power of her example to transform the narrow and bitter adults around her. In either case, belonging actually means conformity; the only question which remains is who is to conform to whom. The more realistic, and not coincidentally, the better-known, books in this tradition accept that the process of adjustment is a mutual one, in which both the stranger and the community are changed by their contact with each other. Adoption, in short, means adaptation.

Lucy Maud Montgomery's *Anne of Green Gables* is one of these more realistic orphan tales. The very title of the book suggests how important belonging is. The heroine's identity is defined not by her deeds, not even by a name which is particularly and essentially individual, but by the name of the household of which she is a part. From its title and from its initial pattern of movement—the entrance of a stranger into a small and literally insular community—the reader may expect the novel to deserve its frequent epithet "heartwarming." For *Anne* is one of those well-loved children's books, the virtues of which are obscured by the very affection in which they are held. Its popular appeal, and its reputation even among those who have not read the book, mean that it requires a strong as well as a sensitive reader to see past the expected patterns to appreciate the subtleties and complexities of the experience the book presents. Any novel, however, which begins with three successive chapters entitled "Mrs. Rachel Lynde is Surprised," "Matthew Cuthbert is Surprised," and "Marilla Cuthbert is Surprised" ought to alert the reader to the possibility that this novel will confound expectation as often as confirm it.

Although the novel does trace stages in the mutual adaptation of individual and community, stages by which the one comes to belong to the other, it exhibits a more complex pattern than one of moving inward, of increasing conformity and stability. Instead, an essential part of belonging is the movement outward, for it is only with the independence made possible by the security of belonging that the fullest meaning of belonging can truly be realized. Beneath its heartwarming popular image, in short, *Anne* presents a vision of the relation between community and individual which is complex as well as close, challenging as well as comfortable.

If the title suggests that individuality is less important than community, the first chapter of the book seems to confirm that suggestion, for it is an introduction not to the eponymous protagonist, but to the community to which she is to belong. What is important to notice about this introduction is twofold: first, it is clear that belonging to Green Gables necessarily means belonging to the larger Avonlea community, and second, it is implied that "belonging" is a more complex relationship than one might initially expect—not one of subordination, possession, or conformity, but of interdependence and tension.

Anne of Green Gables opens with a broad view of Avonlea, both its countryside and its inhabitants, and gradually narrows its focus from the community as a whole, to the Cuthberts, and finally to the as-yet-unidentified orphan on the railway platform. It is a pattern of moving inward, but though the child is the culmination of the pattern, the community is presented first. The child's place is assigned by the Cuthberts, who, in turn, have their assigned place in the community. The pattern, however, is not an orderly one of concentric circles enclosing the child.

That opening overview of Avonlea is instructive: a pattern of concentric rings can only be seen from the outside, but the novel rejects the outsider's perspective. It is through Mrs. Lynde, one of the community members, that the reader is introduced to Avonlea: the outsider is drawn in by the insider who is poised on the physical outskirts of the community:

> Mrs. Lynde lived just where the Avonlea main road dipped into a little hollow . . . ; [she] was sitting at her window keeping a sharp eye on everything that passed, from brooks and children up, and . . . if she noticed anything odd or out of place she would never rest until she had ferreted out the whys and the wherefores thereof. (13)

The immediate impression from the all-seeing, all-encompassing overview is a strong sense of order: even the brook "by the time it reached Lynde's Hollow . . . was a quiet well-conducted little stream, for not even a brook could run past Mrs. Rachel Lynde's door without due regard for decency and decorum" (13). This orderliness is not imposed on Avonlea from the outside; although Mrs. Lynde promotes orderliness, she also embodies it and is properly respected for it:

> Mrs. Rachel Lynde was one of those capable creatures who can manage their own concerns and those of other folks into the bargain. She was a notable housewife; her work was always done and well done; she ran the Sewing Circle, helped run the Sunday School, and was the strongest prop of the Church Aid Society and Foreign Missions Auxiliary. (13)

Even the more questionable side of her attending to her neighbors' affairs is softened by the general respect which is expressed for her undoubted industry even when apparently idle:

Yet with all this Mrs. Rachel found abundant time to sit for hours
in her kitchen window, knitting "cotton warp" quilts—she had
knitted sixteen of them, as Avonlea housekeepers were wont to
tell in awed voices—and keeping a sharp eye on the main road
that crossed the hollow and wound up the steep red hill beyond.
(13-14)

What is remarkable about this portrait of a paragon of domestic
order and virtue, besides the somewhat daunting impression of
Avonlea's orderliness, is that the order is not static: Mrs. Lynde's
leisure is the product of her industry ("her work was always done
and well done") and is accompanied by useful activity of another
sort. At a subtler level, the picture is complex: it is soft and generous
in its images of abundance and cotton quilts, but beneath the
comfortableness is the closely-woven texture of Avonlea life—
"warp," "knitted," "sharp," "crossed," and "wound." Avonlea's
orderliness is not that of simplicity. Similarly, the orderly brook is
acknowledged to have an exuberant and mysterious life: "it was
reputed to be an intricate, headlong brook in its earlier course
through those woods, with dark secrets of pool and cascade" (13).
Though familiar only in its more disciplined form, that energy is
not unknown to Avonlea's inhabitants ("it was reputed"). In fact, as
the reader follows Mrs. Lynde through the first chapter, it becomes
increasingly clear that to be part of the Avonlea community is to be
part of a complex pattern.

That pattern, like Mrs. Lynde's quilts, is apparently comfortable but actually tightly knit: its calm is in fact the tension of energy
and discipline, of activity and order. The order is not fixed and
concentric; it is dynamic and intricate. Even the narrowing focus
of the first chapter is not inexorable: the human focus is thrown off
by the shifting geographical focus. That is, from Mrs. Lynde's
all-seeing vantage point, the human focus narrows successively:
surveying part of the community (Thomas Lynde sowing his late
turnip seed, Matthew Cuthbert who should have been doing the
same, and the other Avonlea folk gathered at Blair's store), penetrating to the heart of the mystery in the Cuthberts' house, and
ending with a glimpse of the child at the station. The geography,
however, resists narrowness. Mrs. Lynde knows what is supposed
to be happening in Avonlea because she has been outside it:

Mrs. Rachel knew that [Matthew] ought [to be sowing his late turnip seed] because she had heard him tell Peter Morrison the evening before in William J. Blair's store *over at Carmody* that he meant to sow his turnip seed the next afternoon. (14, emphasis added)

Similarly, the Cuthberts' "deep-rutted grassy lane" (15) leads not into the heart of Avonlea, but to a house "at the furthest edge of . . . cleared land" (15). Green Gables may be in the community, but only marginally. Its inhabitants are "both a little odd, [from] living away back here by themselves" (15). Finally, to bring into focus the child who is the human center of the story, the reader has to step, not only out of Avonlea altogether, but also out of Mrs. Lynde's consciousness—which is not all-seeing after all: "if she could have seen the child who was waiting patiently at the Bright River station" (20). The child is not yet identified; in fact, she does not really exist in the novel until she encounters the first representative of the community in the person of Matthew Cuthbert.

Exactly what kind of a community the child is entering is carefully introduced. The reader may expect Avonlea to be an idyllic, uncomplicated, pastoral haven, and in fact, early in the chapter, it is described as a remote and secluded place, as sheltered as its name, occupying "a little triangular peninsula jutting out into the Gulf of St. Lawrence, with water on two sides of it" (14). Yet however well-protected it is, surrounded by the deep and brooded over by Mrs. Lynde, Avonlea is not isolated: that first description also points out that people do go "out of it or into it . . . over that hill road" (14). In fact, Avonlea exists in a complex relationship with the outside world; the discussion between Mrs. Lynde and Marilla Cuthbert reveals a tension between suspicion and openness.

On first hearing of the Cuthberts' plan to adopt an orphan, Mrs. Lynde sees Avonlea's safe orderliness dissolving about her, and if Avonlea is unpredictable, so must the universe be: "Well, the world was certainly turning upside down!" (18). She rallies quickly, however, and soon is able to distinguish between familiar and orderly Avonlea and the chaos which is everything beyond, and which now threatens Avonlea. The very idea must be a foreign one—"What on earth put such a notion into your head?" (18). When she has "adjusted her mental attitude to this amazing piece of news" (18), she proceeds vigorously to inform Marilla of the dangers she is about to import in the person of a "strange child . . . and you don't know a single thing about him nor what his disposition is like nor what sort of parents he had nor how he's likely to turn out" (19). She is disturbed first, that is, by his foreignness, and second, by his lack of known identity. Only after expressing her concern about who the child is does she consider what he might do—telling harrowing stories of arson, poisoning and sucking eggs, all of which happen in the chaotic world outside Avonlea, "up west of the Island" (19) or "over in New Brunswick" (20).

Marilla, however, is more open: she does not make so sharp a distinction between here and there; she sees some middle ground between the foreign and the familiar. She reveals that the idea of adoption had originated with a neighbor: "Mrs. Alexander Spencer was up here one day before Christmas and she said she was going to get a little girl from the asylum over in Hopetown in the spring" (18). Nor is Hopetown so alien: "Her cousin lives there and Mrs. Spencer has visited her and knows all about it" (18). Marilla herself distinguishes between such near-familiar places and the entirely foreign: "And then Nova Scotia is right close to the Island. It isn't as if we were getting him from England or the United States. He can't be much different from ourselves" (19). The Island standard is clearly the one to which Marilla adheres, but she knows that familiarity does not necessarily mean safety: "And as for the risk, there's risks in pretty near everything a body does in this world. There's risks in people having children of their own if it comes to that—they don't always turn out well" (19). So it is clear that Matthew's act of going out of Avonlea to fetch the stranger in is the physical expression of the Cuthberts' mental attitude: they are, however tentatively, open to the outside.

Even this conflict between openness and suspicion is more complex than it first seems. The Cuthberts may have been open to "an unheard-of innovation" (17), but they have very narrow and quite selfish expectations of the boy:

> We sent . . . word . . . to bring us a smart, likely boy of about ten or eleven. We decided that would be the best age—old enough to be of some use in doing chores right off and young enough to be trained up proper. We mean to give him a good home and schooling. (18)

It is Mrs. Lynde, so horrified by the idea of the newcomer, who can see past the idea to the human being: "Well, I'm sorry for that poor young one and no mistake. . . . It seems uncanny to think of a child at Green Gables anyhow . . . I wouldn't be in that orphan's shoes for anything" (20).

To be adopted into the Avonlea community by the Cuthberts does not mean a comfortable sinking into conformity. Rather, the entrance of the stranger is both a challenge and a contribution to Avonlea's intricate network of relations, a network which extends outward into the world at large.

Just how closely the community of Avonlea is interwoven with the larger world is suggested in the first chapter and confirmed elsewhere. Avonlea may be pastoral, but it is not a bucolic backwater. Although it is at the end of the road, Avonlea uses its links with the rest of the Island. The railroad runs to within eight miles of Green Gables (21), and links the small communities which are spread along the Gulf shore—White Sands, Bright River, Carmody, Avonlea. There is actual as well as potential intercourse along these communities: Avonlea folk shop in Carmody, and the local entertainment is shared—Diana's cousins come "over from Newbridge in a big pung sleigh to go to the Debating Club concert at the hall" (160). Even the thirty miles to Charlottetown is not so far that it is impossible to go and return in one day (241), though such travel is made easier when "the new branch railway" (291) extends to Carmody. Avonlea residents have relatives outside the immediate area—the Barrys' great-aunt from Charlottetown descends upon her nephew's household for a month at a time (167), and Mrs. Alexander Spencer has visited her cousin in Hopetown (18). Strangers enter the neighborhood too. The hotel at White Sands is the summering-place of rich American ladies and distinguished artists. However exotic these visitors may be at first sight, their world is not entirely alien: the distinguished artist went to school with a man "that [Josie Pye's] mother's cousin in Boston is married to" (283). Moreover, the summer visitors do not merely enjoy the beauty of the Island while exploiting the local people. They are prepared to contribute to the community of which they are peripheral and temporary members: they get up a concert "in aid of the Charlottetown hospital, and [hunt] out all the available amateur talent in the surrounding districts to help it along" (275). Nor is this participation in Island life entirely condescending; although the "white-lace girl kept talking audibly to her next neighbour about the 'country bumpkins' and 'rustic belles' in the audience" (279), the overwhelming impression is of genuine kindness: "the stout, pink lady—who was the wife of an American millionaire—took [Anne] under her wing, and introduced her to everybody; and everybody was very nice to her" (281).

Part of the impression of Avonlea as an open community comes from the fact that real changes in its composition occur. Sensations may be "few and far between" in this "quiet little country settlement" (180), but Avonlea is not static. The community calls a new minister and "opened its heart to [the Allans] from the start" (181). The turnover in schoolteachers is almost brisk: Mr. Phillips is succeeded by Miss Stacy, and yet a third teacher keeps the school before it is given to Anne herself at the end of the book.

Avonlea is not only open to the larger world; it is closely bound to it. The point is made explicitly at the beginning of chapter 18:

> All things great are bound up with all things little. At first glance it might not seem that the decision of a certain Canadian Premier to include Prince Edward Island in a political tour could have much or anything to do with the fortunes of little Anne Shirley at Green Gables. But it had. (149)

The connection is not a direct one: the Premier's visit affects Anne only because he draws all the politically minded adults to town, and thus leaves Anne on her own when a crisis occurs. The necessary link is the adults' interest in politics—an interest which is not that of spectators, but of participants:

> Mrs. Rachel Lynde was a red-hot politician and couldn't have believed that the political rally could be carried through without her, although she was on the opposite side of politics. (149)

These participants relish their party ties, so that politicians are not remote or mysterious, but human beings whom ordinary Avonlea people can claim or criticize:

> "Well, he never got to be Premier on account of his looks," said Marilla. "Such a nose as that man had! But he can speak. I was

proud of being a Conservative. Rachel Lynde, of course, being
a Liberal, had no use for him." (156)

The ties of the outside world which broaden Avonlea's horizons
also make it vulnerable to outside forces. The Cuthberts' security
is destroyed when the Abbey Bank fails; the news is such a shock
that Matthew dies of a heart attack. It is all the result of incompre-
hensible doings in a financial world of which Avonlea receives
news only at second or third hand:

> "Did you hear anything about the Abbey Bank lately, Anne?"
> [asks Marilla].
> "I heard that it was shaky," answered Anne.
> "Why?"
> "That is what Rachel said. She was up here one day last week
> and said there was some talk about it. . . . But Mr. Russell told
> [Matthew] yesterday that the bank was all right." (300-01)

This vulnerability is the more poignant for the link of trust that
had been maintained on the Avonlea side at least.

> "I wanted Matthew to put [our savings] in the Savings Bank in
> the first place, but old Mr. Abbey was a great friend of Father's
> and he'd always banked with him. Matthew said any bank with
> him at the head of it was good enough for anybody."

> "I think he has only been its nominal head for many years," said
> Anne. "He is a very old man; his nephews are really at the head
> of the institution." (300)

Vulnerability is the dark side of the pattern established at the
beginning of the novel, that of surprise and the confounding of
expectation. This darkness had been hinted at previously—a hint
made the more ominous by the several references elsewhere to
Matthew's weak heart:

> When Matthew and I took you to bring up we resolved we would
> do the best we could for you and give you a good education. I
> believe in a girl being fitted to earn her own living whether she
> ever has to or not. You'll always have a home at Green Gables

as long as Matthew and I are here, but nobody knows what is
going to happen in this uncertain world and it's just as well to be
prepared. (252)

Although the moment is swallowed up in Anne's exuberant reaction
to the idea of going to Queen's, the darkness returns with both death
and insecurity foreshadowed in Anne's separation from Diana, who
is not to study for the entrance exam.

"But, oh, Marilla, I really felt that I had tasted the bitterness of
death, as Mr. Allan said in his sermon last Sunday, when I saw
Diana go out alone," she said mournfully that night. ". . . But we
can't have things perfect in this imperfect world, as Mrs. Lynde
says. Mrs. Lynde isn't exactly a comforting person sometimes,
but there's no doubt she says a great many very true things."
(253)

The last main image of the book recognizes the unpredictability
of human experience, but restores the emphasis to opportunity
rather than foreboding, although it requires determination rather
than natural optimism to see it.

When I left Queen's my future seemed to stretch out before me
like a straight road. I thought I could see along it for many a
milestone. Now there is a bend in it. I don't know what lies
around the bend, but *I'm going to believe* that the best does. (312,
emphasis added)

The final description of Anne's situation at the novel's end describes
her newly circumscribed life, but in addition to describing the
consolations of that life, it maintains a link with a larger world, even
if it is only one of dreams.

Anne's horizons had closed in since the night she had sat [at her
window] after coming home from Queen's; but if the path set
before her feet was to be narrow she knew that flowers of quiet
happiness would bloom along it. . . . Nothing could rob her of
her birthright of fancy or her ideal world of dreams. And there
was always the bend in the road! (317)

The novel resists closing in even to the very last sentence, for the cliché at the end, however sentimental, identifies Anne's newly limited life with the entire world: " ' "God's in his heaven, all's right with the world," ' whispered Anne softly" (317).

That this conclusion is the opposite of Mrs. Lynde's first reaction to the news of Anne's coming to Avonlea ("Well, the world was certainly turning upside down!" [18]) is more than a neat rounding-off of the novel. It is the confirmation of a meaning of belonging which only finally becomes clear in that last chapter. Although the novel has throughout portrayed the inevitable inter-connectedness of community and individual, it also demonstrates that this interconnectedness must be acknowledged, must be taken on as a willing responsibility, rather than accepted passively as part of the way things are. In making the commitment to relationship, the individual renounces isolation and attains freedom.

It appears that the pinnacle of belonging is achieved in the penultimate chapter, after Matthew's death, when Marilla explicitly acknowledges the depth of her bond with Anne: "We've got each other, Anne . . . I love you as dear as if you were my own flesh and blood" (305). That acknowledgment, however, is almost more significant to Marilla than to Anne, representing as it does the high point of Marilla's growth to emotional maturity. Nevertheless, Marilla's assertion of that bond is the assurance Anne needs in order to make her own affirmation of belonging. By turning down the Avery scholarship for university studies, and staying home to help Marilla and to teach, Anne acknowledges her bond to be more important than her individual plans, and confirms her place by knowingly taking on the network of responsibilities that belonging entails. "I shall give life here my best," declares Anne, "and I believe it will give its best to me in return" (312). Indeed, that belief is justified, for Anne finds that her commitment to the smaller world does not mean a diminution or a repudiation of the larger. As she tells Mrs. Lynde, "I'm going to study Latin and Greek just the same. . . . I'm going to take my Arts course right here at Green Gables, and study everything that I would at college" (314). As in the very last words of the book, the larger world is comprehended by the smaller. Individuality, then, is established not in contrast to a community, but by a commitment to it, and the individual's freedom is not in the isolation of independence, but in the complexity of connection.

Works Cited

Montgomery, Lucy Maud. *Anne of Green Gables*. 1908. New York: Grosset and Dunlap, 1964.

Journeys of the Mother in the World of Green Gables

Nancy Huse

Nineteenth-century English-speaking women claimed the rights of citizens because of their role as mothers (Reuther). Although feminist psychoanalytic critics today seek to identify the nature of female autonomy, Nancy Chodorow and others have established the importance of recognizing that women are socialized to be mothers. In fact, part of the feminist project is to discover a sane representation of motherhood, one which emphasizes its power without entirely idealizing it or, as in the case of many Oedipal quest narratives, depicting the mother's power as something to be escaped from (Ruddick 345). Like other nineteenth-century women writers, L. M. Montgomery used motherhood as a central theme; unlike many other writers—perhaps because of her island settings—Montgomery filled her Anne books with physical journeys. The orphan's journey, for example, opens the series; and Anne makes many trips, short and long, in the course of her education and adulthood. Two decisive journeys in the books, however, are taken by other female characters: Marilla, Anne's adoptive mother, and Rilla, Anne's biological daughter, who, at the end of the series, likewise becomes a foster or adoptive mother. These two women seem to frame the story of Anne; they likewise— because they are/are not mothers and are/are not Anne herself— offer a way of viewing the female journey of simultaneous relatedness and autonomy (Gallop). Because Marilla's action in mothering Anne is decisive in allowing the Anne stories to exist, and Rilla's action in mothering represents the possibility for a happy ending to that set of stories, these two journeys are of structural interest. As examples of the way motherhood is presented to child readers in her time period, Montgomery's stories of "maidens" who choose to be "mothers" are of historical interest.

Perhaps the most important thing about these journeys is that they can refine our understanding of archetypical patterns as they are found in female experience. The mature female, according to Annis Pratt, is at once maiden/mother/crone, and can employ any one of these roles at any time (172). The Anne books offer an interconnected and simultaneous presence of maiden/mother/crone in Rilla/Anne/Marilla, and moreover the three "stages" are present in the three women as each makes her metaphoric quest. (Anne, for example, sometimes seems "older" than Marilla or "younger" than her own children.) The journeys of Marilla and Rilla, especially, vary the traditional heroic separation/test/reintegration pattern; each journeys away and makes a major decision, yet each is traveling with a child and interacting with that child as she makes her decision. Montgomery thus shows the beginning and the end of the female life cycle not as a place of enviable or unfortunate freedom as in many myths of maidens and crones, but as a state in common with that of mothers themselves, and a condition in which decisions and change, power and the acquisition of power, are intrinsic.

While I do not want to overemphasize the powerful aspects of the maternal journeys in Montgomery's books—Anne herself has too many headaches in the later ones to suit my ideas of adventure—it is clear that the journeys of Marilla and Rilla are both positive and powerful. The powerful aspects of mothering, and the reasons mothers engage in these powerful activities, are described by Sara Ruddick as "maternal thinking," a mode of social practice and theoretical orientation which draws especially on the training in empathy most females acquire in our role as daughters (358). Its most notable characteristic is seeing the *child's* reality with the eye of attention. Maternal thinking focuses on the other in order to preserve life, foster growth, and produce a young adult acceptable to the group. Though the exercise of maternal thinking is prone to the temptation of too-rigid control, the recognition of the child's separate life also calls on the cheerfulness and openness to change necessary to this mode of thought. Reading the journeys of Anne's adoptive/adapting mother and daughter with Ruddick's comments as framework offers some extrinsic justification for viewing the maternal journeys as a representation of female strength not entirely undermined by the negative aspects of power or by the powerless circumstances in which many women mother.

Marilla, at the outset of her decisive journey, is said to be a woman of narrow experience and rigid conscience whose sense of humor is still, though barely, traceable around her lips (*Anne of Green Gables* 5). She thus, in Ruddick's sense, is capable of maternal thinking but in danger of its typical errors of rigidity and conformity. Besides Marilla's humor, another quality equips her to deal with Anne: so fixed is she in her own values and sense of order that she will direct the girl who dyes her hair green into a young adult more than "acceptable" to her group (Ruddick). The journey Marilla takes to return the too-talkative girl might be viewed as predetermined by Matthew's wish to keep Anne, were it not the case as well that Marilla's social context definitely assigns domestic tasks to her, not Matthew—and until she notices Anne's vulnerability by employing the "eye of attention" (Ruddick 358) in the form of questions about Anne's treatment by earlier foster mothers, Marilla herself seems convinced that she is neither interested in nor competent for the "domesticating" of a female orphan. Marilla's rigidity as an older woman committed to her preferences for plain, literal speech and living results in her analysis of Anne's need for preservation when she demands the facts that will enable her to make up her own mind without falling under a "spell" from Anne's charm. As Marilla controls the sorrel mare on the journey away from Green Gables, she also directs the imaginative orphan in behavior that allows Marilla to see the child's reality. Anne does not like to talk about reality, her daily treatment in other families— and this silence empowers Marilla further at the same time that it confirms her awakening empathy.

When Marilla decides to take Anne home with her again, she does so out of a sense of competency and power as well as a conviction of moral responsibility. Watching Anne's "pale face with its look of mute misery—the misery of a helpless little creature who finds itself once more caught in the trap from which it had escaped" (46), she relies on her own judgment of Mrs. Blewitt, the woman who wants to take Anne: "To hand a sensitive, 'highstrung' child over to such a woman! No, she could not take the responsibility for doing that!" (47). Able to appreciate Anne because of the smiles she herself must smother when the child calls Mrs. Blewitt a "gimlet," Marilla does acknowledge the risk in her new task—she may make a terrible mess of it—but claims it as the province of an old maid, not of an old bachelor (49). Through the practice of maternal thinking on this journey, free of Matthew's presence, Marilla alters her own life plan and participates in the openness to change this new life demands. Adept at everything which aids Anne's physical growth, Marilla's mothering will be too rigid in the same areas of female socialization (emphasis on physical beauty and conventional social behavior) which she has rejected for herself. Her eccentric dress code cannot be passed on to Anne if Anne is to marry, and Matthew "puts his oar in" to provide the pretty dresses Anne wants (exercising his gentle and intuitive love, so different from the love Marilla feels for the child she wants to protect and preserve within a world she distrusts). Anne will marry the son of Marilla's youthful love, a plot development which emphasizes the gradual mother/daughter bonding of the spinster and the orphan. Their simultaneous autonomy and symbiosis (Gallop) is also extended into their shared parenting of twin orphans (*Anne of Avonlea*) and then the replacement of Anne as Marilla's companion by Mrs. Rachel Lynde. Marilla's decisive journey home with her foster child has deepened her identity as a woman and preserved, through Anne's responsible adulthood, Marilla's position as householder and citizen. Retaining her steady and even rigid directiveness, Marilla appears in a later book, *Anne's House of Dreams*. Here she repeats religious clichés when Anne's first child dies at birth; Anne resists the conventional thinking of Marilla until she employs the aspects of maternal thinking that were effective in Anne's childhood: Marilla calls Anne back to ordinary reality by reminding her that she, too, has felt pain comparable to the bereaved mother's, perhaps over Matthew's death or Anne's absence from Green Gables. She then invokes the name of Susan, Anne's housekeeper, a guarantee of humor (120) which restores Anne's zest for life.

The story of Anne's daughter Rilla is also replete with humor and with the importance of learning to love an orphan adopted from both duty and a sense of competence. Rilla, however, is a young girl much under the control of others, especially her father, Gilbert. The only one of Anne's children who does not attend college, Rilla describes herself as a "pretty dunce" spending the war years at home learning what she can do for her country. One thing she can do, it seems, is to raise a fine boy and to ground him in an appropriate class setting. Through her role as graceful but unwitting *mater familias,* Rilla grows into a woman who will live in a world forever altered by the First World War. Her story's hints of teenage, unwed motherhood, usually introduced by Susan's references to "your baby" when fifteen-year-old Rilla is entertaining a male visitor (*Rilla of Ingleside* 134), convey some of that change. Rilla's fairy-tale luck and feminine pluck, however, suggest that her maternal journeys bode well for Canada's future. Saving the lower-class, half-English child in his infancy, and then winning a patron, Matilda Pitman, to bequeath funds for his education, show that the diary-writing daughter Anne named for Marilla will exercise a vigorous as well as a pretty presence in adulthood.

The third woman in Montgomery's maternal triad has an open, fluid character. Yet, like her mother before her, Rilla can't tell whose wife she'll be, though this information is obvious to the reader; and like her "Aunt" Marilla, this maiden also resists motherhood. Once Gilbert "induces" her to take care of the baby she has brought home, however, Rilla is as determined as Marilla to brook no interference with her methods. Both Marilla and Rilla contrast with Anne, who—once married—is both an eager mother and one who expects others (Gilbert and Susan) to rear the children with her. Without experience, and silly rather than possessed of traces of humor, young Rilla handles the baby, at first, as though he were a "break-able lizard" (68). She then operates with Jims much the way Marilla had with Anne, moving toward love by resolutely meeting the "creature's" physical needs. Even at fifteen, Rilla can enact what Ruddick calls "maternal power which is benign, accurate, sturdy and sane" (345), called to competence by the helplessness of the infant. Removing the foundling from a potentially abusive foster mother, Rilla performs exactly as Marilla had. She engages in maternal thinking at once, beginning a questioning process that will enable her to save the baby's life. Her questions locate the means to convey the child to Ingleside: she puts him into a soup tureen, his only heirloom, and rides back through hurricane winds with the newborn in her lap. Once her father indicates that the baby will be her responsibility, Rilla continues her thinking, obtaining enough information from Susan to proceed on her own, "beholden to nobody."

Though Rilla lacks Marilla's sense of humor, she does have an openness to change and a resilient, if self-dramatizing, temperament. Ironing the baby's shirts, fretting over his lack of hair, she embarks on the task of producing an acceptable group member (or perhaps two, since she is turning herself, also, into an acceptable female). Like Marilla's love for Anne, Rilla's love for Jims is not immediate, and she recognizes its presence only on the night that she picks him up despite the justification her baby book offers for staying under the covers and letting him cry. Not the act of picking him up, but the baby's laughing response to her, produces something "delightful and yearning and brooding" (94).

Rilla demonstrates her adult potential by fostering Jims, but then faces the problem—as does the novelist—of what is to be his fate. His soldier-father is returning to claim him, with a record of abandonment and shiftlessness. The impending separation is one reason Rilla takes him on a train to visit a friend in Charlottetown. Here, coincidence moves the plot via a Goldilocks sequence in which Rilla and Jims are caught in a stranger's house. The encounter with Matilda Pitman, who makes Jims her heir, follows directly on the equally amazing episode in which the child falls off the train and Rilla instinctively leaps off to protect his fall. On a two-mile walk, at night, to the empty house, Rilla displays her ability to preserve the child's life and foster his growth. This walk and its outcome solves the maternal problem of producing an acceptable group member when Rilla will have no control over Jims' upbringing. Her own flexibility, in focusing on the child when he falls, allows Rilla to welcome the change Jims' new circumstances will bring.

Already a woman because she exercises maternal thinking as well as other domestic and social thought, Rilla is also still the frivolous maiden, and her last word in the text is a lisped "yeth" to Ken's pronouncement of her name as Rilla-*my*-Rilla. Girl, mother, and wise woman conflate to one.

By examining the edges of the Anne books, it is possible to say something about the center as well. Why is Montgomery so preoccupied with mothering that she makes it the task of maidens? Why does Anne mother many children but write few stories, while Montgomery produces two children and more than twenty novels? Gilbert and Gubar have observed that women writers have been the daughters of too few mothers (50); the constant recreation of the forebear as Demeter, as well as the return of the daughter with new knowledge, is a frequent motif in the work of women artists and critics (Seaman) linked to the creation of oneself as an artist. Rarely do women imagine creativity as an act of separation. Montgomery herself was raised by a foster mother (grandmother), and she seems to have found in this dual image of foster and biological connection a way to suggest continuity and power. Confronting the "end" of Anne's story in her marriage to the man who had "spoiled her pen-nib" on the day they met (*Anne of Windy Poplars* 36) Montgomery found a way to extend her narrative by depicting Anne as matchmaker, friend, and the maker of various affiliations in addition to the biological. The journeys of Marilla and Rilla are humorous, adventurous, and interesting examples of motherhood from the point of view of affiliative mothers-by-choice; they frame and extend the story of the redhead destined for Gilbert and submerged in the genteel marriage demanded by plot conventions. In addition, Montgomery seems to have come close to describing the ever-elusive nature of female autonomy—no mean feat.

Works Cited

Chodorow, Nancy. *The Reproduction of Mothering: Psychoanalysis and the Sociology of Gender.* Berkeley, CA: U of California P, 1978.

Gallop, Jane. "The Monster in the Mirror: The Feminist Critic's Psychoanalysis." *Feminism and Psychoanalysis.* Ed. Richard Feldstein and Judith Roof. Ithaca, NY: Cornell UP, 1989.

Gilbert, Sandra M., and Susan Gubar. *The Madwoman in the Attic: The Woman Writer and the Nineteenth-Century Imagination.* New Haven, CT: Yale UP, 1980.

Montgomery, L. M. *Anne of Avonlea.* 1909. New York: Bantam, 1981.

_____. *Anne of Green Gables.* 1908. New York: Bantam, 1981.

_____. *Anne of Windy Poplars.* 1936. New York: Bantam, 1981.

_____. *Anne's House of Dreams.* 1917. New York: Bantam, 1981.

_____. *Rilla of Ingleside.* 1921. New York: Bantam, 1981.

Pratt, Annis. *Archetypal Patterns in Women's Fiction.* Bloomington, IN: Indiana UP, 1981.

Reuther, Rosemary Radford. "Mother as Educator." Illinois Humanities Lecture, Augustana College, 1984.

Ruddick, Sara. "Maternal Thinking." *Feminist Studies* 6 (1980): 342-
    67.
Seaman, Gerda, and Ellen Walker. "The Demeter/Kore Myth as a
    Pattern of Development for the Female Writer." MLA presentation.
    Chicago, 30 Dec. 1985.

The Female *Bildungsroman* in Nineteenth-Century America

Parameters of a Vision

Eve Kornfeld and Susan Jackson

"Oh, don't I wish I could manage things for you as I do for my heroines," Jo March says to her three sisters (146). The joke, however, is between the author and the reader, for this is *Little Women*, the fictionalized autobiography of Jo's real-life prototype, Louisa May Alcott, and she *can* manage the lives of her heroines. Millions of girls have read Alcott's coming-of-age novel of 1868, written in the midst of the most prolific outpouring of women's literature to date. In nineteenth-century America, women made up the majority of the reading public, and the genre commonly known as domestic fiction depicted patterns of behavior with which they could easily identify—life in the home. Within this framework, Jo March and her sisters learn how to manage their lives and prepare for their future as little women. Alcott's novel may be seen as a synthesis of the coming-of-age novel, or *Bildungsroman* (which is usually male-oriented), and domestic fiction, to form the female *Bildungsroman*.

By observing and imitating, adolescents try to forge a sense of self, usually by integrating aspects of the culture to which they are exposed. In writing for adolescents, an author tries to encapsulate the ideologies which she feels will be of most use to her readers in their attempt to define themselves. The moral frameworks provided by the author reflect social assumptions about behavior, including gender relations. *Little Women* was the first well-known American novel written specifically for and about adolescent girls; it depicted them as interesting characters, capable of fun and adventures. While they do enjoy themselves, however, the heroines must also learn how to "govern the kingdom" of the self by learning to be good women.[1] Alcott's model was widely imitated in nineteenth-century America. Study of the female *Bildungsroman* is thus particularly interesting because it was written by women and for girls, and illuminates the social expectations of female life as well as the secret hopes and dreams which might not be revealed in another format.

Much of the energy of feminist literary criticism has been devoted to the issue of the portrayal of women and gender relations. Some critics believe that, on the whole, popular women's literature upheld traditional ideas about women and gender roles, while others think that it subverted them in the hope of creating a new set of expectations and realities for the reader. In his pioneering study of sentimental fiction of 1940, Herbert Brown articulated the former position: "The domestic novels in which these writers sought to glorify the American home were as limited in scope as the narrow sphere of interests of the women readers for whom they were designed. . . . Domestic fiction records few instances of discontent with this circumscribed life" (281).

This critical attitude toward domestic fiction was challenged in the 1950s, however, by Helen Papashvily's initial voice of dissent: "These pretty tales reflected and encouraged a pattern of feminine behavior—quietly ruthless, [and] subtly vicious" (xvii). Papashvily's view of the latent subversiveness of domestic fiction (undermined by those happy endings) was taken up and modified in the 1970s, a period in which the inviolability of the male literary canon began to be questioned. While considerable controversy remains about the impact of domestic fiction on women's consciousness and American culture in general, new attention has been focussed on the possible feminist subtexts of this popular fiction. In the last decade and a half, various feminist scholars have claimed that nineteenth-century American women used the novel as an extension of the self, and as a forum from which to question prevailing gender relations.[2]

The historiographical argument about whether domestic fiction subverted or upheld traditional values of womanhood can usefully be extended to the female *Bildungsroman,* as a subgenre of domestic fiction. A close examination of the most popular examples of the nineteenth-century American female *Bildungsroman* should allow us to determine whether these novels are paeans to the cult of domesticity or subversive texts instructing women about their ability and responsibility to change their situations. The novels examined in this study are the Little Women series by Louisa May Alcott, the Five Little Peppers books by Margaret Sidney (the pseudonym of Harriett Mulford Lothrop), *Rebecca of Sunnybrook Farm* by Kate Douglas Wiggin, and the Anne of Green Gables series by Lucy Maud Montgomery.

As young girls, the heroines of *Little Women* dream impossible dreams. Jo would "have a stable full of Arabian steeds, rooms piled with books . . . do something heroic or wonderful . . . write books, and get rich and famous." Amy's pet wish is "to be an artist, and go to Rome, and do fine pictures, and be the best artist in the whole world." Meg wants "a lovely house, full of all sorts of luxurious things. . . . I wouldn't be idle, but do good, and make everyone love me dearly" (133). These dreams serve two functions. They provide an outlet for young girls trying to come to terms with a prescribed adult identity, and at the same time they reveal a dissatisfaction with the prohibition against entering a male world.

This vague dissatisfaction with a society that offers so few options for women is expressed explicitly at the outset of the novel, in the heroine's wish that she were a boy: "I can't get over my disappointment in not being a boy; and it's worse than ever now, for I'm dying to go and fight with Papa, and I can only stay at home and knit, like a poky old woman" (5). Significantly, Jo is not alone in this sentiment; each of the major examples of the nineteenth-century female *Bildungsroman* begins in much the same vein. Even Rebecca of Sunnybrook Farm echoes the lament: "Boys always do the nice splendid things, and girls can only do the nasty dull ones that get left over" (13). The rest of each book is devoted to the interesting adventures that the heroines have as they learn to become little women.

But they do not learn these hard lessons in the real world. The authors of these nineteenth-century books for girls created a matriarchal society—a feminine utopia. They assumed a power of womanhood not usually found in contemporary American society, and used it as a structure within which a girl could learn to survive, by assimilating the proper values. At the heart of this world, not surprisingly, was the mother.

When the temperamental Louisa May Alcott was ten, she wrote, "I feel sad because I have been cross today, and did not mind Mother. I cried, and then I felt better, and said that piece from Mrs. Sigourney, 'I must not tease my mother'" (*Life, Letters and Journals* 36). Children of this period were taught to worship their mothers, who had given them life and nurture. Indeed, the power of their mother's love on the March girls in *Little Women* is quite remarkable. After they have had an experimental week of "all play and no work," Marmee (Mrs. March) gently shows them the pitfalls of doing only as they please:

> While Hannah [their maid] and I did your work, you got on pretty well, though I don't think you were very happy or amiable, so I thought, as a little lesson, I would show you what happens when everyone thinks only of herself. Don't you feel that it is pleasanter to help one another, to have daily duties which make leisure time sweet when it comes, and to bear and forbear, that home may be comfortable and lovely to us all? (110)

Marmee's gentle reprimand reiterates the necessity of self-discipline. The girls cannot entirely define their own ideal world; they must accept that of their mother, a world devoid of selfishness.

Both *Little Women* and Margaret Sidney's novel of 1878, *Five Little Peppers and How They Grew,* begin with the children's wish that they were rich. Shortly thereafter, however, they learn to count their blessings, by doing something for the mother who works so hard for them. For the Peppers, the occasion is Mamsie's birthday. The family is too poor to afford a working stove, but through sheer force of will, eleven-year-old Polly manages to bake a cake in their old cookstove. Due to the orneriness of the stove the cake turns black with "a depressing little dump" (5), but that is fixed with a posy fortuitously sent by a kind neighbor. Mrs. Pepper wisely expresses enough "delight in the cake . . . to satisfy the most exacting mind" (32). The nineteenth-century fictional mother had to strike a careful balance between love and duty, nurture and reproof.

When his second daughter, Louisa, was born, A. Bronson Alcott wrote to his father-in-law: "Abba [Louisa's mother] is very comfortable, and will soon be restored to the discharge of those domestic and maternal duties in which she takes so much delight, and in the performance of which she furnishes so excellent a model for imitation" (*Life, Letters and Journals* 15). These domestic and maternal duties were what Kate Douglas Wiggin, the author of *Rebecca of Sunnybrook Farm,* called "the crown of womanhood" (97). Women were to provide an example to their daughters of piety and grace and to help them through the difficult task of reaching adulthood.

Interestingly, in these fictional female utopias, the power of the mother's benevolent influence extends beyond the female sphere. In each fictional family, the girls share their mother with male friends who have none. Laurie, the motherless boy-next-door in *Little Women,* discovers a surrogate mother in Marmee; Jasper King, the rich boy who befriends the Pepper children, finds their Mamsie a godsend. When they find out that Jasper has no mother, the Peppers are horrified: "Polly for her life couldn't imagine how anybody could feel without a mother, but the very words alone smote her heart." Throughout the four books about the Peppers, Mamsie provides a restraining and inspirational influence on Jasper, as well as on her girls.

The authors of the nineteenth-century female *Bildungsromans* thus created a power of womanhood not generally found in contemporary American society. The role of males in the novels is correspondingly complex. Harriett Mulford Lothrop (Margaret Sidney's real name; her father thought it improper for women to write and forced her to assume a pen name) wrote that "my judgment told me I must eliminate Mr. Pepper [who has died before *Five Little Peppers* begins] because the whole motif 'to help mother' would be lost if the father lived" (*The Wayside* 156). This comment indicates the fragility of the matriarchal world, even in a fictional setting.

In the real world, of course, men had all of the economic power—a fact that the authors could not deny, even in a utopian situation. It is no coincidence that in each *Bildungsroman* studied, there is a male benefactor who distinctly improves family fortunes. The authors skirt the issue of male power, however, by removing fathers through death and war, and minimizing the direct influence of the male benefactors. Men appear only when they can perform a useful function, and only after it is clear that the women can manage perfectly well on their own, even though circumstances have definitely conspired against them.

There is no room for traditional masculine qualities in this world of women. When Laurie cries with Jo over her sister's impending death in *Little Women,* Alcott editorializes, "it might be unmanly of Laurie to cry, but he couldn't help it and I'm glad of it" (172). The only example in any of the books of a man without any womanly qualities appears in *Rebecca of Sunnybrook Farm:*

> Mr. Simpson spent little time with his family, owing to certain awkward methods of horse-trading, or the "swapping" of farm implements and vehicles of various kinds. . . . After every successful trade he generally passed a longer or shorter term in jail: for when a poor man . . . has the inveterate habit of swapping, it follows naturally that he must have something to swap; and having nothing of his own it follows still more naturally that he must swap something belonging to his neighbors. (73)

An abundance of "good" (feminized) men provide counter examples of behavior in these fictional worlds. Adam Ladd is visiting his aunt when he meets Rebecca of Sunnybrook Farm; his first line is, "I am the lady of the house at present . . . what can I do for you?" (140). Rebecca proceeds to sell him three hundred cakes of soap to benefit the Simpson family, for whose well-being she feels responsible. Adam Ladd is thus doubly acceptable, because he is a thoroughly feminized philanthropist.

Since the ideal of motherhood transcended sexuality and is not necessarily considered to be a biological function, it is possible in these novels for a man to act as a mother. Jeremiah Cobb, the stagedriver who takes Rebecca to live with her aunts (her mother cannot afford to have her live at home), becomes her surrogate mother. He shares this role with his wife Sarah, whom he calls "Mother," a name which, despite her short tenure in that vocation (their only child died at seventeen months), "served at any rate as a reminder of her woman's crown of blessedness" (97). Feminized men and women alike could teach the blessed duties of benevolence and domesticity in this utopian world. Curiously, the worship of domesticity and maternal nurture seems to have overwhelmed even traditional gender boundaries in these novels.

Coincidentally with learning her duties within the domestic sphere, a girl was inculcated in the importance of the community of women through these novels. Anne Shirley, the heroine of Lucy Maud Montgomery's *Anne of Green Gables,* reaches Green Gables having had only make-believe friends. Her first words to her neighbor, Diana Barry, are "Do you think—oh, do you think you can like me a little—enough to be my bosom friend?" (120). Throughout the six volumes of the series the two remain bosom friends, no matter how physically distant they might be. This emphasis on the "bonds of womanhood" permeated the novels. "So sweet is the idea of friendship to the human heart that its name is one of the earliest on our lips, and latest lingers there," wrote Lydia Sigourney in her advice book of 1837, *Letters to the Young Ladies* (97). Sisters are built-in best friends, of course: Polly Pepper's health declines when she and her much younger sister, Phronsie, are separated for the first time. As a result, the entire Pepper family moves in with Polly, who has been taken in by the wealthy King family so that she might learn to play the piano.[3]

As a girl matured, she widened her circle of female friends, but continued to turn to other women for sympathetic support. Rebecca of Sunnybrook Farm, for example, had to move in with her maiden aunts at the age of eleven because her widowed mother could not afford to care for all of her children. Rebecca's aunts are kind in their own way, and Rebecca finds many male and female friends, but she needs "somebody who not only loved but understood; who spoke her language, comprehended her desires, and responded to her mysterious longings" (167). She finds that person in her spinster teacher at the Wareham seminary.

By the late nineteenth century, about ten percent of all American women were spinsters; in the Northeast, the percentage may have been twice as high. Many spinsters appeared in the nineteenth-century female *Bildungsroman.* In these novels, however, the spinsters are portrayed quite differently than in American culture in general: not bitter, disillusioned, or unfulfilled, spinsters in these female utopias are independent financially and mentally; they play an important role in the lives of the heroines and their communities. The vital and interesting role of the spinster in these novels indicates to the reader that a single woman can have a fulfilling life.

Indeed, the heroines of these female *Bildungsromans* who marry do so only after they have established their own independence. Even Marmee, whose bliss is her daughters, proclaims, "better be happy old maids than unhappy wives, or unmaidenly girls, running about to find husbands" (92). The authors take pains to ensure that their heroines will escape what Mary Livermore, in an advice book of 1883, *What Shall We Do With Our Daughters,* called "one of the most serious dangers to which inefficient women are liable—the danger of regarding marriage as a means of livelihood" (62). These authors realized that marriage could be a way of gaining financial security, but they were also aware of its drawbacks.[4]

The marriages in the novels reveal certain patterns: either the couple has to wait for a few years, or else marriage does not separate the heroine from her family. Meg and John Brooke of *Little Women,* for instance, must delay their nuptials until he is able to support her; in the meantime, Meg continues to work as a governess. Gilbert Blythe, who has liked Anne of Green Gables since she was eleven, must wait until he is in medical school for her acceptance. When they finally do marry, however, Anne sacrifices a promising writing career to marry him.

In some instances, both marriage patterns appear. Jasper's father, who has become a surrogate father to the Peppers, sends the youngest Pepper daughter's suitor away in *Phronsie Pepper.* He explains his reasoning to the girl: "Besides [marriage] being decidedly unpleasant for you, it would kill me. . . . I shouldn't live a month if you went off and got married, Phronsie" (19). Duty means, first of all, duty to the family. Phronsie does not even mention her sorrow. In the end, of course, all works out well: Mr. King relents when he learns that Phronsie's suitor is dying. The whole extended family travels to England to nurse him, he and Phronsie marry, and they all return to America to live in Mr. King's house.

Although Jo March at one point wants to "marry Meg [her older sister] myself, and keep her safe in the family" (187), in actuality marriage does not break down the strong female bonds of *Little Women.* Meg, like her real-life prototype Anna, lives near her mother, and the two families spend a great deal of time together. Similarly, Polly Pepper marries her surrogate brother, Jasper, and continues to live with her father-in-law, mother, stepfather, and siblings. The old bonds might be changed, but they are not severed.

For all of this familiarity, however, the language describing marriage in these books tends to be maudlin, metaphorical, and vague:

> [Marriage] was not all Paradise by any means . . . [but in it a woman was] safe from the restless fret and fever of the world, finding loyal lovers in the little sons and daughters who cling to them, undaunted by sorrow, poverty, or age; walking side by side, through fair and stormy weather, with a faithful friend, who is, in the true sense of the good old Saxon word, the "houseband" and learning, as Meg learned, that a wife's happiest kingdom is home, her highest honor the art of ruling it not as a queen, but a wise wife and mother. (364-5)

This is Meg and John's "ideal" marriage—a compromise worked out after a series of marital problems. In fact, Alcott wrote of it somewhat reluctantly. After the publication of the first book of *Little Women,* in which none of the sisters marries, Alcott wrote rather peevishly, "Girls write to ask who the little women marry, as if that was the only end aim of a woman's life" (*Life, Letters and Journals* 201). Her true feelings about marriage manifest themselves in her *alter-ego* Jo's reaction to her sister's marriage.

When she finds the newly engaged Meg and John Brooke together, "Jo gave a sort of gasp, as if a cold shower had suddenly fallen upon her . . . [and rushed] upstairs. . . exclaiming 'Oh, do somebody go down quick; John Brooke is acting dreadfully, and Meg likes it!'" When Laurie announces that he and Amy have married, Jo replies in a similar vein: "Mercy on us! What dreadful thing will you do next?" Whether or not the use of the particular word was intentional, marriage did indeed fill Jo with dread. When told that she is not "giving Meg up," but only "going halves" with John, Jo sighs, "It can never be the same again. I've lost my dearest friend." Jo worries that Meg's marriage will fundamentally alter the structure of her family and its strong female bonds, and objects to this intrusion.

The Peppers react in a similar fashion to the first marriage that encroaches upon their world. In *Five Little Peppers Midway,* "Grandpapa" King gathers them together one day and asks, "'Did you ever think that your mother might marry again?'. . . 'Oh, how can you?' cried Polly passionately . . . 'say such perfectly dreadful things'" (263-4). When they learn, however, that their mother's husband-to-be is Dr. Fisher, an old friend, the young Peppers (in a typically lightning-fast shift of mood) are thrilled. It is curious that Grandpapa, and not Mamsie, should be the one to talk to the children. Perhaps the seriousness (or horror?) of the subject requires a paternal hand.

Alcott refused to marry Jo and Laurie in *Little Women,* even though her readers begged her to do so, but eventually she created the character of Professor Bhaer in response to the demands of her readers and publisher that Jo get married. Alcott also married off Meg and Amy, whose real-life prototypes did marry, but not until they were in their thirties. (May died a year later, and Anna was widowed in ten years.) Alcott herself never married. Her biographer, Edith Cheney, believed that Alcott could not comfortably incorporate the strictures of marriage into her life: "Her heart was bound up in her family, and she could hardly contemplate her own interests as separate from theirs. She loved activity, freedom, and independence. She could not cherish illusions tenderly" (201). There is little doubt that Alcott's own perception of married life as enslavement or an "illusion" was reflected in her novels, with undeniably subversive results.

Distanced from their own adolescences, the authors of female *Bildungsromans* could reinvent girlhood with an eye towards perfection. The "grown-up" life of housewifery, however, could not be portrayed in such a distant, idealized manner. Kate Douglas Wiggin described Rebecca's stint as a housewife in less than glowing terms:

> [She spent] two months of steady, fagging work; of cooking, washing, ironing. . . . No girl of seventeen can pass through such an ordeal . . . without some inward repining and rebellion. She was doing tasks in which she could not be fully happy . . . and like a promise of nectar to thirsty lips was the vision of joys she had had to put aside for the performance of dull daily duty. (306-7)

Perhaps it was because they realized that this was the inevitable future of their heroines that the authors shied away from having them marry; they generally did so only in sequels demanded by the public.

The drudgery of housework aside, a rather grim picture of the state of married life emerges from these novels. None of the heroines comes from an "ideal" family, defined by prescriptive advice books as one in which "the husband will be the breadwinner, and the wife the bread-maker" (Livermore 165-7). Mr. March does not earn a living, and the rest of the fathers are deceased. But the books all have portraits of wronged wives, such as poor Mrs. Winslow, who was left in the forest by her husband, and whose motherless son provided the impetus for the founding of the charitable Riverboro Aunts Association. Rebecca's own mother is another wronged wife: in her effort to keep her family from dissolving after her insolvent husband's death, she ends up "[c]ontent to work from sunrise to sunset to gain a mere subsistence for her children," living "in the future, not in her own present, as a mother is wont to do when her own lot seems dull and cheerless" (170). Again and again, the authors subtly refute the notion that a woman's only place is in the home, and that she should be content with that, by their inability to portray married life as interesting and rewarding.

Alcott and her successors offered something other than housework and childrearing to their readers. In their utopian, fictional world there was an opportunity for "young ladies to make themselves the mistresses of some attainment, either in art or science, by which they might secure a subsistency, should they be reduced to poverty" (Sigourney 32). To some extent, their fiction reflected these authors' unusual lives. Alcott, who felt compelled to support her own family since her father could not, never married. Harriett Mulford Lothrop, the author of the Five Little Peppers series, married her publisher, Daniel Lothrop, when she was thirty-nine; they had one daughter. Kate Douglas Wiggin, the author of *Rebecca of Sunnybrook Farm,* devoted a single page of her 440-page memoir to her first husband, Samuel Wiggin, to whom she was married for eight years; all she recorded about him was that they married and he died. Her second husband was allotted eight pages, as well as numerous letters—throughout most of their marriage they lived in separate countries. Lucy Maud Montgomery, the author of *Anne of Green Gables*, was almost forty when she married. Prior to that she cared for the grandparents who had raised her. Voluntarily or not, the creators of the female *Bildungsroman* in America lived extraordinary lives and, consciously or not, their lives affected their fiction.

For, despite their worship of maternal nurture and family life, these novels all contain some elements subversive to the nineteenth-century cult of domesticity. Most striking, perhaps, is the curious role assigned to men in these matriarchal utopias: traditional gender boundaries are crossed frequently by "feminized" men, if not by "masculine" women; and there seems to be no appreciation for traditional "masculine" qualities. Implicitly, then, these novels contain a deep critique of the male world of money and power, within their exaltation of the value of female nurture. A subtle subversion of the cult of domesticity is also apparent in the treatment of marriage in these books: while spinsters often have positive roles and fulfilling lives, marriage (unlike motherhood) is not portrayed very positively. At least for a while in each series of novels, some alternative to domesticity is offered to the heroines and readers alike. With the bonds of womanhood supporting them, the heroines of these novels exercise some choice over the paths of their lives.

* * * * *

Anne's horizons had closed in . . . but if the path set before her feet was to be narrow she knew that the flowers of quiet happiness would bloom along it. The joys of sincere work and worthy aspiration and congenial friendship were to be hers; nothing could rob her of her birthright of fancy or her ideal world of dreams. And there was always the bend in the road! (429)

At the end of *Anne of Green Gables,* Anne Shirley gives up her university scholarship and takes a job teaching in Avonlea. Matthew Cuthbert, her guardian, has just died, and his sister, Marilla, learns that she is going blind. If Anne left Green Gables, Marilla would lose her home. The decision is not an easy one for Anne. The scholarship she received is very prestigious, and she has always wanted to go to college. But since the womanly virtue of self-sacrifice has been thoroughly inculcated in Anne, she can accept and make the best of this duty.

The boundaries of the feminine utopia can become oppressive after the girl heroine has passed through adolescence. Although she can dream as much as she wants, duty to her family must be her first concern, even if it gets in the way of her own plans. Anne's ambition leads her to desire entrance into the traditionally male world of the university. This desire cannot be realized until she has done her duty in the matriarchal world. And even then, Anne cannot leave home.

The extent of Anne's great sacrifice is evident in the use of the adjective "narrow" to describe her path. According to Herbert Brown, most women in popular domestic fiction were content to have a "narrow sphere of interest." Although Anne accepts her duty, she eagerly looks forward to the "bend in the road." She also rather vehemently states that no one can take away her dreams, and her own ideal world. In a sense, the only power that Anne has is in the world of make-believe.

The authors of the female *Bildungsromans* created a utopia as a framework in which the problems of adolescence could be solved. The nature of this utopia was in part derived from the things denied to women in the real world. The matriarchal culture of nineteenth-century female *Bildungsromans* gave their heroines the freedom of development they would not have found in a male world. They were still, however, precluded from entering this male world fully and finally.

The attraction of fiction is that it allows the author to recreate the world. When Jo March wishes that her sisters were her heroines, Alcott comments on her own position, in which her sisters are her heroines. Eventually, Jo does have "some rich relation leave [her] a fortune unexpectedly," and Amy does "go abroad and come home [married to a rich man] in a blaze of splendor and elegance" (146). Even in the fiction, however, things happen to the characters which Alcott does not want to happen. She is bound by the constraints of domestic fiction and the need to create a credible facsimile of life. The parameters of this world are set by a social reality over which even an author cannot exercise complete control.

Notes

1. Louisa May Alcott, "My Kingdom," in Edith Cheney, ed., *Louisa May Alcott: Life, Letters and Journals* (Boston, MA, 1889).

2. Ann Douglas, *The Feminization of American Culture* (New York: Doubleday, 1977), opened the debate over the impact of domestic fiction on American culture. For a penetrating critique of both Papashvily's assumptions about these novelists' anti-male animus, and Douglas's unsympathetic portrait of domestic fiction as sentimental in the worse sense,

see Nina Baym, *Women's Fiction: A Guide to Novels by and about Women in America, 1829-1870* (Ithaca, NY: Cornell UP, 1978.) Other pioneering studies of nineteenth-century American ideology about womanhood and gender roles include Barbara Welter, "The Cult of True Womanhood, 1820-1860," diss., U of California at Santa Barbara, 1971; and Kathryn Kish Sklar, *Catherine Beecher: A Study in American Domesticity* (New Haven, CT: Yale UP, 1973).

3. For the historical context of this ideal of a female community, see Nancy Cott, *The Bonds of Womanhood: "Woman's Sphere" in New England, 1780-1835* (New Haven, CT: Yale UP, 1977); and Carroll Smith-Rosenberg, "The Female World of Love and Ritual: Relations between Women in Nineteenth-Century America," *Signs* 1 (1975): 1-30.

4. For an interesting new exploration of the lives and attitudes of spinsters in the nineteenth-century Northeast, see Lee Virginia Chambers-Schiller, *Liberty, A Better Husband: Single Women in America: The Generations of 1780-1840* (New Haven, CT: Yale UP, 1984).

Works Cited

Alcott, Louisa May. *Little Women.* 1868. New York: Bantam, 1983.

Brown, Herbert R. *The Sentimental Novel in America, 1789-1860.* Durham, NC: Duke UP, 1940.

Cheney, Edith, ed. *Louisa May Alcott: Life, Letters and Journals.* Boston: Roberts Brothers, 1889.

Livermore, Mary A. *What Shall We Do With Our Daughters, Superfluous Women, and Other Lectures.* Boston: Lee and Shepard, 1883.

Lothrop, Harriett Mulford [Margaret Sidney]. *Five Little Peppers and How They Grew.* 1878. Chicago: Goldsmith, n.d.

_____. *Five Little Peppers Midway.* Boston: D. Lothrop, 1890.

_____. *Phronsie Pepper.* Boston: D. Lothrop, 1897.

_____. *The Wayside: Home of Authors.* New York: American Book Company, 1940.

Montgomery, Lucy Maud. *Anne of Green Gables.* Boston: Page, 1908.

Papashvily, Helen. *All the Happy Endings.* New York: Harper, 1956.

Sigourney, Lydia. *Letters to the Young Ladies.* Hartford, CT: William Watson, 1835.

Wiggin, Kate Douglas. *Rebecca of Sunnybrook Farm.* Boston: Black, 1903.

Anne of Green Gables
A Girl's Reading

Temma F. Berg

While it is impossible to verify the following statement, I do believe it is true: *Anne of Green Gables* was the book that most profoundly influenced me as a child and young adolescent. What I remember most about my childhood reading experience of *Anne* is my sense of total immersion in the story. I was Anne Shirley. I, like Anne, was an orphan. Not literally of course. I had a complete set of parents, but I felt alienated in some undefined way from the world I lived in. I was a lonely, book-ridden child. I had a few friends, but I felt different from them, and when I was among them, I usually preferred to be by myself, reading in a corner, wishing I could be curled up on a window seat like Jane Eyre. Of course, the houses my friends and I lived in did not have window seats, so I read on sofas or chairs, but I might just as well have been hidden in a window seat. I read Anne's books both because I was a reader and because they confirmed my sense of my difference and apartness. They told me it was okay to be different.

Not only did I recognize myself in Anne, but I also used the events of Anne's life as models for my own. I wanted to be as like Anne Shirley as possible. I wanted a bosom friend like Diana Barry. I picked one friend to be my "kindred spirit," but she never seemed to be as good a friend to me as Diana was to Anne. Luckily, though, her mother and my mother did not get along very well, so they *almost* fit the pattern of Marilla and Mrs. Barry. My friend's mother, however, never forbade me her daughter's company, so we never had to make undying vows of friendship in the face of parental opposition, probably the best stimulant for animating ordinary youthful feelings.

While I had difficulty finding a friend like Diana or turning the ones I had into an image of her, I could more easily duplicate Anne's imaginative yearnings and love of reading. I, like Anne, liked to think of myself as a heroine and having a heroine like Anne to model myself on and project myself into made it easier. Just as Anne's reading gave her models, patterns, ways to interpret her experience, Anne and her books gave me models, patterns, ways to interpret and validate my experience. Reading stoked Anne's imagination just as it stoked mine. Though I lived in the city, I used Anne's rural landscape to green my own. I tried to look at the trees along my street and the playground at the end of it through her eyes. I composed long, eloquent descriptive passages as I walked along the streets of my world as a means to enter Anne's. Both by reading the actual books and by reading my own life in their terms, I was able to enter, even if only sporadically, Anne's world.

Recently, the Public Broadcasting System presented a four-part TV movie based on the Anne of Green Gables series, and because the TV movie seemed so faithful to and yet different from my memories of the novel, I found myself reconsidering what the novel meant to me as a child. The TV series seemed more feminist than the novel I remembered. I didn't remember the women in the novel as quite so powerful as the women in the TV show, or Marilla as quite so warm-hearted under her gruff exterior. And I didn't remember the strong-willed woman school teacher at all. Were these and other manifestations of the feminist thought I noticed in the TV series—for example, the obvious comparison between Anne who sought education and her bosom buddy Diana who missed it because her mother thought book-learning was wasted on a girl—present in the novel or simply the addition of a modern screenwriter's sensibility? And, if they were in the novel, why had I not remembered them? What was the significance of that forgetting?

According to Freud, what we do not consciously remember is what most deeply impresses itself on our unconscious. In one of the more intriguing footnotes to *The Interpretation of Dreams,* Freud speculates about this phenomenon:

An important contribution to the part played by recent material
in the construction of dreams has been made by Pötzl (1917) in
a paper which carries a wealth of implications. In a series of
experiments Pötzl required the subjects to make a drawing of
what they had consciously noted of a picture exposed to their
view in a tachistoscope [an instrument for exposing an object to
view for an extremely short time]. He then turned his attention
to the dreams dreamt by the subjects during the following night
and required them once more to make drawings of appropriate
portions of these dreams. It was shown unmistakably that those
details of the exposed picture which had not been noted by the
subject provided material for the construction of the dream,
whereas those details which had been consciously perceived and
recorded in the drawing made after the exposure did not recur in
the manifest content of the dream. The material that was taken
over by the dream-work was modified by it for the purposes of
dream-construction in its familiar "arbitrary" (or, more properly
"autocratic") manner. The questions raised by Pötzl's experiment go far beyond the sphere of dream interpretation as dealt
with in the present volume. (214-15n)

I would agree with Freud's suggestion that Pötzl's experiment
raises questions that go far beyond the sphere of dream interpretation. It carries, for example, a wealth of implications for reading.
What does happen when we read? Are the processes that we cannot
perceive more important than the processes that we can? It would
seem, if we use Pötzl to understand reading, that we would have to
agree that there is much more to reading than meets the eye or inner
ear. Indeed, after going back and rereading *Anne of Green Gables,*
I believe that Pötzl's experiment helped me gain a clearer understanding of my childhood reading experience of that novel. It would
seem that the feminism I must just have missed—consciously—
when as a young girl I read Anne's story, all the more deeply
embedded itself in my unconscious. The power of *Anne of Green
Gables* may indeed come as a result of the subtle pervasiveness of
its feminism.

The feminism of the novel is present in a variety of ways: in its
portrayal of Anne as an independent, creative, and strong-willed
heroine; in its emphasis on her extraordinary imaginative powers
and on the way imagination can empower women; and in its

forward-looking view of the dialectic that exists between men and women and within each human being.

Anne is definitely not a typical girl. She is, as Janet Weiss-Townsend has suggested, aggressive, independent, and practical (12). However, while I would agree with this estimation and with much in Weiss-Townsend's discussion of *Anne,* I do not agree with her assertion that *Anne* has more in common with boys' books than with a feminist novel like *Surfacing.* Anne's story is very different from a typical boys' adventure story. While the boy hero usually seeks autonomy, separation, and freedom from social restraints, Anne desperately wants to belong: "You see," she tells Matthew on her first ride to Green Gables, "I've never had a real home since I can remember. It gives me that pleasant ache again just to think of coming to a really truly home" (18). When she sees Green Gables, she immediately feels a sense of belonging. When she learns she must leave because she is not the boy they expected, she hesitates to allow herself to grow any fonder of the place. She even refrains from going outside to play. Anne is no rebel; she is not in conflict with her society. She does not seek to engage her reader's antisocial sympathies. Anne wants to be accepted and she makes wanting to be accepted not only acceptable, but courageous and as worthwhile as it is difficult. Susan Drain suggests that one of the most important themes in *Anne of Green Gables* is this drive towards community: "the process of adjustment is a mutual one, in which both the stranger and the community are changed by their contact with each other. Adoption, in short, means adaption" (15).

Though Anne is not a rebellious boy-child seeking to demonstrate his independence from authority and refusing to conform to the expectations of others, Anne is not, as the novel indicates over and over again, ordinary. She is unusual and one of her most distinguishing features is her imagination. Like a character in a Dickens novel Anne has her identifying phrase: she needs "scope for her imagination." Her mental agility quickly sets her apart from everyone else in the book. Intrigued by her imagination and the unexpectedness of her mercurial musings, shy Matthew and caustic Marilla are quickly bewitched by her. They, like the reader, are caught in the trap of looking forward to what happens next, because whatever Anne does, it is bound to be unexpected. As Drain so aptly put it, "Any novel . . . which begins with three successive chapters entitled 'Mrs. Rachel Lynde is Surprised,' 'Matthew Cuthbert is

Surprised,' and 'Marilla Cuthbert is Surprised' ought to alert the reader to the possibility that this novel will confound expectation as often as confirm it" (16).

There is, in *Anne of Green Gables,* a wonderfully complex attitude toward reading and the uses of the romantic imagination. While usually Anne's imagination and reading supply her with ways to cope with the world's cruel unfairness, at other times they cause her uneasiness. In a chapter suggestively entitled "A Good Imagination Gone Wrong," Anne describes in detail three of her imaginative speculations and in the process learns to be wary of the power of the imagination. The first two incidents concern minor housekeeping errors—forgetting a pie and starching Matthew's handkerchiefs. Anne tells Marilla she forgot the pie because "an irresistible temptation came to me to imagine I was an enchanted princess shut up in a lonely tower with a handsome knight riding to my rescue on a coal-black steed" (159). A rather pedestrian romantic image, which leads to an equally pedestrian housekeeping mishap. Likewise, the second incident lacks serious consequences: Anne starches Matthew's hankies because she is trying to think of a name for a new island she and Diana discovered. She tells Marilla she finally settled on the name Victoria Island because they found it on the Queen's birthday.

The third example of Anne's imagination gone wrong is, unlike the preceding two instances, extremely suggestive of the extent of the negative power of the imagination. When Marilla asks Anne to go to Diana's house to bring back an apron pattern from Diana's mother, Anne protests, for, she says, she will have to go through the Haunted Wood. Unlike "Victoria Island," an imaginative name which emphasized female power, the name "Haunted Wood" paradoxically demonstrates both female power and powerlessness. Now that Anne has named the wood (an exercise of her power), she cannot enter it after dark for fear she will see what she has imagined: a wailing woman in white, the ghost of a little murdered child and a headless man (becoming the powerless victim of her own powerful imagination). Marilla, predictably unsympathetic, insists Anne go. She goes and learns bitterly to "repent the license she had given to her imagination" (162). Although Anne goes on to tell Marilla that she will now be content with commonplaces after this dreadful experience, she of course does not long remain so. She has, however, learned a very important lesson: if using one's imagination can be salutary, it can also be dangerous.

In a later chapter, Anne proves how well she has learned her lesson when she gives up reading a Gothic novel, at her teacher's request, even before finishing it. "It was one Ruby Gillis had lent me," she explains to Marilla, "and, oh, Marilla, it was so fascinating and creepy. It just curdled the blood in my veins. But Miss Stacy said it was a very silly unwholesome book, and she asked me not to read any more of it or any like it" (234). Though Anne finds it agonizing to have to give back the book without knowing how it ends, she does do so. She has, in other words, successfully learned to resist the incredible hold that "what happens next" has on the unwary reader. Though her own ability to wield that power may have led Matthew and Marilla to keep her at Green Gables and may keep her own reader interested in her, she now knows that such power must occasionally be resisted. Actually what Anne learns— to be a resisting reader—is the basic lesson of feminist criticism, for women readers need to be especially cautious as they assimilate and project the images that fiction gives them.[1]

Though naming can sometimes get Anne in trouble, it usually empowers her. Coming to *Anne* after having read Lacan, I now realize just how important that power to name is. Fatherless (and motherless) Anne takes upon herself the power of the father—signification. Lucy Montgomery obviously never read Lacan, but she instinctively knew the power that comes from naming and she must have endowed Anne Shirley with that power deliberately. Even as a young naive reader, I knew that naming was a powerful act. The title Montgomery gave her book—*Anne of Green Gables*—was testimony to the effectiveness of that power. Though the Cuthberts might threaten to return Anne to the orphanage, because of the title I knew she was bound to stay. Naming is indeed a powerful act, both inside and outside the text.

Anne's imagination empowers not only her but others. For example, Marilla. Marilla's longstanding friendship with the town gossip, Rachel Lynde, has, it seems, depended upon Marilla's silent acquiescence before the sharpness of Rachel's tongue. After Anne responds with rage to Rachel's ruthlessly candid estimation of her as "skinny," "ugly," "freckled," and "red-headed," however, Marilla finds herself, evidently for the first time in her life, criticizing Rachel. Twice Marilla rebukes Rachel, although she is surprised

at herself both times for doing it. When Anne finally goes to
Rachel's house to apologize for her angry retort, she wins the
woman over and, on her return home with Marilla, is so pleased
with herself and her apology that Marilla again feels shaken out of
her characteristic seriousness: "Marilla was dismayed at finding
herself inclined to laugh over the recollection [of Anne's apology].
She had also an uneasy feeling that she ought to scold Anne for
apologizing so well; but then, that was ridiculous!" (73). Anne not
only awakens Marilla's imagination but she goes on to awaken
other dormant feelings as well: "Something warm and pleasant
welled up in Marilla's heart at touch of that thin little hand in her
own—a throb of the maternity she had missed, perhaps. Its very
unaccustomedness and sweetness disturbed her" (74). Likewise,
when Anne goes to visit Diana's Aunt Josephine, who has always
been self-sufficient and independent, the young orphan girl causes
that older woman to perceive a lack where she had never felt one
before:

> "I thought Marilla Cuthbert was an old fool when I heard she'd
> adopted a girl out of an orphan asylum," she said to herself, "but
> I guess she didn't make much of a mistake after all. If I'd a child
> like Anne in the house all the time I'd be a better and happier
> woman." (229)

Anne is a spirit that awakens and disorients. Ugly, skinny, freckled,
and red-haired she may be, but she is also a powerful force of
release.

When I read the book as a young girl, I don't remember that I
was aware of just how much force Anne exerted, especially over
Marilla:

> Marilla felt helplessly that all this [Anne's satirical impressions
> of Sunday School] should be sternly reproved, but she was
> hampered by the undeniable fact that some of the things Anne
> had said, especially about the minister's sermons and Mr. Bell's
> prayers, were what she herself had really thought deep down in
> her heart for years but had never given expression to. It almost
> seemed to her that those secret, unuttered critical thoughts had
> suddenly taken visible and accusing shape and form in the person
> of this outspoken morsel of neglected humanity. (81)

Very different from the boy heroes we are given in classical children's literature, Anne does not rebel by attacking authority— religious or educational—directly, but by bewitching others into recognizing their own covert dissatisfaction with the institutions they have always overtly abided by. A revolutionary force, Anne does not engage in useless vituperation or antagonism; she uses her imagination to arouse the sleeping imaginations of others. The imagination becomes linked in *Anne* with our emotional self, our repressed, hidden, often subversive unconscious. However, I cannot agree with Carol Gay that Anne's imaginative and romantic way of looking at things is distinctively "feminine" (12), although much in the novel and in current French feminist theory might confirm this speculation.[2]

Whether or not the force Anne represents can be defined as or confined to the feminine, certainly the feminine in *Anne* resists confinement. In many ways, the town of Avonlea seems to be a town of Amazons. Women play a much larger role in it than men. When the prime minister comes to town, it is the women (even if they cannot vote for him) who go off to meet him, whether to admire or condemn him. Rachel Lynde has the greatest power of observation of anyone in the town, and though Diana has two parents, Mrs. Barry is the one we keep meeting. It is she who forbids and finally readmits Anne to Diana's friendship. Likewise, the only Barry relative Anne ever meets is Aunt Josephine. When a new minister comes to town, it is his wife who draws Anne's admiration. Also, the new teacher is a woman, and she is as revolutionary a force as Anne: "[Miss Stacy] led her class to think and explore and discover for themselves and encouraged straying from the old beaten paths to a degree that quite shocked Mrs. Lynde and the school trustees, who viewed all innovations on established methods rather dubiously" (245). Both she and Mrs. Allan (the minister's wife who teaches the Sunday School) prove to be the most significant influences in Anne's life. Overall, women support, direct, and serve Anne as models throughout her life. As Gay so aptly puts it, "Anne lives in a woman's world" (10).

Though in many ways *Anne of Green Gables* seems to be setting up separate worlds for men and women and finding the worlds of women and girls far more interesting than the worlds of men and boys, there is one plot in the novel—the story of Gilbert Blythe's relationship with Anne—which complicates any attempt to see this novel as dividing the sexes into two separate spheres. In fact, it could be demonstrated that Montgomery uses Anne and Gilbert to embody and, at the same time, seek a different solution to the problem that Carol Gilligan poses in her classic study of development, *In A Different Voice*. Montgomery was a keen observer of the world in which she lived, and just as she seems to have anticipated and revised Freudian and Lacanian notions, she seems to have anticipated and, in the process, revised Gilligan. According to Gilligan, while men value separation, integrity and justice, women value interdependence, caring, and responsibility. These different values lead men and women to speak "in different voices," which, in turn, leads to misunderstandings. Gilligan hopes that once we understand the difference, we will be able to revise some of our thinking about human development: "This dialogue between fairness and care not only provides a better understanding of relations between the sexes but also gives rise to a more comprehensive portrayal of adult work and family relationships" (174). Though Gilligan sees some lessening of the difference between men and women as they mature, the poles of the dialectic remain gender-determined. Men and women are inherently different. Lucy Montgomery, on the other hand, presents a far more radical version of this dialectic between our desire for integrity and our desire to connect with others.

While Gay would seem to see Montgomery's work as confirming Gilligan's division into women's and men's worlds—"[s]he created through her Avonlea series a world where the traditional women's values of love, warmth, sensitivity, imagination, and quiet endurance survive and overcome" (12)—I would like to suggest that Montgomery seeks to displace rather than validate the Victorian concept of "separate spheres." Anne moves between both poles of the dialectic Gilligan describes. She is loving and intuitive, but she is also ambitious. She works hard to get to college and to win a scholarship once she is there: "Wouldn't Matthew be proud if I got to be a B.A.? Oh, it's delightful to have ambitions. I'm so glad I have such a lot. And there never seems to be any end to them—that's the best of it. Just as soon as you attain to one ambition you see another one glittering higher up still. It does make life so interesting" (273). Anne does win the scholarship but her desire to continue her education quickly comes into conflict with her sense of responsibility. When Marilla says she will have to sell Green

Gables because she cannot care for it and herself now that Matthew is dead and her eyesight failing, Anne does not hesitate to sacrifice the scholarship she has won to stay in Avonlea and help the woman who took her in so long ago. But Anne is not the only one to sacrifice. When Gilbert Blythe learns of Anne's decision, he gives up the teaching position in Avonlea he has been given so that Anne will get it and thus be better able to care for Marilla and Green Gables. To do so is a financial sacrifice on his part, for now he will have to pay board to take another teaching post out of town. He has, moreover, already made a sacrifice similar to Anne's and also given up a scholarship in order to stay at home to help his father. In *Anne of Green Gables,* if there are two poles to the dialectic, the dialectic works itself out in each individual, not between individuals. Men and women alike have to wrestle with contrary impulses.

Significantly, in the TV movie, Anne's interest in Gilbert Blythe is intensified at various points by his ostensible interest in other girls—Josie Pye, an unnamed girl at a ball, and another unnamed girl at college—and by Diana Barry's undying interest in him. In the book, however, Anne's interest in him is never a matter of sexual rivalry. Once she forgives him for teasing her about her red hair (and it takes her long enough to do that!), she seeks his friendship because he stimulates her intellectually:

> There was not silly sentiment in Anne's ideas concerning Gilbert. Boys were to her, when she thought about them at all, merely possible good comrades. If she and Gilbert had been friends she would not have cared how many other friends he had nor with whom he walked. (275)

Unlike Ruby Gillis, Anne does not seek a beau in Gilbert Blythe, she seeks a friend.

Anne does not accept conventional roles for either men or women. She sets no limits on the capacities of either group. Men are more than objects of sexual interest to her, and women, Anne tells the shocked Rachel Lynde, would make good ministers.

Though Rachel Lynde may disagree with Anne about woman's role, it is Rachel, who has the last word to say about nearly everything in Avonlea, who provides the best last word to define and demonstrate Anne's special power:

I never would have thought she'd have turned out so well that first day I was here three years ago. . . . Lawful heart, shall I ever forget that tantrum of hers! When I went home that night I says to Thomas, says I, "Mark my words, Thomas, Marilla Cuthbert'll live to rue the step she's took." But I was mistaken and I'm real glad of it. I ain't one of those kind of people, Marilla, as can never be brought to own up that they've made a mistake. No, that never was my way, thank goodness. I did make a mistake in judging Anne, but it weren't no wonder, for an odder, unexpecteder witch of a child never was in this world, that's what. There was no ciphering her out by the rules that worked with other children. It's nothing short of wonderful how she's improved these three years, but especially in looks. She's a real pretty girl got to be, though I can't say I'm overly partial to that pale, big-eyed style myself. I like more snap and color, like Diana Barry has or Ruby Gillis. Ruby Gillis's looks are real showy. But somehow—I don't know how it is but when Anne and them are together, though she ain't half as handsome, she makes them look kind of common and overdone—something like them white June lilies she calls narcissus alongside of the big, red peonies, that's what. (241)

What better evidence of the power Anne Shirley has than this tribute by the one woman in the novel ordinarily most immune to imagination and innovation. Even she has learned to think in "flowery" metaphors!

If we define feminism as belief in a woman's power to change the world that threatens to confine her, then Anne Shirley and the books that tell her story convey a subtle but revolutionary feminism which has empowered generations of young girls. And, let us hope that they continue to do so.

Notes

1. Significantly, many feminist critics have focused on the particular dangers of Gothic fiction. Imaging enthrallment, it reinforces feminine passivity. In "The Gothic Mirror," Claire Kahane offers a feminist psychoanalytic interpretation of Gothic fiction to revise the conventional view of the Gothic as the story of "a helpless daughter confronting the erotic power of a father or brother, with the mother noticeably absent" (335). Kahane substitutes for this Oedipal paradigm the possibility that

Gothic fiction serves as a mirror within which the female reader can confront her feminine identity, her link with her mother, her lack of autonomy. Kahane is able to suggest ways in which the Gothic empowers the woman: "the heroine's active exploration of the Gothic house in which she is trapped is also an exploration of her relation to the maternal body that she shares, with all its connotations of power over and vulnerability to forces within and without" (338). See Shirley Nelson Garner, Claire Kahane, and Madelon Sprengnether, eds., *The (M)other Tongue: Essays in Feminist Psychoanalytic Interpretation* (Ithaca, NY: Cornell UP, 1985).

2. Elsewhere, I have argued that the subversive imagination, the irrational unconscious, the primal and primary poetry of the dream is to be linked with the bisexuality that Freud always suspected was the ground of psychic life. See "Suppressing the Language of Wo(Man): The Dream as a Common Language," in *Engendering the Word: Feminist Essays in Psychosexual Poetics* (Champaign, IL: U of Illinois P, 1989).

Works Cited

Drain, Susan. "Community and the Individual in *Anne of Green Gables*: The Meaning of Belonging." *Children's Literature Association Quarterly* 11 (1986): 15-19.

Freud, Sigmund. *The Interpretation of Dreams*. Trans. James Strachey. New York: Avon Books, 1965.

Gay, Carol. "'Kindred Spirits' All: Green Gables Revisited." *Children's Literature Association Quarterly* 11 (1986): 9-12.

Gilligan, Carol. *In A Different Voice: Psychological Theory and Women's Development*. Cambridge, MA: Harvard UP, 1982.

Lacan, Jacques. *Ecrits: A Selection*. Trans. Alan Sheridan. New York: Norton, 1977.

Montgomery, Lucy M. *Anne of Green Gables*. 1908. New York: Grosset and Dunlap, 1935.

Weiss-Townsend, Janet. "Sexism Down on the Farm?: *Anne of Green Gables*." *Children's Literature Association Quarterly* 11 (1986): 12-15.

Suggestions for Further Reading

A Guide to the Research and Criticism
on *Anne of Green Gables*

Bibliographies

This reading list is confined to material about the first of L. M. Montgomery's novels, *Anne of Green Gables*. It was this novel that established her reputation as a writer and that endures as a classic of its type; it is also the book most written about. Montgomery, however, published a total of twenty novels, a collection of poems, and more than 400 stories during her career. The entry on Montgomery in the *Dictionary of Literary Biography* (volume 92) includes a convenient checklist of first editions of Montgomery's work in Canada, the United States, and Great Britain. For a full list of editions and details on the publication history of Montgomery's books, refer to the 1986 bibliography compiled by Ruth Weber Russell, D. W. Russell, and Rea Wilmshurst. This bibliography also cites film and stage adaptations of *Anne of Green Gables;* it remains the most complete list of works by and about Montgomery. The results of Wilmshurst's search for Montgomery's stories were first published separately in 1983. Barbara Garner's and Mary Harker's bibliography of *Anne of Green Gables* materials (1989) annotates scholarly and critical pieces, unpublished theses, and some of the articles and reviews that have appeared in popular periodicals.

Garner, Barbara Carman, and Mary Harker. "*Anne of Green Gables*: An Annotated Bibliography." *Canadian Children's Literature* 55 (1989): 18-41.

New, W. H., ed. *Canadian Writers, 1890-1920. Dictionary of Literary Biography.* Vol. 92. Detroit, MI: Gale Research, 1990.

Russell, Ruth Weber, D. W. Russell, and Rea Wilmshurst. *Lucy Maud Montgomery: A Preliminary Bibliography.* Waterloo, ON: U of Waterloo Library, 1986.
Wilmshurst, Rea. "L. M. Montgomery's Short Stories: A Preliminary Bibliography." *Canadian Children's Literature* 29 (1983): 25-34.

The Series

At the same time that the Pages of Boston agreed to publish *Anne of Green Gables,* they asked L. M. Montgomery to write a sequel featuring the irrepressible, red-haired orphan. Montgomery completed the manuscript of *Anne of Avonlea* just six weeks after she had received a copy of the first book. She did not like her new Anne book as well as the first, she confided in a letter to Ephraim Weber, and hoped she was not "to be dragged at Anne's chariot wheels the rest of my life" (Eggleston 74). But Anne proved so popular with her readers that Montgomery's publishers continued to press her for additional novels long after she felt she had written all she could about the character. By the time she was working on *Anne of the Island* in 1913, she complained in a letter to her long-time correspondent G. B. MacMillan that Anne "is something I have outgrown and find out of fashion with my later development" (Bolger and Epperly 68). In her journal a month later she speculates that her "forte is in writing humour," but that young women "in the bloom of youth and romance," unlike children and old people, "should be sacred from humour" (2:133). Despite Montgomery's qualms about moving her heroine past childhood, however, she catered to the demands of her public and publishers, producing a total of eight novels following Anne's careers as girl, young woman, teacher, wife, and mother. The last two of these novels fill in periods of Anne's life mentioned only in passing in the other novels. Listed in the order of the events of the character's life, this is the series: *Anne of Green Gables* (1908), *Anne of Avonlea* (1909), *Anne of the Island* (1915), *Anne of Windy Poplars* (1936), *Anne's House of Dreams* (1917), *Anne of Ingleside* (1939), *Rainbow Valley* (1919), and *Rilla of Ingleside* (1920). All of the novels have been published in a number of formats. The complete series is available at present from Seal Books of Canada, Bantam Books of the United States, Angus and Robertson of Australia, and Harrap of Great Britain.

Anne of Windy Poplars is entitled *Anne of Windy Willows* in the English and Australian series.

Life and Letters

Before *Anne of Green Gables* was six months old, Montgomery received a letter from her publishers asking her to send "a personal sketch" of how she came to write the book, because of the many inquiries directed to them (*Journals* 1:339). Since that time, interest in Montgomery's life and its relation to her fiction has continued unabated.

A prolific letter writer and diarist, Montgomery herself provided much of her life's story as it is commonly told. Between June and November of 1917, Montgomery's memoirs were published in six installments by the Toronto women's magazine, *Everywoman's World*. The installments were collected and appeared in book form as *The Alpine Path* in the same year; these memoirs were reissued in 1974. Many of the most frequently repeated anecdotes about Montgomery's life and the creation and publication history of *Anne* can be found in her reminiscences. Those reminiscences seem, in fact, to have been the primary source for Hilda Ridley's retelling of Montgomery's life in *The Story of L. M. Montgomery* (1956). Ridley focuses on Montgomery's childhood, adolescence, and young womanhood, apparently because she is interested in demonstrating the similarities between Montgomery and her most popular literary heroines, Anne and Emily.

Wilfrid Eggleston's collection in 1960 of letters from Montgomery to Ephraim Weber, a Mennonite homesteader who began the correspondence by writing Montgomery a fan letter, tends to confirm the opinion that Montgomery's fiction is autobiographical, because the letters are selected only from the years Montgomery lived at Cavendish. In the *Dalhousie Review* shortly after her death in 1942, Weber himself commented on the nature and much wider extent of his correspondence with Montgomery; in Eggleston's collection, however, Montgomery does not appear as a resident of rural Ontario, a mother, or a minister's wife.

Monographs published by women's groups during the 1960s provide more anecdotes and details about two periods of Montgomery's life. Margaret Mustard, one of Ewan Macdonald's parishioners in rural Ontario, compiled local recollections of Montgomery as minister's wife; the Women's Institute of Springfield, P.E.I., included reprints of some of Montgomery's early essays and poems in its celebration of *The Island's Lady of Stories.*

Francis Bolger's *The Years Before* Anne (1974), published by the Prince Edward Island Heritage Foundation to mark the centenary of Montgomery's birth, also takes as its focus Montgomery's early life. But Bolger's extensive use of family history and genealogy serves to emphasize the difficulty of equating Anne and Montgomery. Quite unlike Anne, Montgomery's roots in "the Island" were old, substantial, and profound. Bolger also documents Montgomery's development as a writer in the years leading up to the publication of *Anne* by reproducing much of Montgomery's juvenilia, including school essays, poetry, her first published essays, and her letters to a P.E.I. girlfriend written during the year she lived with her father and stepmother in Prince Albert, Saskatchewan.

Bolger further complicated the easy equation of Montgomery and Anne when, in 1980, he and Elizabeth Epperly published selected letters from Montgomery to her other long-time correspondent, Scottish writer George Boyd MacMillan. Unlike Eggleston, Bolger and Epperly reproduce letters from all four decades of the epistolary friendship. The span of the material, as well as the fact that Montgomery regularly discussed her emotional and creative life with MacMillan, make this collection invaluable as a source of biographical information.

The letters, both published and unpublished, and interviews with people who knew Montgomery are the basis for Mollie Gillen's 1975 biography of Montgomery, entitled *The Wheel of Things.* Gillen's biography is the fullest account of Montgomery's life available to date. She did not, however, have access to the journals Montgomery kept throughout her life; as a result, her observations usually repeat rather than challenge standard interpretations and assessments of Montgomery and her work. In 1978, a condensed version of Gillen's biography appropriate for use in elementary classrooms was published as *Lucy Maud Montgomery.* Blanche Norcross summarizes the same material for a juvenile audience in her outline of Montgomery's life and writing in *Pioneers Every One: Canadian Women of Achievement* (1979).

The ongoing publication of *The Selected Journals of L. M. Montgomery* by Mary Rubio and Elizabeth Waterston should change the scholarly and critical study of Montgomery and her work permanently. The first two volumes of the private journals, which cover the years 1889-1910 and 1910-1921 respectively, were published in 1985 and 1987; the third volume is scheduled for release in 1992. The material already available gives readers an opportunity to hear Montgomery's voice differently. For example, close reading makes it clear that Montgomery's fiction for children was not a direct translation of her experience as a girl. Montgomery seems, in fact, to have felt that her regard for her audience sometimes required her to betray what she knew about childhood. The adjustments Montgomery made from private voice to public voice are often the subject of journal entries. Commenting in November 1908 that she has had a letter from a Toronto journalist who has been assigned "to write a special article" about her, for example, Montgomery remarks:

> Well, I'll give him the bare facts he wants. He will not know any more about the real *me* or my real life for it all, nor will his readers. The only key to *that* is found in this old journal. (1:342)

The continuities and disjunctions between the diarist's voice and the epistolary voice can be documented by comparing the treatment of various subjects in the journals and the letters.

Writing, however, is only one of Montgomery's occupations. Although it is the activity that often sustains her, it also seems at times an empty achievement. The entry of December 3, 1908, for example, registers such a response to the success of *Anne of Green Gables:*

> The mail, as usual, brought me a grist of letters about my book and a bunch of favorable reviews—hard, cold, glittering stones to a soul that is asking vainly for the homely bread of a little human companionship and tenderness in its hard hours. (1:343)

While it seems certain that readers will persist in questioning the correlation between Anne and her creator, the availability of Montgomery's journals makes it possible to set that question in broader contexts. It also seems certain that Montgomery's own words—from the journals, letters, memoirs, or novels—will continue to provide the basic shape of the readings of her life.

Bolger, Francis W. P. *The Years Before* Anne. [Charlottetown]: Prince
 Edward Island Heritage Foundation, 1974.

_____, and Elizabeth R. Epperly, eds. *My Dear Mr. M.: Letters to G. B.
 MacMillan from L. M. Montgomery.* Toronto: McGraw-Hill, 1980.

Eggleston, Wilfrid, ed. *The Green Gables Letters from L. M. Montgomery to Ephraim Weber 1905-1909.* 1960. 2nd ed. Ottawa: Borealis,
 1981.

Gillen, Mollie. "Lucy Maud Montgomery." *The Canadians.* Don Mills,
 ON: Fitzhenry, 1978.

_____. *The Wheel of Things.* Don Mills, ON: Fitzhenry, 1975.

Lucy Maud Montgomery: The Island's Lady of Stories. Springfield, PE:
 Women's Institute, 1963.

Montgomery, L. M. *The Alpine Path: The Story of My Career.* 1917.
 Don Mills, ON: Fitzhenry, 1974.

Mustard, Margaret. *L. M. Montgomery as Mrs. Ewan Macdonald of
 Leaskdale Manse 1911-1926.* Leaskdale, ON: St. Paul's Women's
 Association, 1965.

Norcross, E. Blanche. *Pioneers Every One: Canadian Women of
 Achievement.* Don Mills, ON: Burns, 1979.

Ridley, Hilda M. *The Story of L. M. Montgomery.* London: Harrap;
 Toronto: McGraw-Hill, 1956.

Rubio, Mary, and Elizabeth Waterston, eds. *The Selected Journals of
 L. M. Montgomery, Volume I: 1889-1910.* Toronto: Oxford
 UP, 1985.

_____, eds. *The Selected Journals of L. M. Montgomery, Volume II:
 1910-1921.* Toronto: Oxford UP, 1987.

Weber, E. "L. M. Montgomery as a Letter-Writer." *Dalhousie Review*
 22 (1942-43): 300-10.

Early Reviews

Writing to Ephraim Weber on September 10, 1908, Montgomery comments that "there has been some spice in my life so far this
summer reading the reviews" of *Anne of Green Gables* (71). She
informs Weber that she has received more than sixty reviews to date
and quotes phrases from nineteen of them: the novel is called
"wholesome and stimulating" by the *Philadelphia Inquirer* and "a
delightful story" by the *Boston Herald;* Anne is described as
"positively irresistible" by the *Boston Transcript* and as possessing
"the elusive charm of personality" by the *Milwaukee Free Press*

(71). In her letter of August 31, 1908, to MacMillan, Montgomery counts sixty-six reviews and categorizes them by tone: "sixty were kind and flattering beyond my highest expectations . . . two were a mixture of praise and blame, two were contemptuous and two positively harsh" (39). She records her surprise that the reviewers "take the book so seriously" and her disappointment that there is so little agreement among the reviewers as to the faults of the book. "What one critic praises as the most attractive feature in the book another condemns as its greatest fault—and there am I no wiser than before," she laments.

Locating the reviews of *Anne* has proven a difficult process for Montgomery bibliographers. In the journals, Montgomery mentions the reviews only in passing and, for the most part, in general terms. While there are scrapbooks of newspaper and magazine clippings collected by Montgomery housed both at the Confederation Centre of the Arts in Charlottetown, P.E.I., and at the University of Guelph, none contains the reviews to which Montgomery refers in her letters.* Moreover, book reviews from the early years of the century can be difficult to locate because of the lack of indices. Magazine pieces such as the *Bookman* and *Canadian Magazine* reviews are listed in the *Combined Retrospective Index to Book Reviews in Humanities Journals: 1802-1974.* Reviews which appeared in newspapers are more difficult to find: if these are indexed at all, it is only by the paper itself. Finding these reviews of *Anne* requires bibliographers to search through the runs of newspapers between June 1908, when the novel was published, and September 1908, when Montgomery wrote to Weber.

The reviews that have been found and documented confirm Montgomery's reports to MacMillan and Weber that response to the novel was overwhelmingly enthusiastic. Of the nine reviews listed by Barbara Garner and Mary Harker, only the *New York Times* review could be called "contemptuous." Although the *Times* reviewer admits the story "had in it quaint and charming possibilities," he complains that the main character knows too much. Anne is young and unschooled, but talks "as though she had borrowed

---

*For accounts of their searches for early reviews, see Garner and Harker 20-21, and Russell, Russell, and Wilmshurst xii.

Bernard Shaw's vocabulary, Alfred Austin's sentimentality, and the reasoning powers of a Justice of the Supreme Court." Such inconsistencies make her "altogether too queer" for this reviewer. Moreover, he finds little character development in the novel, "no real difference between the girl at the end of the story and the one at the beginning of it," although the other characters seem "human enough" to him.

The other reviews that have been found, all decidedly "kind and flattering," discuss a number of the features critics continue to identify as aspects of the novel's appeal. The *Montreal Herald* lauds the "local coloring" and judges the novel to be "one of the few Canadian stories that can appeal to the whole English-speaking world." This view that the combination of particular details and universal values is the key to the success of the story is echoed by the *Canadian Magazine*. The environment of the novel is said to be "thoroughly Canadian" at the same time that the story appeals "to the best human sympathies."

Both the *Toronto Globe* and the *Spectator* of London, England, also underscore the novel's wholesome human values, with the reviewer in the *Spectator* recommending the novel to "all novel-readers weary of problems, the duel of sex, broken Commandments, and gratuitous suicides." Such a recommendation might appear to contemporary readers to be based on a reading of the novel as escapist and conservative fiction; the reviewer in the *Spectator*, however, judges the problem novels to be "hackneyed" and Montgomery's "sylvan glories" to be "an alternative entertainment." The reviewer in the *Toronto Globe* echoes this opinion, believing that the novel encourages "every Canadian boy and girl" who "has had ambitions to be something different to the ordinary individual" and "is worth a thousand of the problem stories with which the bookshelves are crowded today." The reviewer in the *St. John Globe*, to the contrary, suggests that Anne is "not by any means an unusual girl," although she is "truly delightful."

Many other reviewers applaud Montgomery's skilful realization of the character of "that Anne-girl." "She is certainly one of the most attractive figure [*sic*] Canadian fiction has yet produced," says the *Montreal Herald*. The *Canadian Magazine* agrees: "Anne is indeed a most interesting and entertaining person, and she might well be placed with the best character creations in recent fiction."

To the *American Library Association Booklist* reader, Anne seems "lovable, impulsive, imaginative but obedient." Murray in the *Montreal Daily Star,* and the reviewers for the *Outlook,* the *Toronto Globe,* and the *Spectator* all link the success of Anne as a character to Montgomery's mixture of the humorous with the pathetic. The *Spectator* develops this idea most fully:

> Anne is a creature of irresistible loquacity when we first meet her, and meeting with kindness and consideration for the first time after years of poverty and neglect, she expands in a way that is at once ludicrous and touching. Perhaps her literary instinct is a little overdone, but otherwise Miss Montgomery shows no disposition to idealise her child heroine. . . .

In their assumptions about audience, these early reviewers reveal attitudes quite different from those of recent commentators on the novel. The *Spectator* reviewer specifically reads *Anne* in the context of the problem novels for adults popular in the last decades of the nineteenth century; several other reviewers also assume that the novel will be read by an adult audience. The "whole English-speaking world" is the audience the *Montreal Herald* envisages, although the book is seen as "an ideal volume for growing girls." George Murray maintains in the *Montreal Daily Star* that the novel, "by its humor and pathos, will inevitably draw laughter and tears from every member of the gentler sex" and the *Canadian Magazine* judges the novel within "the whole range of Canadian fiction." Many recent discussions assume that the fact that *Anne* is a novel for children is of central importance in understanding and evaluating Montgomery's story. While a number of the early reviewers specifically take note of *Anne* as fiction directed to children, they tend to see this as either irrelevant or incidental to their judgment of the novel. The *Toronto Globe* most clearly considers the fiction in its relationship to a specialized audience, with its observation that young Canadian readers with ambitions to be different from other people will particularly enjoy this book. The *Outlook* believes "it will please grown-up people quite or nearly as well as the school-girls for whom it is primarily designed" and "ought to have a wide reading"; the *American Library Association Booklist* suggests that "all girls from 12 to 15, and many grown-ups" will enjoy Anne's story.

While these reviewers paid little attention to identifying a restricted readership for the novel, they recognized that Montgomery's story resembled other novels. The reviewer from the *Boston Herald* remarks on the similarity between *Anne* and Alice Hegan Rice's *Mrs. Wiggs of the Cabbage Patch*, a connection the Page company considered impressive enough to use in promoting Montgomery's book in the *Nation*.* Both the *Outlook* and the *Spectator* see *Anne* as a variation of Kate Douglas Wiggin's *Rebecca of Sunnybrook Farm*; both reviewers hasten to add, however, that "the book is by no means an imitation" (*Outlook*) and that "[t]here is no question of imitation or borrowing" (*Spectator*). The *Spectator* and the *Saint John Globe* reviewers also mention the similarities between Montgomery's book and Louisa May Alcott's Little Women novels. All of these books continue to be discussed in relation to one another as examples of a genre usually called either "the family story" or "girls' books."

Montgomery's language and style is singled out for praise in a number of the reviews. The commentator in the *Canadian Magazine* suggests that the story is "excellent in technique, development, and consistency," and that Montgomery writes "in a piquant literary style, full of grace and whole-heartedness." The description of Montgomery's style as graceful is repeated in various ways by the *Montreal Herald:* the story is said to be "charmingly told," the local coloring "delicately placed," the characters drawn "with a delicate touch." The delicacy and charm, however, do not make the novel artificial, for this reviewer also praises Montgomery's "manner" as "marvellously natural" and singles out as a chief attraction of the book "the author's love of nature which finds expression everywhere, without once appearing exaggerated or forced." The connection between a natural style and a love of nature is apparently assumed as well by the *Montreal Daily Star:* Montgomery, Murray notes, "is evidently a keen student of both nature and human nature." The *Saint John Globe* similarly praises the story both for its prettiness and its "naturalness."

Despite the Montgomery revival that is under way in Canada, it is difficult to imagine that any critic or reviewer, even one concerned exclusively with children's literature, would promote

---

*Garner and Harker cite and annotate this advertisement.

Anne of Green Gables as "the most fascinating book of the season," as George Murray did in the *Montreal Daily Star,* or proclaim that "the novel easily places the author . . . in the first rank of our native writers," as the *Canadian Magazine* did. In 1908, however, these were among the responses of Montgomery's first, adult readers in literary magazines and mainstream newspapers. Montgomery herself was both thrilled and puzzled by the audience she had attracted. By October 1908, with *Anne* in its fifth edition, Montgomery confides to her journal, "I *can't* believe that such a simple little tale, written in and of a simple P.E.I. farming settlement, with a juvenile audience in view, can really have scored out in the busy world" (1:339).

But there are questions among those raised by the novel's first reviewers which continue to fuel critical commentary today. Does Montgomery's "simple little tale" score with readers who live "out in the busy world" because it is regressive, wish-fulfillment fantasy? Or does its popularity suggest a hunger in both its first and subsequent audiences for recognition of "something other," for the validation of ways to be that are different from the ways of "the ordinary individual"?

"A Heroine from an Asylum." Rev. of *Anne of Green Gables,* by L. M. Montgomery. *New York Times Saturday Review* 18 July 1908: 404.

"In the World of Books." Rev. of *Anne of Green Gables,* by L. M. Montgomery. [Toronto] *Globe* 15 Aug. 1908: 5.

Murray, George. Rev. of *Anne of Green Gables,* by L. M. Montgomery. *Montreal Daily Star* 8 Aug. 1908: 2.

Rev. of *Anne of Green Gables,* by L. M. Montgomery. *American Library Association Booklist* 4.8 (1908): 274.

Rev. of *Anne of Green Gables,* by L. M. Montgomery. *Montreal Herald* 21 July 1908: 4.

Rev. of *Anne of Green Gables,* by L. M. Montgomery. *Outlook* 22 Aug. 1908: 957-58.

Rev. of *Anne of Green Gables,* by L. M. Montgomery. *Saint John Globe* 8 Aug. 1908: 10.

Rev. of *Anne of Green Gables,* by L. M. Montgomery. *Spectator* 13 March 1909: 426-27.

"The Way of Letters." Rev. of *Anne of Green Gables,* by L. M. Montgomery. *Canadian Magazine* Nov. 1908: 87-88.

Contexts and History of Reception

At the time Montgomery was writing *Anne of Green Gables,* there was little consensus among Canadian literary critics as to what Canadian literature might be, if indeed there was a Canadian literature at all. Archibald MacMurchy, in the preface to his *Handbook of Canadian Literature (English)* in 1906, notes that the common opinion of "men who ought to know" was that "'Canada had no literature of its own . . .'" (iii). He writes the *Handbook* to demonstrate that "the literary production of the people of the Dominion is proportionately equal, in quantity and quality, to that of any like part of the English-speaking race" (iv). During the economically and culturally buoyant decade following the First World War, MacMurchy's opinion was endorsed by a number of other literary commentators. In tracing the development of a national literature, each mentioned the contribution of L. M. Montgomery. She is usually linked in these accounts to a group of novelists who began to write between 1880 and 1920 and who produced "regional" or "community" novels. These writers, according to J. D. Logan and Donald French in *Highways of Canadian Literature* (1924), "began to realize that life around them was as interesting" as that in England or the United States (298). Logan and French choose to date the "Second Renaissance in Canadian fiction" from 1908, in part because it was the year *Anne of Green Gables* was published. Lorne Pierce in *An Outline of Canadian Literature (French and English)* (1927) is equally enthusiastic. Montgomery is given a place as a member of "the first authentically Canadian, self-conscious school of national literature" (13) and her first novel named "deservedly a classic of its kind, not because of its excellence of style or plot, but because of the altogether charming character, Anne" (38). Lionel Stevenson in *Appraisals of Canadian Literature* (1926) agrees that Montgomery's characterization is the outstanding achievement of *Anne of Green Gables* and uses the novel as the preeminent example of a type of Canadian fiction he defines as "a whimsical, sympathetic portrayal of a naive character in everyday surroundings" (129). Vernon Rhodenizer in 1930 judges the Anne series "a *comédie humaine* unparalleled in Canadian fiction" (101). Archibald MacMechan's assessment is more measured. Although he recognizes the historical significance of Montgomery's books in *Headwaters of Canadian*

Literature (1924), MacMechan compares *Anne* unfavorably with *Little Women,* the first being merely "a clever book," while the second is "a masterpiece" (211). Like the early reviewers, none of these literary historians takes much notice of the fact that *Anne* was written for a juvenile audience, considering it, rather, in terms of its place in Canadian literature.

E. K. Brown, writing in 1942, refuses to consider Montgomery's novels as literature in any sense at all. Along with a number of other "best-selling writers," Montgomery is dismissed by him as an "aggressively unliterary" writer of "Canadian books" as distinct from Canadian literature (5). Brown's censure is tempered somewhat by Desmond Pacey in *Creative Writing in Canada* a decade later, but the same distrust of popularity is evident in his equation of "the age of brass," as he names the first two decades of the twentieth century, with "an era of best sellers" (82). Pacey agrees with the earlier Canadian literary historians that regional novelists such as Montgomery contributed to "a good national literature" by "becoming aware of the artistic possibilities of their own place"; he sees this group of writers as failures, however, in that they refuse to challenge "the values of the new industrial society," seeking "merely to turn the clock back" (95). In fact, Pacey suggests that *Anne of Green Gables* was popular precisely because it "had all the features of the kind of escape literature which a materialistic and vulgar generation craved" (106). What virtues Pacey allows the novel—it has a "quaint, naive perfection," a pleasantly whimsical tone, an "implicit and unobtrusive" didacticism, and a "sentimentalism a little less cloying than is usual in books of its type"—are conceded because "it would be silly to apply adult critical standards" to a children's book (106). Arthur Phelps's assessment of Montgomery in *Canadian Writers* (1951) is more tentative. "By the standards of discriminating literary criticism," Phelps agrees, no critic could consider popular writers such as Mazo de la Roche, Ralph Connor, or Montgomery important. But, having just re-read Montgomery's novels, he wonders, if *Anne of Green Gables* "can create a character with capacity to enter alive into the imaginations of hundreds of thousands of readers, may one not say also of that novel that it must possess some of the vital qualities of style and plot that suggest a respectable artistic achievement?" (89).

In another context, the *Literary History of Canada,* edited by
Carl Klinck (1965; rev. 1976), Pacey notes that the publication of
Brown's *On Canadian Poetry* was one of the final events "in the
long-drawn-out campaign to make Canadian literature academi-
cally respectable" (1:16). Academic respectability evidently dic-
tated scorn of literature such as Montgomery's, which was not only
popular but also written for children. It was a respectability culti-
vated by commentators during the next decades of the Canadian
mapping of literary history. The demand for rigor in judging home-
grown writers clearly informs Sheila Egoff's evaluation of Montgomery in her influential history of Canadian children's literature,
The Republic of Childhood (1967). Egoff quotes Brown's condemnation of Montgomery's professionalism with approval and sighs
over the inexplicably bad taste of the populace:

> To denigrate the literary qualities of *Anne of Green Gables* is as
> useless an exercise as carping about the architecture of the
> National War Memorial. Anne arrived and she has stayed. . . . It
> is sad but true that the Anne books continue to evoke great
> nostalgia from many adults to whom much vastly superior
> modern Canadian writing is unknown. (304)

Egoff is somewhat more generous in a piece on children's literature
written for the 1976 edition of the *Literary History of Canada,* in
which she acknowledges that, although the success of such senti-
mentalists as Montgomery "was more commercial than artistic,"
these writers were nevertheless "important for their part in estab-
lishing the image of the Canadian [as] . . . close to nature, vigorous,
and wholesome" (2:138). The astringency of Egoff's tone, however, is evident when her piece is set beside the chapter on children's
books written by Marjorie McDowell for the first edition of
Klinck's history. Montgomery's work is described by McDowell as
possessing "whimsical humour and gentle idealism," a setting
which is "a true Arcadia," a tone of "delight in living," and a
"powerful unity of mood" (627). Montgomery is also discussed
briefly under the heading of "Writers of Fiction 1880-1920" in both
the 1965 and 1976 editions of the *Literary History,* where it is
suggested that her letters "reveal an intellectual depth and a specu-
lative mind which is seldom evidenced in her fiction" (331; 1:345).

Montgomery goes virtually unmentioned in the thematic overviews of Canadian fiction that appeared during the 1970s and into the 1980s. There is, for example, no mention of her work in D. G. Jones's *Butterfly on Rock* (1970), in Northrop Frye's *The Bush Garden* (1971), in John Moss's *Patterns of Isolation* (1974), or in Gayle McGregor's *The Wacousta Syndrome* (1985). Margaret Atwood includes Marilla in her list of "powerful, negative old women in Canadian fiction" (205) in *Survival: A Thematic Guide to Canadian Literature* (1972), but otherwise ignores Montgomery. George Woodcock, in *The World of Canadian Writing* (1977), remarks only that *Anne* shows "how far the manipulation of authentic detail to give local colour to a formulaic kind of romance might be stretched in a direction opposite to that of true realism" (23).

The silence of these commentators regarding Montgomery might be taken to suggest a general acceptance of the judgment of Klinck's *Literary History* that Montgomery's fiction is shallow and simpleminded. It might, alternatively or additionally, reflect the fact that fiction written for children had become a special area of study by this time. This would seem to be the reason Elizabeth Waterston gives scant attention to *Anne of Green Gables* in *Survey: A Short History of Canadian Literature* (1973), although she begins her book by acknowledging that she first became interested in Canadian literature when she read Ralph Connor and Montgomery as a child. In fact, an article by Waterston initially published in 1966 marks the beginning of the detailed critical study of *Anne;* Waterston continues to work with Mary Rubio on editing the Montgomery journals. Montgomery is read thoughtfully by Clara Thomas in her general study of Canadian literature geared to a middle school audience, entitled *Our Nature—Our Voices* (1972). Jon Stott and Raymond Jones judge *Anne of Green Gables* to be "often funny and always moving" and Montgomery's characters to be "deftly, vividly portrayed" in their 1988 guide to Canadian children's books.

Within the last few years, Montgomery's fiction has been taken up in mainstream histories of Canadian literature again. Thomas MacLulich discusses her work at length in *Between Europe and America: The Canadian Tradition in Fiction* (1988), arguing that Montgomery is among the writers early in the century who "start to free themselves from a highly class-conscious or European view of literature, and begin to create a body of fiction that is thoroughly

North American in spirit" (9). William New, in his 1989 *A History of Canadian Literature,* reads Montgomery as struggling "to match experience with the conventions of romance, or to free experience from them" (100). To New, *Anne of Green Gables* is "[i]ronic and engaging," trenchant, and "in some degree espouses the cause of women's education" (101).

In 1990, in *The New Republic of Childhood,* Sheila Egoff and Judith Saltman also read the sentimentality of Anne's story as ironic. Montgomery is accorded considerably more attention in this edition than in the first two—eight of her novels are mentioned by name and Montgomery scores twenty entries in the index—and her staying power is attributed to the novel's "sharp look at adults and small-town community relationships that have probably not changed all that much" (21).

The Oxford Companion to Canadian Literature (1983) specu- lates that *Anne of Green Gables* is "perhaps the best-selling book by a Canadian author" (14). That success is a result of Montgomery's popularity outside as well as inside Canada. *Anne* was first published by the Page company of Boston in 1908 and was available in a British edition the same year. The novel, although frequently discussed in both American and British guides to children's literature, seems to have entered the children's literary tradition of those countries without exciting the extremes of praise and deprecation it has met in Canada. This is perhaps because it is invariably read as an example of a common type of fiction, rather than an unique phenomenon. For example, Dora Smith, in a Na- tional Council of Teachers of English guide of 1963, links *Anne* with both English and American girls' books series as symptomatic of a "rash" which "broke out at the turn of the century" (3). Bernice Cullinan in *Literature and the Child* (1981) lists *Anne of Green Gables* as one of the favorites of the girls' stories in her historical survey chapter, along with novels by Wiggin, Frances Hodgson Burnett, and Porter; and May Arbuthnot and Zena Sutherland mention *Anne of Green Gables* in *Children and Books* (1977) as one example of the increasingly realistic fiction for children pub- lished at the turn of the century. Alleen Nilsen and Kenneth Donel- son diverge somewhat from the critical practice of lumping together all girls' books in *Literature for Today's Young Adults* (1985). They discuss *Anne* and *Rebecca of Sunnybrook Farm* as successful books within a genre that usually produces characters "so stickily and uncomplainingly good that they drowned in goodness while readers either drowned or gagged" (557).

But, probably because Montgomery's novel is seen as just one of many books of its type, *Anne of Green Gables* is ignored in many of the comprehensive American guides to children's literature. The novel goes unmentioned in Donna Norton's *Through the Eyes of a Child: An Introduction to Children's Literature*, Charlotte Huck's *Children's Literature in the Elementary Classroom*, Bernard Lonsdale's and Helen Mackintosh's *Children Experience Literature*, Joan Glazer's and Gurney Williams's *Introduction to Children's Literature*, and *A Critical History of Children's Literature* by Cornelia Meigs, Anne Eaton, Elizabeth Nesbitt, and Ruth Viguers.

Montgomery's novel seems to be a standard choice in studies and surveys of children's literature published in Great Britain. John Rowe Townsend in *Written for Children* (1965) compares Wiggin's *Rebecca* with Montgomery's Anne (84). Sheila Ray discusses family stories in her handbook for librarians (1972) and suggests that *Anne of Green Gables, Little Women*, and Susan Coolidge's *What Katy Did* are the North American examples girls are most likely to have read (70); *Anne*, particularly, is in "continuous demand" (134). Peter Hollindale lists the novel as a classic of children's literature in his guide, *Choosing Books for Children* (1974). His definition of "great books" as "splendid, highly inconvenient books" which were "composed from a complex of interests and motives" and have an "unstable, multiple appeal" (123) does seem relevant to *Anne*. The changing evaluations and contexts of evaluation of the novel in the years since its first publication suggest that its appeal is indeed "unstable" and "multiple."

Arbuthnot, May Hill, and Zena Sutherland. *Children and Books*. 5th ed. Glenview, IL: Scott Foresman, 1972.

Atwood, Margaret. *Survival: A Thematic Guide to Canadian Literature*. Toronto: Anansi, 1972.

Brown, E. K. *On Canadian Poetry*. 1942. 2nd ed. Toronto: Ryerson, 1943.

Cullinan, Bernice E., with Mary K. Karrer and Arlene M. Pillar. *Literature and the Child*. San Diego, CA: Harcourt, 1981.

Egoff, Sheila. *The Republic of Childhood: A Critical Guide to Cana-*

dian Children's Literature in English. 1967. 2nd ed. Toronto:
    Oxford UP, 1975.
_____, and Judith Saltman. *The New Republic of Childhood: A Critical
    Guide to Canadian Children's Literature in English.* Toronto:
    Oxford UP, 1990.
Hollindale, Peter. *Choosing Books for Children.* London: Paul Elek,
    1974.
Klinck, Carl F., ed. *Literary History of Canada: Canadian Literature in
    English.* [Toronto]: U of Toronto P, 1965.
_____, ed. *Literary History of Canada: Canadian Literature in En-
    glish.* 2nd ed. 4 vols. Toronto: U of Toronto P, 1976.
Logan, J. D., and Donald G. French. *Highways of Canadian Literature:
    A Synoptic Introduction to the Literary History of Canada (English)
    from 1760 to 1924.* Toronto: McClelland and Stewart, 1924.
MacLulich, T. D. *Between Europe and America: The Canadian Tradi-
    tion in Fiction.* Toronto: ECW P, 1988.
MacMechan, Archibald. *Headwaters of Canadian Literature.* Toronto:
    McClelland and Stewart, 1924.
MacMurchy, Archibald. *Handbook of Canadian Literature (English).*
    Toronto: William Briggs, 1906.
New, W. H. *A History of Canadian Literature.* Macmillan History of
    Literature. Houndmills and London: Macmillan Education, 1989.
Nilsen, Alleen Pace, and Kenneth L. Donelson. *Literature for Today's
    Young Adults.* 2nd ed. Glenview, IL: Scott Foresman, 1985.
Pacey, Desmond. *Creative Writing in Canada: A Short History of
    English-Canadian Literature.* Toronto: Ryerson, 1952.
Phelps, Arthur L. *Canadian Writers.* Toronto: McClelland and Stewart,
    1951.
Pierce, Lorne. *An Outline of Canadian Literature (French and En-
    glish).* Toronto: Ryerson, 1927.
Ray, Sheila G. *Children's Fiction: A Handbook for Librarians.* 2nd ed.
    Leicester: Brockhampton, 1972.
Rhodenizer, V. B. *A Handbook of Canadian Literature.* Ottawa:
    Graphic, 1930.
Smith, Dora V. *Fifty Years of Children's Books, 1910-1960: Trends,
    Backgrounds, Influences.* Champaign, IL: National Council of
    Teachers of English, 1963.
Stevenson, Lionel. *Appraisals of Canadian Literature.* Toronto: Mac-
    millan, 1926.

Stott, Jon C., and Raymond E. Jones. *Canadian Books for Children: A Guide to Authors and Illustrators*. Toronto: Harcourt, 1988.

Thomas, Clara. *Our Nature—Our Voices: A Guidebook to English-Canadian Literature*. Toronto: New P, 1972.

Townsend, John Rowe. *Written for Children: An Outline of English-Language Children's Literature*. 1965. New York: Lippincott, 1983.

Toye, William, ed. *The Oxford Companion to Canadian Literature*. Toronto: Oxford UP, 1983.

Waterston, Elizabeth. *Survey: A Short History of Canadian Literature*. Toronto: Methuen, 1973.

Woodcock, George. *The World of Canadian Writing: Critiques and Recollections*. 1977. Vancouver: Douglas and McIntyre, 1980.

Scholarship and Criticism

Many of the critical and scholarly articles written about *Anne of Green Gables* mention the novel's popularity with readers during the ten decades since its publication. Several pieces are principally concerned with documenting this enthusiastic readership. Montgomery's correspondent Ephraim Weber refutes the criticism that *Anne* is "'the nadir of Canadian fiction'" in the *Dalhousie Review* in 1944 by outlining the wide range of readership Montgomery's novel attracts. In an overview of the reception of the novel in the first sixty years of its history, Helen Fitzpatrick (1969) lists statistics of book sales and quotes responses from such well-known readers as Mark Twain and Bliss Carman. Mary Vipond (1979) maps the reading habits of Canadians more generally in the early part of the twentieth century by analyzing lists of best-sellers between 1899 and 1918. As one of the biggest successes of the book-selling trade, Montgomery's novel is mentioned by Vipond along with other examples of "domestic" or "family" fiction. Anne's popularity in Japan since the 1952 translation of the novel into Japanese is outlined by Yuko Katsura in *Canadian Children's Literature* in 1984; in 1987 in the same journal, Barbara Wachowicz traces the symbolic importance of Montgomery's character to Polish readers since the first appearance of the novel in Polish in 1912.

Another group of critics documents the history of *Anne of Green Gables* by placing the novel within established literary categories. These critics do not read the novel as unusual and therefore popular, but rather as typical and therefore popular. Frances Frazer (1976), for example, identifies three "dominant strains" in the literature of Prince Edward Island: folklore, "rowdy parochialism," and romance. *Anne* and Montgomery's other novels are discussed as the best-known illustrations of the last category. In a piece first published in 1985 and reprinted in this volume, Thomas MacLulich positions Montgomery in terms of the literary debate between realism and idealism current at the turn of the century. MacLulich also discusses *Anne* as a "regional idyll," suggesting that the novel stands "at the head of a tradition that has given rise to some of the most memorable works of Canadian fiction," among them those of Hugh MacLennan and Margaret Laurence. This argument, published first in the *Dalhousie Review* in 1983, has been amplified in MacLulich's recent study of Canadian literature, *Between Europe and America* (1988). Janice Kulyk Keefer (1987) argues that "the more original and reflective" Maritime writers, among them Montgomery in *Anne*, undercut their idyllic texts with subversive subtexts.

As an example of children's literature, *Anne* is seen by Mac-Lulich (1985) as one of several girls' novels featuring "literary heroines" and psychologically attuned to children's needs. Janet Weiss-Townsend (1986) in the article reprinted here also discusses *Anne* as a girls' book; unlike MacLulich, however, she concludes that the designation is not a useful one. Mary Rubio, in a 1975 article, compares Montgomery's novels with Mark Twain's two novels for boys, in order to make a case for *Anne* as a realistic, rather than romantic or sentimental, novel.

Several critics define *Anne* as an "orphan novel"; for at least four of these discussions, that term is central to the critic's understanding of the novel and its appeal to readers. Gillian Thomas's (1975) and Susan Drain's (1986) articles, linking the success of the novel with Anne's lack of a family, are reproduced in this collection. Claudia Mills (1987) finds three distinct types of orphan novels in the twentieth century. The exuberant orphans of the early decades of the century, of which *Anne* is an example, are replaced in mid-century by polite orphans who must learn to become "more childlike." By contrast, the orphans and foster children of recent fiction are angry children. Gillian Avery (1989) dates the tradition of orphan tales from Samuel Richardson's *Pamela* and considers nineteenth-century children's versions of the tradition. Such mid-nineteenth-century heroines as Elsie Dinsmore and Ellen Montgomery are compared and contrasted with late-century heroines, among whom Avery includes Rebecca of Sunnybrook Farm and Anne of Green Gables.

Reviewing novels for adolescents about the development of the female artist, Sarah Smedman (1989) sketches a tradition beginning with *Jane Eyre* of depicting the roles played in that development by two types of teachers, the classroom tyrant and the "advocate of truth, justice, and compassion." *Little Women* and *Anne of Green Gables* are among the novels mentioned by Smedman. In the same issue of *Children's Literature in Education,* Charlene Gates discusses teaching as a rite of passage in the novels of Montgomery and Laura Ingalls Wilder. In both series, the main character's belief that teachers are absolutely good or bad must yield to a more complicated understanding of the imperfections of human nature, Gates argues.

Several commentators isolate specific literary techniques or elements of fiction to judge the success or failure of Montgomery's work. Montgomery's borrowings from other literature have been the subject of several articles. Joyce-Ione Coldwell (1980) admires Montgomery's use of the techniques of oral storytelling, particularly in *The Story Girl* and *The Golden Road.* Lesley Willis (1976) decries what she sees as Montgomery's misuse of myth and fairy tale in *Anne of Green Gables.* Constance Classen (1989) repeats the observation that Montgomery's first novel resembles Wiggin's *Rebecca of Sunnybrook Farm* and gives examples of verbal echoes, similarities in characterization, and parallels in plotting. Rea Wilmshurst (1989) lists the sources of Montgomery's recitations, quotations, and literary allusions in the Anne series as "a first step toward understanding her use of remembered phrases." Forty-one references in *Anne of Green Gables* are identified.

The article in this collection by Marilyn Solt (1984-85) argues that Montgomery's use of setting is central to the success of the novel. Many other recent critics agree with the early reviewers, who suggested that it is the spirited character of Anne that sets the novel apart from others of its type. Muriel Whitaker (1975) develops this argument at length in the article reprinted here, by comparing Montgomery's portrait of Anne with other of her less successful heroines. Rosamond Bailey (1989), however, sees streetwise and

ungrammatical Mary Vance of *Rainbow Valley* as a more successful, because more realistic, version of Anne.

By examining such questions of technique, most of these critics
defend, at least in a limited sense, the literariness of *Anne of Green
Gables*. According to Perry Nodelman (1979), whose article is
reprinted here, and Mary Cadogan and Patricia Craig in *You're a
Brick, Angela!* (1976), literary qualities play no part in the appeal
of girls' books such as *Anne*. This appeal, while undeniable, is
defined in both discussions as regressive, the articulation of a desire
not to grow up. Cadogan and Craig identify nostalgia for Victorian
values and "misdirected sexuality" as the shared features of a group
of North American books which also includes Wiggin's *Rebecca*,
Gene Stratton Porter's *Girl of the Limberlost*, Porter's *Pollyanna*,
and Jean Webster's *Daddy-Long-Legs*.

That *Anne* evokes an adolescent girl's state of mind is the
argument as well of several pieces of psychoanalytic criticism on
the novel, although these critics celebrate that evocation. In 1966,
in a survey of Montgomery's life and work for a University of
Toronto Press volume on Canadian women and their times, Elizabeth Waterston suggests that Montgomery "structured" her life
story "into mythical patterns" and considers how "[m]odern psy-
chology explains some of the hidden power of L. M. Montgomery's
books." Although Montgomery was routinely mentioned in Canadian literary histories from the beginning of the century,
Waterston's essay marks the commencement of serious critical
interest in the fiction. The piece was reprinted in the 1975 Montgomery issue of *Canadian Children's Literature*, which was itself
reprinted as a collection of essays by John Sorfleet. Mary Rubio,
both in the article (1985) appearing in this collection and in a 1984
article, similarly argues that Montgomery's skillful reworking of
the tensions in her life have resulted in a novel that recreates the
experience of adolescence. Jacqueline Berke (1978) works with the
similarities among a group of novels rather than the relationship
between biography and fiction in her examination of the self-sufficient heroine. By applying, to novels by Montgomery, Wiggin,
Porter, Burnett, Johanna Spyri, and Carolyn Keene, Freud's theory
that a child learns to master the environment by turning passive
experiences into active ones, Berke explains that the effect of the
absence of mothers and grandmothers from popular girls' fiction is
to allow daughters to try out mothering roles.

Many of Montgomery's critics mention the cultural background and the reception of her work; the cultural functioning of Montgomery's novel is considered explicitly by a number of them. Montgomery's achievements as a woman writing for girls is, in particular, a subject of growing interest and scholarship.

Shirley Wright (1982) begins her study of multiculturalism in English Canadian children's literature by mentioning the negative attitudes toward minorities in *Anne of Green Gables*. Laura Weaver (1988) considers how being a member of a minority group within the dominant culture determined her position as a reader of girls' books. Aritha Van Herk (1985) suggests that girls themselves become "othered" in children's literature; novels such as Montgomery's seem to offer opportunities for change but, in fact, merely close escape routes. The autobiographies of nineteenth-century American women confirm the experience of childhood represented in girls' books such as *Anne of Green Gables,* argues Anne Scott McLeod (1984). For girls, childhood is a period of freedom followed by a "closing of the doors as the girl neared puberty." Nancy Huse (1986), in the paper reprinted here, sees motherhood defined as the experience of simultaneous relatedness and autonomy in the Anne series.

Jane Burns (1977) suggests that Montgomery's attitudes toward women, as revealed in her life and letters, were highly conventional, although the girls in her novels do aspire to be more than wives and mothers. Isobel McKenna (1974) discusses Montgomery's representation of Anne as an example of the growing opportunities for women in fiction. Catherine Ross (1979), in the article reprinted here, suggests that Montgomery, among other Canadian women writers, specifically parodies earlier representations of women in fiction. Elizabeth Waterston (1984) contrasts the women in Canadian novels by men with the heroines of Canadian novels by women. The article by Carol Gay in this volume (1986) considers Montgomery's novel as a female utopia. In another article reprinted here, Eve Kornfeld and Susan Jackson (1987) argue that the nineteenth-century female *Bildungsroman* simultaneously worships maternal nurture and subverts the cult of domesticity.

The most recent adaptation of *Anne of Green Gables* to film has prompted further analysis of the cultural uses of Montgomery's story. Susan Drain (1987) argues that the Sullivan Productions film version of Anne has reduced *Bildungsroman* to romance in order to comply with popular expectations of television stories. Temma Berg, in the article reprinted here, suggests, to the contrary, that the film manifests the feminist concerns of the novel.

Anne of Green Gables has repeatedly roused such diametrically opposite interpretations from critics. If, as Frank Kermode has suggested in *Forms of Attention* (Chicago: University of Chicago Press, 1985), a text continues to be read if it is the subject of interpretative argument, then it is likely that Montgomery's "simple little tale" will generate new readings as critics develop other strategies or shift the terms of their studies. A number of critics, among them McLeod, MacLulich, Huse, Kornfeld and Jackson, have taken account of the findings of recent cultural and historical scholarship in building their arguments. A few critics, such as Ross, Keefer, and Berg, have made intriguing observations about Montgomery's purposes and methods in crafting the language of her narrative. But much more work could be done in reading *Anne* by the light of recent theories of culture, language, and subjectivity. Such a development might well have pleased Anne herself, for she is not only a creature but also a theorist of words.

Avery, Gillian. "'Remarkable and Winning': A Hundred Years of American Heroines." *The Lion and the Unicorn* 13.1 (1989): 7-20.

Bailey, Rosamond. "Little Orphan Mary: Anne's Hoydenish Double." *Canadian Children's Literature* 55 (1989): 8-17.

Berke, Jacqueline. "'Mother I can do it myself': The Self-Sufficient Heroine in Popular Girls' Fiction." *Women's Studies* 6.1 (1978): 187-203.

Burns, Jane. "Anne and Emily: L. M. Montgomery's Children." *Room of One's Own* 3.3 (1977): 37-48.

Cadogan, Mary, and Patricia Craig. "Orphans and Golden Girls." In *You're a Brick, Angela!: A New Look at Girls' Fiction from 1839 to 1975.* London: Gollancz, 1976. 89-110.

Classen, Constance. "Is *Anne of Green Gables* an American Import?" *Canadian Children's Literature* 55 (1989): 42-50.

Coldwell, Joyce-Ione Harrington. "Folklore as Fiction: The Writings of L. M. Montgomery." In *Folklore Studies in Honour of Herbert Halpert: A Festschrift.* St. John's, NF: Memorial U of Newfoundland, 1980. 125-36.

Drain, Susan. "'Too Much Love-Making': *Anne of Green Gables* on Television." *Lion and Unicorn* 11.2 (1987): 63-72.

Fitzpatrick, Helen. "Anne's First Sixty Years." *Canadian Author and Bookman* 44.3 (1969): 5-7, 13.

Frazer, Frances M. "Island Writers." *Canadian Literature* 68-69 (1976): 76-87.

Gates, Charlene E. "Image, Imagination, and Initiation: Teaching as a Rite of Passage in the Novels of L. M. Montgomery and the Novels of Laura Ingalls Wilder." *Children's Literature in Education* 20 (1989): 165-73.

Katsura, Yuko. "Red-Haired Anne in Japan." *Canadian Children's Literature* 34 (1984): 57-60.

Keefer, Janice Kulyk. "Pigs in the Pinewoods: Self-Destructing Regional Idylls." In *Under Eastern Eyes: A Critical Reading of Maritime Fiction.* Toronto: U of Toronto P, 1987. 186-210.

MacLeod, Anne Scott. "The Caddie Woodlawn Syndrome: American Girlhood in the Nineteenth Century." In *A Century of Childhood: 1820-1920.* Ed. Mary Lynn Stevens Heininger. Rochester, NY: Margaret Woodbury Strong Museum, 1984. 97-119.

MacLulich, T. D. "*Anne of Green Gables* and the Regional Idyll." *Dalhousie Review* 63 (1983): 488-501.

_____. "L. M. Montgomery and the Literary Heroine: Jo, Rebecca, Anne, and Emily." *Canadian Children's Literature* 37 (1985): 5-17.

McKenna, Isobel. "Women in Canadian Literature." *Canadian Literature* 62 (1974): 69-78.

Mills, Claudia. "Children in Search of a Family: Orphan Novels Through the Century." *Children's Literature in Education* 18 (1987): 227-39.

Rubio, Mary. "L. M. Montgomery: Where Does the Voice Come From?" *Canadiana: Studies in Canadian Literature/Etudes de Littérature Canadienne. Proceedings of the Canadian Studies Conference.* Ed. Jorn Carlsen and Knud Larsen. Aarhus, Denmark: Department of English, 1984. 109-19.

_____. "Satire, Realism, and Imagination in *Anne of Green Gables.*" *Canadian Children's Literature* 3 (1975): 27-36.

Smedman, M. Sarah. "Not Always Gladly Does She Teach, Nor Gladly Learn: Teachers in *Künstlerinroman* for Young Readers." *Children's Literature in Education* 20 (1989): 131-49.

Sorfleet, John Robert, ed. *L. M. Montgomery: An Assessment.* Guelph, ON: Canadian Children's P, 1976.

Van Herk, Aritha. "An (Other) Third World: Girls in Children's Literature." *Komparatistische Hefte* 12 (1985): 33-37.

Vipond, Mary. "Best Sellers in English Canada, 1889-1918: An Overview." *Canadian Fiction* 24 (1979): 96-119.

Wachowicz, Barbara. "L. M. Montgomery: At Home in Poland." *Canadian Children's Literature* 46 (1987): 7-36.

Waterston, Elizabeth. "Lucy Maud Montgomery: 1874-1942." In *The Clear Spirit: Twenty Canadian Women and Their Times*. Ed. Mary Quale Innis. Toronto: U of Toronto P, 1966. 198-220. Rpt. in *Canadian Children's Literature* 3 (1975): 9-26.

———. "Women in Canadian Fiction." *Canadiana: Studies in Canadian Literature/Etudes de Littérature Canadienne. Proceedings of the Canadian Studies Conference*. Ed. Jorn Carlsen and Knud Larsen. Aarhus, Denmark: Department of English, 1984. 100-08.

Weaver, Laura. "'Plain' and 'Fancy' Laura: A Mennonite Reader of Girls' Books." *Children's Literature* 16 (1988): 185-90.

Weber, E. "L. M. Montgomery's *Anne*." *Dalhousie Review* 24 (1944): 64-73.

Willis, Lesley. "The Bogus Ugly Duckling: Anne Shirley Unmasked." *Dalhousie Review* 56 (1976): 247-51.

Wilmshurst, Rea. "L. M. Montgomery's Use of Quotations and Allusions in the Anne Books." *Canadian Children's Literature* 56 (1989): 15-45.

Wright, Shirley. "Images of Canada in English Canadian Literature for Children, or, After *Anne of Green Gables*." In *Sharing: A Challenge for All*. Ed. John G. Wright. Kalamazoo, MI: Western Michigan U, 1982. 179-95.

Contributors

Temma F. Berg is assistant professor of English at Gettysburg College, Pennsylvania, where she also teaches in the Women's Studies program. She has published extensively on the subject of reading and reader-response theory and is editor of *Engendering the Word: Feminist Essays in Psychosexual Poetics,* published by the University of Illinois Press. She is currently researching the work of early women theorists.

Susan Drain is a visiting professor at the University of Toronto. Her academic home is Mount Saint Vincent University in Halifax, Nova Scotia, where she is able to combine and pursue many of her critical and research interests: children's literature, women's studies, Victorian studies, composition, and hymnology.

Carol Gay was professor of English and Director of Graduate Studies in English at Youngstown State University, Ohio. She published widely in colonial American literature, the Transcendentalists, women's studies, and children's literature, and was a charter member and the first archivist of the Children's Literature Association. She died in December 1985.

Nancy Huse teaches English at Augustana College, Illinois, where she is involved in both women's studies and family life studies. She has published articles on a variety of topics in children's literature and is at work on developing a feminist approach to the criticism of children's literature.

Susan Jackson earned an A.B. in History and American Studies from Princeton University in June 1986. She is currently working as an editor and journalist in New York and Japan.

Eve Kornfeld is an associate professor of history at San Diego State University, California. She has published a series of interdisciplinary articles on feminism and gender relations in American culture, and has a special interest in the intersection of history and literature.

T. D. MacLulich is both a poet and a scholar. His history of Canadian literature, *Between Europe and America: The Canadian Tradition in Fiction,* appeared in 1988. In 1967 he was awarded the University of Toronto's E. J. Pratt Medal for Poetry. He has taught English at the University of Victoria, British Columbia.

Perry Nodelman, a former editor of the *Children's Literature Association Quarterly,* has written articles and papers on all aspects of children's literature. He has published *Words About Pictures: The Narrative Art of Children's Picture Books,* with the University of Georgia Press and *The Pleasures of Children's Literature* with Longman. He is professor of English at the University of Winnipeg, Manitoba.

Mavis Reimer is a Ph.D. candidate in English at the University of Calgary, Alberta. For her dissertation, she is studying the girls' school story in late Victorian and Edwardian England. She has taught and published articles in children's literature.

Catherine Ross is associate professor in the School of Library and Information Science at the University of Western Ontario. She teaches Canadian literature, children's literature, and reference and research methods, and has published articles in Canadian studies and children's literature.

Mary Rubio is editor of *Canadian Children's Literature* and a member of the English department at the University of Guelph, Ontario. She is joint editor of L. M. Montgomery's journals, published by Oxford University Press.

Marilyn Solt is an associate professor of English, emerita, of Bowling Green State University, Ohio. She is the joint author of *Newbery and Caldecott Medal and Honor Books,* published by G. K. Hall.

Gillian Thomas has taught children's literature at the University of Victoria, California State University, and Dalhousie University. She is a professor of English at Saint Mary's University in Halifax, Nova Scotia, and the author of *Harriet Martineau,* published by G. K. Hall. *A Position to Command Respect: Women Contributors to the Eleventh Britannica* is forthcoming from Scarecrow Press.

Janet Weiss-Townsend, when not studying literature at the University of Winnipeg, acts as Technical Services Co-ordinator for a large Canadian consulting engineering firm.

Muriel A. Whitaker is Professor Emeritus, Department of English, University of Alberta. Internationally known as a medievalist, she has also published in the areas of children's literature and the illustration of children's books.

Index